The History of the Great and Mighty Kingdom of China and the Situation Thereof, Issue 15

You are holding a reproduction of an original work that is in the public domain in the United States of America, and possibly other countries. You may freely copy and distribute this work as no entity (individual or corporate) has a copyright on the body of the work. This book may contain prior copyright references, and library stamps (as most of these works were scanned from library copies). These have been scanned and retained as part of the historical artifact.

This book may have occasional imperfections such as missing or blurred pages, poor pictures, errant marks, etc. that were either part of the original artifact, or were introduced by the scanning process. We believe this work is culturally important, and despite the imperfections, have elected to bring it back into print as part of our continuing commitment to the preservation of printed works worldwide. We appreciate your understanding of the imperfections in the preservation process, and hope you enjoy this valuable book.

WORKS ISSUED BY

The Hakluyt Society.

MENDOZA'S HISTORIE OF THE KINGDOME OF CHINA.

VOL. II.

M.DCCC.LIV.

THE HISTORY

OF THE

GREAT AND MIGHTY

KINGDOM OF CHINA

AND

The Situation Thereof.

COMPILED BY THE PADRE

JUAN GONZALEZ DE MENDOZA.

AND NOW REPRINTED FROM THE EARLY TRANSLATION OF R. PARKE.

EDITED BY

SIR GEORGE T. STAUNTON, Bart.

With an Introduction

BY

R. H. MAJOR, ESQ.,

OF THE BRITISH MUSEUM,
HONORARY SECRETARY OF THE HAKLUYT SOCIETY.

VOL. II.

LONDON:
PRINTED FOR THE HAKLUYT SOCIETY.
M.DCCC.LIV.

LIBRARY
LELAND STANFORD JUNIOR
UNIVERSITY

137068

THE HAKLUYT SOCIETY.

SIR RODERICK IMPEY MURCHISON, G.C.St.S., F.R.S., Corr. Mem. Iust. Fr., Hon. Mem. Imp. Acad. Sc. St. Petersburgh, &c., &c., PRESIDENT.

The EARL OF ELLESMERE. } VICE-PRESIDENTS.
CAPT. C. R. DRINKWATER BETHUNE, R.N., C.B.
REAR-ADMIRAL SIR FRANCIS BEAUFORT, K.C.B., F.R.S.
CAPTAIN BECHER, R.N.
CHARLES T. BEKE, Esq., Phil. D., F.A.S.
WILLIAM DESBOROUGH COOLEY, Esq.
BOLTON CORNEY, Esq., M.R.S.L.
THE RIGHT REV. LORD BISHOP OF ST. DAVID'S.
RT. HON. SIR DAVID DUNDAS.
SIR HENRY ELLIS, K.H., F.R.S.
JOHN FORSTER, Esq.
R. W. GREY, Esq.
JOHN HOLMES, Esq.
JOHN WINTER JONES, Esq.
SIR CHARLES LEMON, BART., M.P., F.R.S.
P. LEVESQUE, Esq., F.A.S.
SIR JOHN RICHARDSON, M.D.
THE EARL SOMERS.
SIR GEORGE STAUNTON, BART. F.R.S.

R. H. MAJOR, Esq., F.R.G.S., HONORARY SECRETARY.

THE SECOND PART

OF THE

HISTORIE

OF THE

MIGHTIE KINGDOME OF CHINA,

THAT IS DIUIDED INTO THREE PARTS.

The first containeth such thinges as the fathers, frier Martin de Herrada, prouinciall of the order of Saint Augustine, in the Ilands Philipinas, and his companion fryer Geronimo Martin, and other souldiers that went with them, did see and had intelligence of in that kingdom.

The second containeth the miraculous voiage that was made by frier Pedro de Alfaro, of the order of S. Francis, and his companions, vnto the said kingdome.

The third containeth a briefe declaration by the said frier, and of frier Martin Ignacio, that went out of Spaine vnto China, and returned into Spaine againe by the Orientall India, after that he had compassed the world. Wherein is contained many notable things that hee did see and had intelligence of in the voiage.

THE ARGUMENT OF THE FIRST PART.

WHEREIN is declared the cause that moued frier Martin de Herrada and frier Geronimo Martin, and such souldiers as went in their companie, for to passe from the Ilands Philipinas, vnto the kingdome of China, in the yeare 1577; and of the entrie they made therein, and what they did see there for the space of foure monethes and sixteene daies that they remained: and of what they vnderstood, and of al things that happened vnto them, till they returned againe vnto the ilands from whence they went: all the which are notable and strange.

THE HISTORIE
OF THE
MIGHTIE KINGDOME OF CHINA.

SECOND PART.

CHAP. I.

The Spanyards departe from Mexico vnto the Ilandes Phillipinas, where they had intelligence of the mightie kingdome of China.

GOUERNING in the kingdom of Mexico, Don Luys de Velasco, who was viceroye, and lieftenant in that place for the Catholike king Don Philip king of Spaine, was commanded by his maiestie to prepare a great armie in the South Sea, and to leuie souldiers necessarie for the same, and to send them to discouer the ilands of the west, those which that famous captaine Magallanes did giue notice of when he did compasse the world in the ship called the Victorie.

The viceroy with great care and diligence did performe the kinges commandement. This fleete and armie being prepared readie (which was not without great cost), hee caused them to depart out of the port at Christmas time in the yeare of 1564; and sent, for general of the same fleet and for gouernour of that countrie which they should discouer, the worthie Miguel Lopez de Legaspi, who afterwarde died in the said Ilande with the title of Adelantado, a yeare after that the fathers Fryer Martin de Herrada and Fryer Geronimo Marin and their companies did enter into China.

So after that our Spaniardes hadde discouered the sayde ilandes, and some of them populared to the vse of his maiestie, but in especiall that of Manilla, which is fiue hundred leagues in circuit; in the which is situated the citie of Luson, and is also called Manilla, and as the metropolitane of all the iland, whereas the gouernours haue ordeined their place of abiding euer since the first discouery. They haue also founded in that citie a cathedrall church, and erected a bishopricke.

And for bishops of the same, his maiestie did ordaine the most reuerend fryer Don Domingo de Salazar, of the order of preachers, in whom was comprehended some holinesse, good life, and learning, as was requisite and necessarie for that prouince: and was consecrated in Madrid the yeare of 1579.

At this present there be three monasteries of religious men in that iland, the one of the order of S. Austen, and were the first that by the commandement of his maiestie did enter into this iland, preaching the law of the gospell, which was great profit vnto those soules, yet great trauaile vnto them, and cost many of them their liues in dooing it: the other monasterie is of barefoote fryers of the order of S. Francis, of the prouince of S. Joseph, who haue beene great examples, with great profit vnto them of those portes. The third are of the order of S. Dominicke or preachers, who haue done their dutie in all things so well as the other. These three orders were alonely in those ilands for certaine yeares, till now of late time haue gone thither Jesuites, which haue bin a great aide and helpe vnto their religion.

When these Spaniardes were come vnto these ilands, they had strightwaies notice of the mightie kingdome of China, as well by the relation of them of the ilands (who tolde vnto them the maruels thereof), as also within a fewe daies after they did see and vnderstand, by ships that came into those ports with marchants, that brought marchandise and other things of great curiositie from that kingdome, and did particularly declare the mightinesse and riches thereof: all which haue been declared vnto you in the first three bookes of this historie. This beeing knowen vnto the religious people of S. Austin, who at that time were alone in those ilands, but in especiall vnto the prouinciall, Frier Martin de Herrada, a man of great valour and wel learned in all sciences, who seeing y® great capacitie or towardnesse which the Chinos had more than those of the Ilandes in all things, but in especiall of their gallantnesse, discretion, and wit, he straightwaies had a great desire to go thether with his fellow to preach the gospell vnto those people, of so good a capacitie to receiue the same: who with a pretended purpose to put it in vse and effect, he began with great care and studie to learne that language, the which he learned in a few daies, and did make thereof a dictionarie. Then afterwards, they did giue great entertainment and presents vnto the merchants that came from China, for to procure them to carie them thether, and many other things, the which did shew their holie zeale; yea, they did offer themselues to bee slaues vnto the marchants, thinking by y^t meanes to enter in to preach: but yet none of these diligences did take effect, till such time as the diuine maiestie did discover a better way, as shalbe declared vnto you in this chapter following.

CHAP. II.

A rouer of this kingdome of China called Limahon, doth make himselfe strong at the sea, and doth ouercome an other rouer of the same countrie called Vintoquiam.

The Spaniards did enioy their new habitation of Manilla in great quietnesse, voide of all care of any accident that might disquiet them, or any strange treasons of enimies for to offend them; for that those Ilandes were in great quietnes, and in obedience vnto the Christian king Don Phillip, and in continuall traficke with the Chinos, which seemed vnto them a sufficient securitie for the continuance of the quietnesse they liued in. And againe, for that they vnderstoode that they had a law amongst them (as hath bin told you in this historie), y^t it was forbidden to make any wars out of their owne countrie. But being in this security and quietnes, vnlooked for, they were beset with a mightie and great armada or fleete of ships, by the rouer Limahon, of whose vocation there are continually on y^t coast, the one by reason y^t the country is full of people, wheras of necessitie must be many idle persons; and the other and principall occasion, by reason of the great tyranny y^t the gouernors doo vse vnto the subjects. This Limahon came vpon them with intent to do them harme, as you shal vnderstand. This rouer was borne in the citie of Trucheo, in the prouince of Cuytan, which the Portingals do call Catin. He was of mean parentage, and brought vp in his youth in liberty and vice: hee was by nature warlike and euill inclined. He would learne no occupation, but all giuen to robbe in the high waies, and became so expert that many came vnto him and followed that trade. He made himself captain ouer them which were more then two thousand, and were so strong y^t they were feared in all that prouince where as they were. This being knowen vnto the king and to his councell, they did straight way command the viceroy of the prouince where as the rouer was, that with all the haste possible he should gather together all the garrisons of his frontyers, to apprehende and take him, and if it were possible to carrye him aliue vnto the citie of Taybin, if not his head. The uiceroy incontinent did gather together people necessarie and in great haste to followe him.

Where Limahon was borne.

The which being knowen vnto Limahon the rouer, who saw that, with the people he had, he was not able to make resistance against so great a number as they were, and the eminent danger that was therein, he called together his companies, and went from thence vnto a port of the sea, that was a few leagues from that place; and did it so quickly and in such secret, that before the people that dwelt therein could make any defence (for that they were not accustomed to any such assaultes, but liued in great quietnesse), they were lordes of the port and of all such ships as were there: into the which they imbarked themselues straightwaies, wayed anker and departed to the sea, whereas they thought to bee in more securitie than on the lande (as it was true). Then hee seeing himselfe lorde of all those seas, beganne to robbe and spoyle all shippes that he could take, as well strangers as of the naturall people: by which meanes, in a small time, hee was prouided of mariners and other things which before hee lacked, requisite for that new occupation. He sacked, robbed, and spoyled all the townes that were vpon the coast, and did verie much harme. So he finding himselfe verie strong with fortie shippes well armed, of those he had out of the port, and other that he had taken at the sea, with much people such as were without shame, their handes imbrued with robberie and killing of men, hee imagined with himselfe to attempt greater matters, and did put it in execution: he assaulted great townes, and did a thousand cruelties: in such sort, that on all that coast whereas hee was knowen, he was much feared, yea and in other places farther off, his fame was so published abroad. So he following this trade and exercise, he chanced to meete with an other roouer as himselfe, called Vintoquian, likewise naturally borne in China, who was in a port voide of any care or mistrust, whereas Limahon finding opportunitie, with greater courage did fight with the shippes of the other: and although they were threescore ships great and small, and good souldiers therein, hee did ouercome them, and tooke fiue and fiftie of their ships. So that Vintoquian escaped with

One rouer robbed another.

8 A DISCOURSE OF THE

five ships. Then Limahon, seeing himselfe with a fleete of nintie fiue shippes well armed, and with many stout people in them, knowing that if they were taken, they should be all executed to death: they therefore setting all feare a part, gaue themselues to attempt new inuentions of euill, not onely in robbing of great cities, but also in destroying of them.

CHAP. III.

The kinge of China doth arme a fleete of shippes against the rouer Lymahon, who withdraweth himselfe to Touzuacaotican, whereas he hath notice of the Philippinas.

The complayntes increased euerie day more and more vnto the king and his counsell, of the euils doone vnto the Chinos by this rouer Lymahon. For the which commandement was giuen straightwaies vnto the uiceroy of that prouince (whereas he vsed to execute his euill), that with great expedition he might be taken (for to cut off this inconuenience), who in few dayes did set foorth to sea, one hundred and thirtie great shippes well appointed, with fortie thousand men in them, and one made generall ouer them all, a gentleman called Omoncon, for to go seeke and followe this rouer, with expresse commandement to apprehende or kill him, although to the executing of the same he put both shippes and men in danger.

<small>One hundred and thirtie great ships of warre with fortie thousand men.</small>

<small>They do more esteeme honour than losse of ships or men.</small>

Of all this prouision, Lymahon had aduertisement by some secrete friends, who seeing that his enemies were many, and he not able to counteruaile them, neither in shippes nor men, determined not to abide the comming, but to retire and depart from that coast: so in flying he came vnto an ilande in secrete called Touznacaotican, which was fortie leagues from the firme land, and is in the right way of nauigation to the Ilands Philippinas.

In this iland was Lymahon retyred with his armie a certaine time, and durst not returne to the firme land, for that he knew that the kinges fleete did lie vpon the coast to defende the same. And although he did send foorth some ships a robbing, yet did they not doo any thing of importance, but rather came flying away from the mightie power of the kinges. From this ilande they did goe foorth with some of their ships, robbing and spoyling al such as they met with marchandice and other things that they carried from one ilande to an other, and from the iland vnto the firme, and comming from thence amongst them all, they caused to take two ships of China which came from Manilla, and were bound to their owne countrie. And hauing them in their power they searched them vnder hatches, and found that they had rich things of golde, and Spanish ryalles, which they had in truck of their marchandice the which they carried to the ilandes. They informed themselues in all points of the state and fertilitie of that countrie, but in particular of the Spaniardes, and how many there were of them in the citie of Manilla, who were not at that present aboue seuentie persons, for that the rest were separated in the discouering and populing of other ilands newly found; and vnderstanding that these few did liue without any suspition of enimies, and had neuer a fort nor bulwarke, and the ordinance which they had (although it was very good), yet was it not in order to defend themselues nor offend their enemies, hee determined to goe thither with all his fleete and people, for to destroy and kill them, and to make himselfe lorde of the saide ilande of Manilla and other adiacent there nigh the same. And there he thought himselfe to be in securitie from the power of the king, which went seeking of him.

And so, as he was determined, he put it in vre[1] with as much expedition as was possible.

CHAP. IV.

This rouer Limahon goeth to the Ilands Philippinas, and commeth to the citie of Manilla.

This rouer Limahon determining to goe and to take the Ilands Philippinas, and to make himselfe lord and king ouer them all, but first to kill the Spaniardes, which hee thought easely to be done, for that there was so few. And there he pretended to liue in securitie, without feare that before he had of the kings great fleete, for that it was so farre distant from the firme lande. So with this determination hee departed from those ilandes whereas he was retyred, and went to sea, and sayling towardes the Ilandes Philippinas they passed in sight of the Ilandes of the Illocos, which had a towne called Fernandina,[2] which was newe founded by the captaine John de Salzedo, who at that instant was in the same for lieutenant to the gouernour. Foure leagues from the same they met with a small galley, which the said John de Salzedo had sent for victuals. There was in her but 25 souldiers besides y*e* rouers, so that with the one and the other they were but a fewe in number; for that as they thought they did trauaile in places of great securitie, and without any suspition to meete enemies. So soone as Limahon had discouered the galley, hee cast about towardes her, and with great ease did take her, and did burne and kill all that was in her, and pardoned one of them.

[1] "Use", supposed to be contracted from the Latin word "usura", usage.
[2] The Illocos, Ilocos, Ylocos, or Hilocos, here erroneously called "islands", is the name of a province on the west side of the Island of Luzon.

This being done, he did prosecute his voyage according vnto his determination, and passed alongest, but not in such secret but that hee was discouered by the dwellers of the towne of Fernandina, who gaue notice thereof vnto the lieutenant of the gouernor aforesaide, as a woonder to see so many shippes together, and a thing neuer seene before at those ilands. Likewise it caused admiration vnto him, and made him to thinke and to imagine with great care what it might bee; hee sawe that they did beare with the citie of Manilla, and thought with himselfe, that so great a fleete as that was could not goe to the place which they bare in with, for any goodnesse towardes the dwellers therein, who were voide of all care, and a small number of people as aforesaid. Wherewith hee determined with himselfe with so great speede as it was possible, to ioyne togither such Spaniards as were there, which were to ye number of fiftie foure, and to depart and procure (although they did put themselues in danger of inconuenience) to get the forehande of them, to aduertise them of Manilla, and to ayde and helpe them to put their artilerie in order, and all other thinges necessarie for their defence.

This determination the captayne did put in vre verie speedily, which was the occasion that the citie and all those that were in it was not destroyed and slayne: yet they could not eschue all the harme, for that the shippes that carried them were small, and a few rouers and not very expert, for that the suddennesse of their departure would not afforde better choice, as also they went from one place to an other procuring of victuals: all which was the occasion that they did not come thither in such time as they desired, and as was conuenient.

This Lymahon was well prouided of prouision and al other thinges necessarie, and hauing the wind fayre, he was alwaies in the fore front, and came in the sight of Manilla vppon Saint Andros Eue, in the yeare 1574, whereas he came to an anker that night with all his whole fleete. And he seeing that the end of his pretence consisted in expedition before that they should be seene of those of the citie, or discouered by them on the coasts: the nightes at that time being very darke, which was a great helpe vnto them, he chose foure hundred of his best souldiers, such as hee was fully perswaded of their valour and stout courage, and put them in small vessels, and charged those that went with them for captaines, to make such expedition that they might come vnto the citie before it was day; and the first thing that they did was to set fire on the citie, and not to let escape one man liuing therein, promising them that at the break of the day he would be with them to giue them aide and succour if neede did require, which they did. But for that nothing is done without the will and permission of God, it went not with Limahon and his foure hundred souldiers according as he did make reckoning; for that all that night the winde was of the shoore, and the more the night came on, the more the wind encreased, which was such a contradiction vnto their expectation, that they could not by night disembarke themselues, although they did procure by all meanes possible by policie and force for to do it. Which of certaintie and without all doubt, if this had not beene (at great ease), they had brought to a conclusion their euill pretence, with the spoyle and losse of the citie and all that dwelt therein: for their pretence was for to destroy and beat it downe, as it might well appeare by the commandement hee gaue vnto his captaines.

CHAP. V.

Limahon doth send 400 souldiers before for to burne the citie of Manilla, and they were resisted by other men.

For all the contradiction of the winde this same night, the foure hundred Chinos did put themselues within a league of the citie, vpon S. Andrewes day, at eight of the clocke in the morning, whereas they left their boates and went a land, and in great haste beganne to march forwardes in battaile a raye deuided in two partes, with two hundred hargabuses afore, and immediatly after them other two hundred pickemen: and by reason that they were manie and the countrie verie plaine, they were straightwayes discouered by some of the citie, who entered in with a great noyse, crying, Arme, arme, arme, the enemies come! The which aduice did little profite, for that there was none that would beleeue them: but beleeued that it was some false larum doone by the people of the countrie for to mocke them. But in conclusion the enemies were come vnto the house of the generall of the fielde, who was called Martin de Goyti, which was the first house in all the citie that wayes which the enemies came. And before that the Spaniardes and souldiers that were within the towne could bee fully perswaded the rumour to be true, the enemies had set fire vpon his house, and slewe him and all that were within, that none escaped but onely the goodwife of the house, whom they left naked and verie sore wounded, beleeuing that she had beene dead: but afterwards shee recouered and was healed of her woundes. In the meane time that they were occupied in their first crueltie, they of the citie were fully resolued of the trueth, although all of them, with this successe unlooked for, were as people amased and from themselues; yet in the end they sounded to armour, and did provide to saue their liues. Some souldiers went foorth vppon the sandes, but in ill order as the time did permitte, and slewe all the Chinos that they did meete, and none escaped : which was the occasion that the rest did ioyne themselues together, and put themselues in order to make some resistance against their enemies, who with great furie entred into the citie, burning and destroying all before them, and crying victorie.

This is the proper resistance of the Spaniardes when they doo finde themseluas in such like perilles : and this was doone with such great courage, that it was sufficient to stay the furie of those which vnto that time had the victorie: and to make them to retyre, although there was great difference in number betwixt the one and the other.

<small>A good praise of others.</small>

The Chinos in retyring lost some of their souldiers, but vnto the Spaniardes no great harme, and in this their defence did notable actes. This being considered of the Chinos, and that their boates were farre off, for that time would not giue them place to bring them any nearer, they did resolue themselues to leaue assault in the state that it was in, and put themselues in couert, and there to refresh themselues of the trauaile past, and afterwarde to returne with their generall Captaine Lymahon, to prosecute their intent, which they thought to bee comprehended with great ease. So when they came vnto their boates, to avoyde any danger that might happen, they embarked themselues and returned vnto their fleete whereas they left them. And not long after they were departed, they might see them rowe with great furie towardes their shippes, and when they came vnto their captaine Limahon, they did aduertise him in particular of all that had happened, and how that by reason of the contrarie winde, they could not come thether in time as he had commanded them, and according vnto their desire, which was the occasion that they could not bring to passe their pretence, and that by reason of his absence they had referred it till a better occasion did serue. Their captaine did comfort them, and gaue them great thankes, for that which they had done, promising them in short time to bring to effect their euill intent; and straightway commanded to weigh anker, and to enter into a port called Cabile, which is but two leagues from the citie of Manilla. Thither they of the citie might plainely see them to enter.

CHAP. VI.

The gouernour of Manilla purposeth himselfe to abide the assault of the Chinos, to whom they gaue the repulse: then Limahon returned and planted himselfe vppon the plaine nigh the riuer Pagansinan.

At this time, by the order of his majestie, was elected for gouernour of these Ilandes Philippinas, Guido de Labacares, after the death of Miguel Lopez de Legaspi, who understanding the great fleete and power of Lymahon the rover, and the small resistance and defence that was in the citie of Manilla, with as much speede as was possible he did call together all their captaynes and dwellers therein: and with a generall consent they did determine to make some defence for to resist them as well as they could (for the time that the enemie did remaine in the port aforesaide): for to the contrarie the Spaniardes should loose great credite, if that they should forsake and leaue the towne, so long as their liues did indure. For in no other place in all the ilandes there about, they could haue any securitie. With this determination they put this worke in execution, and spared no person, of what qualitie and degree so euer he was, but that his hande was to helpe all that was possible, the which indured two dayes and two nightes, for so long the rouer kept his shippes and came not abrode: for these woorthie souldiers vnderstoode, that remayning with their liues their labour and trauaile would soone be eased.

In which time of their continuall labour, they made a fort with pipes and bordes filled with sande and other necessaries thereto belonging, such as the time would permit them: they put in carriages foure excellent peeces of artilerie that were in the citie. All the which being put in order, they gathered together all the people of the citie into that little fort, which they made by the prouidence of God our Lorde, as you may beleeue, for that it was not his pleasure that so many soules as were in those ilands, baptised and sealed with the light and knowledge of his holy faith, should returne againe to be ouercome with the deuill: out of whose power hee brought them by his infinite goodnes and mercie: neither would hee that the friendship should be lost that these ilands had with the mightie kingdome of China. By which meanes we may coniecture that the diuine power had ordained the remedie of saluation for all that countrie. The night before the enemie did giue assault vnto the citie, came thether the captayne John de Salzedo, lieutenant vnto the gouernour of the townes of Fernandina, who, as aforesayde, came with purpose to ayde and helpe the Spaniardes that were then in Manilla. Whose comming, without all doubt, with his companions, was the principall remedie, as well vnto the citie, as vnto all those that were within it: for considering that they were but fewe, and the great paines they tooke in making the last resistance, and the labor and trauaile they had in the ordayning of the fort for their defence, with other necessaries, against that which was to come, ioyning therewith the feare that was amongst them of the assalt past: surely they had neede of such a succour as this was: and surely by the opinion of all men, it was a myracle of God, doone to bring them thether. So with the comming of this captaine with his people, they all recouered newe courage, with great hope valiantly to resist their enemies: for the which incontinent they did put all thinges in good order, for that the rouer the morning following, before the breake of the day (which was the second day after hee gaue the first assalt), was with all his fleete right against the port, and did put a lande sixe hundreth souldiers, who at that instant did set vppon the citie, the which at their pleasure they did sacke and burne (for that it was left alone without people, as aforesayde by the order and commaundement of the gouernour, which for their more securitie were retyred into the fort).

So hauing fired the citie, they did assalt the fort with great crueltie, as men fleshed with the last slaughter, thinking that their resistance was but small. But it fell not out as they did beleeue, for that all those that were within were of so valiant courage, that who so euer of their enemies that were so bolde as to enter into their fort, did paye for their boldnesse with the losse of their liues. Which being seene by the Chinos they did retire, hauing continued in the fight almost all the day, with the losse of two hundreth men, that were slaine in the assalt, and many other hurt; and of the Spaniardes were slaine but onely two, the one was the Ancient bearer, called Samho[1] Hortiz, and the other was the bayliefe of the citie, called Francisco de Leon. All which being considered by Lymahon the rouer, who being politike and wise, and saw that it was losse of time and men, to goe forwardes with his pretence against the valiauntnesse of the Spaniardes (which was cleane contrarie vnto that which had proued vnto that day), he thought it the best way to embarke himselfe and to set sayle, and goe vnto the porte of Cabite from whence he came. But first hee gathered together all his dead people, and after did burie them at the ilande aforesaid, where as he stayed two dayes for the same purpose.

That being doone, he straightwayes departed from thence and returned the same way that he came, till he ariued in a mightie riuer, fortie leagues from the citie of Manilla, that is

[1] Misspelt for Sancho.

called Pangasinan, the which place or soyle did like him verie well, and where he thought he might be sure from them, who by the commaundement of the king went for to seeke him.

There hee determined to remayne, and to make him selfe lorde ouer all that countrie, the which hee did with little trauaile, and built himselfe a fort one league within the ryuer, where as he remayned certayne dayes, receauing tribute of the inhabitants there abouts, as though he were their true and naturall lorde: and at times went foorth with his ships, robbing and spoyling all that he met vpon the coast. And spred abroade that hee had taken to him selfe the Ilandes Philippinas, and howe that all the Spaniardes that were in them, were eyther slaine or fledde away: wherewith hee put all cities and townes bordering there aboutes in great feare, and also how that he had setled himselfe upon this mightie riuer Pangasinan, whereas they did receiue him for their lord, and so they did obey him, and paide him tribute.

CHAP. VII.

The generall of the fielde, called Salzedo, doth set vppon Limahon, he doth burne his fleete, and besiege his fort three moneths, from whence this rouer dooth escape with great industrie.

The gouernour vnderstanding by the ilanders, and of those that dwelt in the citie of Manilla, of the fame that the rouer Limahon did publish abroad in all places where as he went, howe that he had ouerthrowen and slaine the Spaniardes; and being of them well considered, that if in time they did not preuent the same, it might be the occasion of some great euill, that afterwardes they should not so easely remedie as presently they might: and those which were their friendes and subiectes in all those ilandes, giuing credite vnto that which the rouer declared, might be an occasion that they should rebell against them, by reason that the naturall people were many and they but a few: for that vnto that time they had sustained themselues onely by the fame to be inuincible. With this consideration they entred into counsell, and did determine to ioyne together all the people they could, and being in good order, to follow and seeke the rouer, for that they vnderstood of necessitie he must abide and repayre himself in some place nigh there aboutes, for that he durst not goe vnto China for feare that he had of the kings fleete; and fearing that they should vse such policies as hee hath vsed, they might come on him vnwares, and destroy him as he had done others. And seeming vnto them (that although they could not destroy him altogether) yet at the least they should be reuenged of the harme that they had receiued, and thereby to giue to vnderstand that the fame that he hath giuen out of himselfe was a lie, and should be an occasion for to remaine in their old securitie, and also had in better estimation and opinion of the dwellers there abouts, as also to cause great friendship with the King of China, for that it is against a traytor and one that hath offended him.

This determination they put in vre and effect according as the time would permit: in which time they had certaine newes howe that the rouer was in the river of Pagansinan, and there did pretende to remaine. These newes were very ioyfull vnto the Spaniardes. Then the gouernours commanded to be called together all people bordering there abouts, and to come vnto the citie where as hee was. Likewise at that time he did giue aduice vnto such as were lordes and gouernours of the ilandes called Pintados,[1] com-

---

[1] More correctly, the Islands of Painted Men. Martinière, in his "Dictionnaire géographique, historique, et critique," thus speaks of these Pintados in his article "Philippines":—" Ceux qu'on appelle Bisayas et Pintados dans la Province de Camerinos, comme aussi à Leyte, Samar, Panay, et autres lieux, viennent vraisemblablement de Macassar,

manding them to come thither, with such shippes and people as they could spare, as well Spaniardes as the naturall people of the countrie. All this was accomplished and done with great speede; the people of the countrie came thither with great good will, but in especiall those of the ilandes of the Pintados. After the death of Martin de Goyti, who was slaine in the first assault of the Chinos as aforesayde in the citie of Manilla, the governour did ordaine in his roome for generall of the field, in the name of his maiestie, John de Salzedo, who with all this people, and with those that were in the citie, went foorth (leauing the gouvernor no more ayde then that which was sufficient for the defence of the citie and the fort that they had new made, which was verie strong), and carried in his company two hundred and fifty Spanish souldiers, and two thousand five hundred Indians their friends. All which went with great good will and courage to be revenged on the iniurie receiued, or to die in the quarrell. All which people were embarked in small ships and two foygattes[1] that came from the ilandes there borderers, for that the shortnes of time would not permit them to prouide bigger shipping, neyther should they haue found them as they would, for at such time as the inhabitants therabouts did see the rouer in assalt against the citie, they did set fire on a small galley and other bigge ships that were in the same port, and did rise against the Spaniards, beleeuing that it had not been possible for them to escape so great and mightie a power: although since the first entrie of the Spaniardes in those ilandes they were verie subiect. The generall of the fielde with the people aforesaide, did depart from Manilla the three and twentieth day of March anno 1575, and arrived at the mouth of the river Pagansinan vpon tenable[2] Wednes-

où l'on dit quil y a plusieurs peuples qui se peignent le corps comme ces Pintados."

[1] Misspelt for frigattes.
[2] Ash Wednesday: the Wednesday *to be kept* holy.

day in the morning next following, without being discouered of any, for that it was doone with great aduice, as a thing that did import verie much. Then straightwaies at that instant the generall did put a lande all his people and foure peeces of artilerie, leauing the mouth of the riuer shutte vp with his shipping, inchayning the one to the other, in such sort that none could enter in, neyther yet goe foorth to give anie aduice vnto the rouer of his ariuall: hee commaunded some to goe and discouer the fleete of the enimie, and the place whereas hee was fortified, and charged them verie much to doo it in such secrete sort that they were not espied, for therein consisted all their whole worke. The captaines did as they were commanded, and found the rouer voyde of all care or suspition to receiue there any harme, as he found them in the citie of Manilla when he did assault them.

This securitie that hee thought himselfe in did proceede from the newes that hee had from his friendes at the China, that although they did prouide to sende against him, yet could they not so quickly haue any knowledge where hee was, neyther finde out the place of his abiding: and againe, hee knewe that the Spaniards of the Phillippinas remained without shippes, for that they had burnt them as you haue heard, and that they had more need to repayre themselues of their ill intreatie the yeare past, then to seeke any reuengement of their iniuries receiued.

The generall of the fielde being fully satisfied of his negligence and voide of care, and giuen to vnderstande of the secretest way that was to goe vnto the fort whereas the rouer was, he commaunded the captayne Gabriell de Ribera that straightwayes he should depart by lande, and that vppon a suddaine, he should strike alarum vpon the enimie, with the greatest tumult that was possible. Likewise he commanded the captaynes Pedro de Caues[1] and Lorenso Chacon, that either of them with fortie souldiers should goe vp the riuer

---

[1] Chabes in original.

in small shippes and light, and to measure the time in such sort, that as well those that went by lande, as those that went by water, should at one instant come vppon the fort, and to give alarum both together, the better to goe thorough with their pretence: and he himselfe did remaine with all the rest of the people to watch occasion and time for to ayde and succour them if neede required. This their purpose came so well to passe, that both the one and the other came to good effect: for those that went by water did set fire on all the fleete of the enemie, and those that went by lande at that instant had taken and set fire on a trench made of tymber, that Lymahon had caused to be made for the defence of his people and the fort: and with that furie they slewe more then one hundreth Chinos, and tooke prisoners seuentie women which they founde in the same trench; but when that Lymahon vnderstoode the rumour, he tooke himselfe straightwayes to his fort, which he had made for to defend himselfe from the kinges navie, if they should happen to finde him out: and there to saue his life vpon that extremitie, he commaunded some of his souldiers to goe foorth and to skirmish with the Spaniardes, who were verie wearie with the trauaile of all that day, and with the anguish of the great heate, with the burning of the ships and the trench, which was intollerable, for that they all burned together.

The captaines seeing this, and that their people were out of order, neither could they bring them into any, for that they were also weary (although the generall of the field did succour them in time, the which did profite them much), yet did they sound a retraite, and did withdraw themselues with the losse of fiue Spaniards and thirtie of the Indians their friends, and neuer a one more hurt. Then the next day following the generall of the fielde did bring his souldiers into a square battle, and began to march towards the fort, with courage to assalt it if occasion did serue thereunto: he did pitch his campe within two hundreth paces of the fort, and founde that the enimie did all that night fortifie himselfe verie well, and in such sort that it was perilous to assalt him, for that he had placed vpon his fort three peeces of artilerie, and many bases,[1] besides other ingins of fire worke. Seeing this, and that his peeces of artilerie that hee brought were very small for to batter, and little store of munition, for that they had spent all at the assalt which the rouer did giue them at Manilla, the generall of the fielde and the captaines concluded amongst themselues, that seeing the enimie had no ships to escape by water, neither had hee any great store of victuals, for that all was burnt in the ships, it was the best and most surest way to besiege the fort, and to remaine there in quiet vntill that hunger did constraine them either to yeeld or come to some conclusion, which rather they will then to perish with hunger.

This determination was liked well of them all, although it fell out cleane contrarie vnto their expectation; for that in the space of three monethes that siege indured, this Limahon did so much that within the fort he made certaine small barkes, and trimmed them in the best manner he coulde, wherewith in one night hee and all his people escaped, as shall bee tolde you: a thing that seemed impossible, and caused great admiration amongst the Spaniards, and more for that his departure was such that he was not discouered, neither by them on the water nor on the lande. What happened in these three monethes, I doo not here declare, although some attempts were notable, for that my intent is to declare what was the occasion that those religious men and their consorts did enter into the kingdome of China, and to declare of that which they said they had seene: for the which I haue made relation of the comming of Limahon, and of all the rest which you haue heard.

[1] In the original Spanish *versete*. A "base" was the smallest piece of ordnance made.

CHAP. VIII.

Omoncon, captain of the king of China, commeth to seeke Limahon, and doth meete with Spaniards.

In the meane time that the siege indured at the fort, as you haue vnderstood, there went and came certaine vessels which brought victuals and other necessaries from the cittie of Manilla, which was but fortie leagues from the mouth of that riuer of Pagansinan, as hath beene tolde you. It happened vppon a day that a shippe of Myguel de Loarcha, wherein was frier Martin de Herrada, provinciall of the Augustine friers, who was come vnto the riuer Pagansinan for to see the generall of the fielde, and in the same shippe returned vnto Manilla to hold Capitulo, or court, in the saide ilande and port of Buliano. Seuen leagues after they were out of the mouth of Pagasinan, they met with a shippe of Sangleyes, who made for the port, and thinking them to bee enimies, they bore with them (hauing another shippe that followed them for their defence), and had no more in them but the saide prouinciall and fiue Spanyards, besides the mariners. This shippe of Sangley, seeing that hee did beare with them, would haue fledde, but the winde woulde not permit him, for that it was to him contrarie; which was the occasion that the two shippes wherein the Spanyards were, for that they did both saile and rowe, in a small time came within cannon shot. In one of the shippes there was a Chino called Sinsay, one who had beene many times at Manilla with merchandise, and was a verie friend and knowne of the Spanyards, and vnderstoode their language; who knowing that shippe to be of China, and not to be a rouer, did request our people not to shoote, neither to doo them any harme, vntill such time as they were informed what they were in that same shippe.

This Sinsay went straight wayes into the fore shippes, and demanded what they were, and from whence they came: and being well informed, he vnderstoode that he was one of the ships of warre that was sent out by the king of China, to seeke the rouer Limahon, who leauing the rest of the fleet behinde, came forth to seeke in those ilands to see if he coulde discouer him to be any of them: and the better to be informed thereof, they were bounde into the port of Buliano, from whence they came with their two shippes: from whome they woulde haue fledde, thinking they had beene some of the rouers shippes. Being fully perswaded the one of the other, they ioyned together with great peace and friendshippe: the Spanyards straightwayes entred into their boate and went vnto the shippe of the Chinos, and carried with them the aforesaid Sinsay for to be their interpreter, and to speake vnto the Chinos. In the saide shippe came a man of great authoritie who was called Omoncon, who brought a commission from their king, and shewed it vnto the Spanyards and vnto the father prouinciall: in the which the king and his councell did pardon all those souldiers that were with Limahon, if that forthwith they would leaue him and returne vnto the kings part; and likewise did promise great gifts and fauour vnto him that did either take or kill the aforesaid rouer. Then did Sinsay declare vnto him of the comming of the rouer vnto the ilands, and all that happened in the siege of the cittie, as aforesaide: and howe they had him besieged in the riuer of Pagansinan, from whence it was not possible for him to escape.

The captaine generall of the king of China.

The captain Omoncon reioyced very much of these newes, and made many signes of great content, and did embrace the Spanyards many times, and gaue other tokens whereby he did manifest the great pleasure he receiued, and woulde therewith straightwaies depart vnto the rest of the fleet. And for that they looked euery day for the death or imprisonment of the rouer, the better to informe himselfe, hee deter-

26   A DISCOURSE OF THE

mined (for it was so nigh hand) to go and see the generall of the fielde in Pagansinan, and carry with him Sinsay, one that was knowne both of the one and the other : by whose meanes they might treate of such things that best accomplished the confirmation of the peace and friendship betwixt the Chinos and the Spaniards, as also of the death or imprisonment of Limahon. With this resolution the one departed vnto Pagansinan, whereas they arriued the same day, and the others vnto Manilla, whether they went for victuals.

CHAP. IX.

Omoncon is well receiued of the generall of the field, and lodged in Manilla with the gouernor, whereas they doo conclude the going of the fathers of Saint Augustine to China.

When that the generall of the field vnderstood wherfore the comming of Omoncon was, hee did entertaine him with great curtesie ; and after that hee had giuen him to vnderstand in what extremitie he had brought the rouer (which was a thing impossible for him to escape, except it were with wings), hee did counsell him, that for the time till hee brought his purpose to effect (which could not be long) that he would go vnto Manilla, which was not farre from thence, and there to recreate and sport himselfe with the gouernor and other Spaniards that were there, for that hee alone was sufficient to accomplish his pretence, without the comming thither of the kings fleete, neither for to remoue out of the port whereas they were in securitie. And for his going thither he should haue a shippe of his the which did row, and was for to bring victuals and other prouision ; and he shoulde go in the company of the captaine Pedro de Chaues that was bound vnto Manilla, and promised him that within few dayes he would giue him the rouer aliue or deade, which vnto the iudgement of all men coulde not bee long.

Omoncon, considering that this offer might come well to passe, did put it straight wayes in vre, and did imbarke himselfe in the company of ye captain, and sent his ship wherein he came alone by sea, because it was big and drew much water: the which was constrained to turne backe againe into the part from whence he went, by reason of stormie windes and wether, and was no impediment in the other with ores, for that hee went alongst the shoare and was shrowded with the land from the force of the wind, so that in few dayes they arriued in the port of the cittie of Manilla, whereas they were well receiued and feasted of the gouernor. Omoncon remained ther certaine dayes, after the which, he seeing that the siege did long endure, and that his staying might cause suspition of his death; and againe, that the whole fleete did tarrie his comming to his intelligence of the rouer, being fully perswaded and certaine that hee coulde not escape the Spaniards hand, they had him in such a straight, and that they would without all doubt sende him vnto the king aliue or dead (as they promised him), hee was determined to returne vnto China with the good newes that he had vnderstood, with a determinate intent, to returne againe and carrie the rouer after that they had him prisoner. With this resolution, in the end of certaine dayes, he went vnto the gouernor, certifying him of his pretence, whereby he might giue him license to put it in execution. The gouernor did like wel of his pretence, and did promise him the same the which the generall of the fielde did offer vnto him: and which was, so soone as the rouer should be taken prisoner or slaine, to sende him vnto the king without any delay, or else to put him whereas he should be foorth comming, and to giue them aduertisement to send for him, or come himself: and did offer him, more, that for his voyage he should be prouided forthwith of all things necessarie, without lacking of anything. Omoncon did give him great thankes for the same, and in recompence therof did promise vnto the gouernor, for that he understoode and had intelligence of the fathers of S. Augustine, that his honor, and his antecessor and the Adelantado Miguel Lopez de Legaspi, had desired many times to send vnto the kingdome of China some religious men, to intreat of the preaching of the gospel, and to see the wonders of that kingdome, and howe that they neuer coulde put this their desire in execution; for that those Chinos which came thither, although they did offer them whatsoeuer they would demand, fearing the punishment that should be executed on them according vnto the lawes of the kingdome: he did promise him that he would carrie them with him vnto China, such religious men as his honour would command, and some souldiers such as would go with them: hoping with the good newes that hee carried, to runne in no daunger of the law, neither the vizroy of Aucheo to thinke euill thereof; and for a more securitie that they should not be euill intreated, hee woulde leaue with him pledges to their content.

Omoncon promiseth to carry the friars vnto China.

The gouernor reioyced verie much at this his offer, for that it was the thing that he and all those of the ilands most desired of long time since, and did straightwayes accept his offer; saying that he did clearely discharge him of his pledges, for that he was fully satisfied of his valor and worthines, and that hee would not doo the thing that should not be decent vnto his person and office. The gouernor being verie ioyful of these newes, did therewith sende for the prouinciall of the Augustine friers, who was elected but fewe dayes past: his name was frier Alonso de Alvarado, a man of a sincere life, and one of them that was sent by the emperor in the discouerie of the newe Guinea, vnto whome hee declared the offer that the captaine Omoncon had made vnto him: whereat he reioyced so much, that being an old man, hee would himself haue gone thither: to which the gouernor would not consent in respect of his age, and other particularities, but entred in counsel who were best to go, and to finde one that were fitte to execute that which they had pretended (which was, as wee haue saide, to bring in and plant in that kingdome the holie Catholike faith): they determined that there shoulde go but two religious men, by reason that at that time there was but a fewe of them, and two souldiers in their companie. The religious men shoulde bee frier Martin de Herrada of Pamplona, who left off the dignitie of prouinciall, and was a man of great learning and of a holy life: and for the same effect had learned the China tongue, and manie times for to put his desire in execution did offer himselfe to bee slaue vnto the merchants of China, onely for to carrie him thither: and in companie with him should go frier Hieronimo Martin, who also was verie well learned, and of the cittie of Mexico. The souldiers that were appointed to beare them companie, were called Pedro Sarmiento, chiefe sargeant of the cittie of Manilla, of Vilorado; and Miguel de Loarcha, both principall men and good Christians, as was conuenient for that which they tooke in hand. These fathers did carrie them for this purpose, that if they did remaine there with the king preaching of the gospell, then they shoulde returne with the newes thereof to giue the gouernour to vnderstande of all that they had seene and happened vnto them; and likewise vnto the king of Spaine, if neede did so require.

This offer of the captaine Omoncon, and the appointment which was made by the gouernour and the prouinciall, was knowne throughout al the citie; and after that they had made great reioycings and feasts for the same, it was approued of all men, that those that were named were principall persons, as aforesaid, and were fully certified that there should nothing be neglected of that they did commaunde them: neither let passe any occasion, for that it was that which they did all desire, but in particular for the seruice and honor of God, and for the benefite and profite that shoulde redowne vnto them all by the mutuall contractation betwixt the one nation and the other: and also giue the king to vnderstande of so good newes as this is. The gouernor did straightwayes call those persons that were named and appointed to come before the captain Omoncon, and tolde them what was determined: the which they did accept with great ioy, and gaue great thankes; and the gouernor in token of gratitude, did giue vnto the captaine Omoncon, in the presence of them all, a gallant chaine of golde, and a rich robe of crimson in graine: a thing that hee esteemed verie much, and much more esteemed in China, for that it is a thing that they haue not there. Besides this, they did ordaine a reasonable present for to sende vnto the gouernor of Chincheo, he that dispatched Omoncon by the commandement of the king to go and seek the rouer: also another present for the vizroy of the prouince of Ochian, who was at that present in the citie of Aucheo.

A token that fine cloth is esteemed.

And for that Sinsay shoulde not finde himselfe agreeued (who was a merchant well knowne amongst them, and perhappes might bee the occasion of some euill and disturbance of their pretence), they gaue vnto him also another chaine of golde, as well for this, as also for that hee was euer a sure and perfite friend vnto the Spaniards. Then straightwayes by the commaundement of the gouernor, there were brought togither all such Chinos as were captiue and taken from Limahon out of the fort aforesaide at Pagansinan, and gaue them vnto Omoncon to carrie them free with him; and gaue likewise commaundement that the generall of the fielde, and all such captaines and souldiers that were at the siege of the forte, shoulde giue vnto him all such as did there remaine; binding himselfe to pay vnto the souldiers, to whome they did appertaine, all whatsoeuer they should be valued to be worth: all the which being done, he commanded to bee put in a redinesse all that was necessarie for the voyage, and that in ample manner, the which was doone in a short time.

CHAP. X.

Omoncon departeth with certificate, in what perplexitie he left Limahon the rouer, and doth carrie with him the fathers of S. Augustine.

The twelfth day of June, in the yeare of our Lord 1575, being Sunday in the morning, the aforesaid gouernor and all that were in the cittie did ioyne and go together vnto the monasterie of saint Augustine, where was deuout prayers made vnto the Holy Ghost, and after they had all of them requested of God so to direct the voyage, that it might be to the honor and glorie of his diuine majestie, and to the saluation of the soules of that kingdome, whome Lucyfer had so long possessed, Omoncon and Synsay did take their leaue of the gouernour, and of the rest, giuing them thankes for their good entertainment that they made them, and did promise them, in recompence thereof, to bee alwayes their assured friends, as shall appeare by his works, and to carry them, whome he did request of his owne good will, with securitie as vnto himselfe, and that he would first suffer wrong himselfe, before any should be done vnto those whom he had on his charge. The gouernor and all the rest did thankfully accept his new offer, giuing him to vnderstand that they were fully perswaded that his word and deede should be all one, and therewith they tooke their leaue of them, and of the religious men with the two souldiers their companions, not lacking teares to be shed on both parts.

Then did they al imbarke themselues in a ship of the ilands which was made readie for the same effect, and went out of the port in the company of another shippe with merchants of China that were at Manilla, into the which Sinsay put himselfe with all their victuals, for to carry it vntill they came vnto the port of Buliano, whereas was the great shippe of Omoncon, wherin they should make their voyage; which was that which was forced to returne backe againe by reason of foule wether: they aryued at the same port the Sunday following, for that the winde was somewhat contrarie, and had lost the shippe that carried their victuals, but after founde her at an anker in the port, for that she was the bigger shippe and sailed better: they founde also in her two Spanish souldiers, whom the generall of the fielde had sent from Pagansinan, for that, from the place whereas he was, he did see the saide ship to enter into the port, with commandement for to carrie them vnto him. This did cause vnto the religious men and souldiers a suspition that the generall of the fielde woulde procure to stay them vntill such time as he did see the ende of the siege of the fort, which euerie day was looked when they would yeelde, for that they shoulde carry with them Limahon the rouer aliue or dead. Uppon the which almost euery one gaue his iudgement, that it were better to depart without obeying his commandement, neither to take their leave of him, but to prosecute their voyage so much desired, for they thought euerie houre of their staying to bee a whole yeare: fearing that euerie thing would be an impediment to disturbe their intent and purpose: but better persuading themselues, knowing the good condition and great Christianitie of the generall of the fielde, whom frier Martin had alwayes in place of his sonne, for that he was the neuew vnto the Adelantado Legaspi, the first gouernor and discouerer of the said Philippinas, whom he brought with him from Mexico, being but a child: they were agreed to go vnto him, and shewe their obedience, and to take their leaue of him and of all the rest of their friends that were in the camp. So with this determination they put their shippe into the river Pagansinan, which was but seuen leagues from the saide port. They had not sailed three leagues but a contrary winde so charged them, that they were constrained to returne into the port from whence they came, and there concluded amongst themselues to send

Pedro Sarmiento in the barke wherein came the two souldiers aforesaid; for that it was little and went with oares, they might with lesse daunger enter into the riuer of Pagansinan, rowing vnder the shoore: and that hee in the name of them all should conferre with the generall of the field, and so take his leaue of him and of all the rest of their friends, whome they did request that they would not forget them in their prayers, to commend them vnto God to bee their aider and helper in this their pretence, so much desired of them all: and gave him great charge to bring with him the interpreter that they should carrie with them, which was a boy of China that was baptised in Manilla, and could speake Spanish very well; he was named Gernando.[1] This Pedro Sarmiento came thither, and did accomplish all that was commended vnto him verie faithfully: but the generall of the field was not therewith satisfied, neither the captaines and souldiers that were with him, for that the father friers were very wel beloued of them, for they deserued it: so they determined to send for them, and to request them to come thither and see them, being so nigh as they were. They being vnderstood by the friers (not without the suspition aforesaid), and seeing that they could not excuse to go vnto them to accomplish their commandement and gentle request, they departed out of Buliano with a faire wind, for that the storme was done, although the sea was a little troubled; and therewith they ariued at Pagansinan whereas they were well receiued of the generall of the fielde, and of all the rest with great ioy and pleasure. Their suspition fell out cleane contrarie as they thought, for that the generall of the fielde would not stay them, but did dispatch them with all speede possible, and did deliuer vnto them at the instant all such captiues as the gouernor had commanded, and the souldiers that had them did with a verie good will deliuer them, seeing to what intent it did extende, and also the interpreter, with all other thinges

---

[1] Misprint for "Fernando."

that was necessarie and requisite for the voyage; and writ a letter vnto Omoncon, who remained in Buliano, that hee would fauour and cherish them as he did not thinke to the contrarie: and did ratifie that which the gouernour had promised him, for to sende the rouer aliue or deade, after they had ended their siege by one meanes or other. He also requested of frier Martin de Herrada that he would carrie with him one Nicholas de Cuenca, a souldier of his company, for to buy for him certaine things in China, who did accept the same with a verie good wil, and promised to intreat him as one of his owne, and haue him in as great regard: and therewith they departed and went vnto the port of Buliano from whence they came, taking their leaue of the generall of the field and of all the rest of the campe, with no lesse teares then when they departed from Manilla. He sent to beare them company til they came vnto the port, the sergeant maior, who carried with him a letter vnto the captaine Omoncon, and a present of victuals and other things; and other two letters, the one for the gouernor of Chincheo, and the other for the vizroy of the prouince of Ochian, wherein he doth giue them to vnderstand how that he hath burnt al the fleete of Limahon, and slaine many of his companions, and howe that he hath besieged him so straightly that it is not possible for him to escape, neither indure long without yeelding of himselfe; and then either aliue or dead he would send him, as the gouernor of Manilla had writ and promised. These two letters were accompanied with two presents, wherein was a basen and an ewre of siluer, and certaine robes of Spanish cloth, the which the Chinos doo esteeme very much, as also other things of great valew that they have not in their country, and craving pardon because he did not send more. The occasion was for that he was in that place, and all his goods in the cittie of Manilla. The same day with a faire winde they came vnto the port Buliano, whereas they found Omoncon abiding their comming, and receiued all such things as the sergeant maior did carrie him in the name of the generall of the field, and rendered vnto him great thanks, and made a new promise to accomplish that offer made vnto the gouernor.

CHAP. XI.

The Spaniards do depart with the captain Omoncon from the port of Buliano, and ariue at the firme lande of China.

The desire was so much of this father frier Martin de Herrada to be in China, as well for to preach in it the holy gospel, as also for to see the wonders that haue beene reported to be in that countrie, that although he was dispatched by the gouernor and generall of the fielde, yet he thought that their voyage would be interrupted: and therefore to see himselfe free from this feare and suspition, so soon as he came vnto the port of Buliano to the captaine Omoncon, hee requested him with great vehemencie, that he would straightwayes set saile, for that the winde serued well for their purpose. Then Omoncon, who desired no other thing, but thought euery houre that he tarried to be a whole yeare, commanded forthwith the mariners to make all thinges in a redinesse to set saile, and to bring home all their ankers, and ride apicke, redie to depart after midnight: the which was done as hee had commanded. So vppon a Sunday at the break of day, being 25. of June, they took a Spaniard souldier into their companie, who was called John de Triana, and vsed him in their seruice, for that hee was a mariner. So at the same time, after they had praied vnto God to direct their voyage, they set saile with a prosperous winde. There was with the friers, souldiers, and men of seruice, twentie persons, besides the Chinos that were captiues, and the people of the captaine

They departed towards China.

Omoncon. They were not so soone off from the coste, but the winde abated and they remained becalmed certaine dayes: but afterwards they had a lustie gale, that carried them forwards. The Chinos doo gouerne their ships by a compasse deuided into twelue partes, and doo vse no sea cardes, but a briefe description of Ruter,[1] wherewith they doo nauigate or saile: and commonly for the most part they neuer go out of the sight of land. They maruelled very much when that it was told them, that comming from Mexico vnto Philippinas, they were three monethes at the sea and neuer sawe land. So it pleased God, that although it was verie calme and little winde stirring, that we made but little way, yet, upon the Sunday following, which was the thirde of July, we had sight of the land of China: so that we found all our voyage from the port of Buliano, from whence we departed, vnto the firme land, to be one hundred and fortie leagues; and twenty leagues before they came in the sight thereof, they had sounding at three score and tenne, and fourscore fathome, and so waxed lesse and lesse vntill they came to the lande, which is the best and surest token they haue to be nigh the land. In all the time of their voyage, the captain Omoncon with his companie shewed such great curtesie and friendship to our men, as though they had been the owners of the saide ship: and at such time as they did imbarke themselues, he gaue his own cabin y^t was in the sterne to ye friers, and vnto Pedro Sarmiento and to Miguel de Loarcha, he gaue another cabin that was very good, and commanded his company in the ship that they should respect them more then himselfe; the which was in such sort, that on a day, at the beginning of their voyage, the fathers founde them making of sacrifice vnto their idols, and told them that all which they did was a kinde of mockage, and that they shoulde worshipe but onely one God: and willed them to

---

[1] More commonly spelt Rutter or Ruttier, a direction book. The word is derived from "Routier," a road book.

doe so no more. Who, onely in respect of them, did leaue it off, and not vse it after in all the voyage: whereas before they did vse it euerie day manie times.

Besides this, they would worshippe the images that the friers did carrie with them, and kneele vpon their knees with great shew of deuotion; who nowe hauing sight of the firme lande in so short time, and passed that small gulfe so quietly, which was wont to bee verie perilous and full of stormes, they did attribute it vnto the orations of the friers, their companions and souldiers. The like curtesie was shewed vnto them by Sinsay, who was the seconde person in the shippe, and hee that did best vnderstande that nauigation and voyage. So, as they drewe nearer the land, they might discouer from the sea a verie gallant and well towred cittie, that was called Tituhul, whereas the king hath continually in garrison tenne thousande souldiers, and is vnder the gouernement of the prouince of Chincheo.

They leaue the worshipping of one idol to worship another.

So the next day following wee came vnto a watch towre, which was situated vppon a rocke at the entrie into a bay, who had discouered our shippe, and knew the standart or flagge to bee the kings: and made a signe vnto seuen shippes which were on the other side of the point, which was part of a company ordeined for to keepe and defende the cost, which were more then foure hundred. Straightwayes the captaine of the seuen shippes came foorth to knowe what we were, and what chanced shalbe told you in this chapter following.

CHAP. XII.

The captaine Omoncon is come to the prouince of Chincheo, but before he doth come vnto an anker, he dooth passe some trouble with another captaine of the sea.

This captaine Omoncon, when he saw that the ships did make towards him, hee cast about his shippe and passed alongst by the watch towre, making his way towards the towne, where he was a natural subiect and nigh at hand, being but two leagues from the point: which being perceiued by the generall of that bay which was in a redinesse, who imagined by his working that it should be some shippe of euill demeanor and their enimies, without any delation hee issued forth from behind the point with three ships, that did row with oares verie swift: and gaue them chase, cutting them off from their pretence: and when he came nigh vnto them, hee shot at them to make them to amaine: the which Omoncon would not doo, for that hee supposed (as afterwards hee did confesse) that hee should be some man of little estimation, and not the generall of the coste. But as he drew nigher vnto him, hee did know him by the flagge he bare on the sterne in the foist[1] wherein he was himselfe with his souldiers, and straightwayes caused to amaine[2] his sailes, and tarried for him. The generall did the like, and stayed behinde, sending a boate for to bring the captaine vnto him, and to declare what he was and from whence he came. Omoncon did forthwith imbarke himself into his boate without any resistance, but rather with feare that hee should be punished for that hee did flie from him. The generall, when hee saw him, did straightwayes know him (and in that the fathers did vnderstand by signes), hee was verie glad of his comming, and gaue him good entertainment.

[1] A small craft: from Fusta—*Span.*
[2] To let fall or lower at once: from Amainar—*Span.*

This generall was a goodly man of person, and was verie well apparelled, and did sit in a chaire in the sterne of his ship, the which was all couered to keepe away the sunne: hee commanded the Captaine Omoncon to sit downe by him vpon the hatches, without chaire or any other thing, who did obey him, although first hee did refuse it with great modestie, as not woorthie to haue that honour, which was not esteemed a little. After that he was set, he gaue him to vnderstand in effect of all his voyage and successe, and in what extremitie he left Limahon, and also howe that hee carried with him the friers and other Spaniards, which went to carrie the newes, and to intreate of peace with the vizroy of Aucheo: vnto whome, and vnto the gouernor of Chincheo, hee carried presents, sent from the gouernor and generall of the fielde of the Ilands Philippinas. When the generall had heard this relation, he commanded the boate to returne and to bring them before him, that hee might see what manner of men they were of person and the vse of apparell, and likewise to satisfie himselfe of other desires that came into his mind by that which Omoncon had saide of them. The fathers and their companions did obey the commandement, and did imbarke themselues in the boate (although it were with some feare), and came vnto the shippe, whereas the generall receiued them with great curtesie after his fashion, and shewed them a good countenance, and tokens that he very much reioyced to see them and the vse of their apparell they ware. But after awhile hee commanded that they shoulde bee put vnder hatches, which was the occasion to augment the feare they conceiued when they were sent for: and the more when they saw that they were commanded to be shut vp in a cabin with the interpreter that they brought with them.

This being done, they were in great care howe they might vnderstand the generals pretence; and at a close doore that was before the cabin whereas they were, uppon a sudden they might see that all those that were in the shippe did arme themselues in great haste, and the Captaine Omoncon amongst them: then they heard bases and harqubus shot, with a great noise of people, which did verie much alter them: in such sort that they looked euery moment when they should come and cut of their heads. Whilst that our people were in this agonie and great feare, Omoncon considered of them and of the charge that he had to bring them thither: therewith he sent one of his seruants to giue them to vnderstand of all that they had heard and seene, wherewith they did quiet themselues, and put away al the feare that they had conceiued with their suddain putting downe in the cabine, and the shooting off of those peeces. The which the better to giue you to vnderstand, I will first declare vnto you the occasion (and then after the rest). Limahon had not so soone taken his course towards the ilands, but straightwaies it was knowne in the kingdome of China: and the vizroy of Ochian, by the order that he had from the roiall counsell, did command all gouernors of such cities that were nigh vnto the coast, to dispatch away shipping for to go follow and seeke him, with aduertisement that hee who did accomplish this diligence with the first, should be very wel rewarded and esteemed, for that they feared that if the rouer should ioine with ye Castillas (for so they do cal the Spaniards in that country, of whom they haue had great notice), might thereby grow some great harme and inconuienence, which afterwards could not be well remedied: which was the occasion that they made the more haste, for that if it were possible to take him, or else to spoile his shipping before that he should come vnto the said ilands. In accomplishing of this commandement, the gouernor of Chincheo did prouide shipping, and did sende the captaine Omoncon with them: but yet he could not prouide them of souldiers and other necessaries till certaine daies after that he was gone foorth: so he went till hee came and met with the Spaniards, nigh vnto Buliano (as aforesaid).

They call the Spaniards Castilias.

About the same time the general of the bay that was there to defend the cost, did dispatch another ship for to enquire and know where the rouer was, and to bring relation therof, that straightwayes they might go and assalt him with all the whole armie. This ship was the fathers of Sinsay, he that was friend vnto the Castillas, who came in companie with the friers from the ilands (as it is said), and he went in the said ship for pilot; who, although hee went out of the port with great speede, yet with greater hast hee returned againe without mastes or yardes, for that they lost them in a great storme and torment that tooke them in the gulfe, whereas they thought to haue beene lost.

At the same time that the friers departed from Buliano to Pagansinan, being requested to come thither by the master of the field (as aforesaid), there was in the same port a ship of China, that came vnto the ilands to traficke; and being well informed of all things, as well in what extremity the Spaniards had the rouer, as also of ye going of Omoncon, and how that he carried vnto the firme lande the aforesaide friers and their companions. The said shippe departed in a morning very secretly, ten dayes before that Omoncon did make saile, and came to the firme land the saide ten daies before, and gaue notice thereof vnto the gouernor of all that they had vnderstood, as wel by relation as by sight; and how that ther came with Omoncon and the Spaniards, Sinsay, who was he that in al things touching Limahon was the dooer, and that whatsoeuer shall happen good in this relation, they ought to giue the praise and thanks vnto him, and not vnto Omoncon. This he spake for the good affection he had vnto Sinsay by way of friendship, for that he was of the same profession, a merchant.

The gouernour of the bay being verie desirous to haue the rewarde and thankes of the king, with occasion to say that the sonne of him whom he sent to follow and seeke Limahon was the chiefe and principall meanes of that good successe. Straight wayes, so soone as hee heard the newes of the shippe that ariued there tenne dayes before (as aforesaide), he commaunded sixe shippes to goe foorth of the baye to the sea, with order and commission to bring the ship to an anker in the sayd bay, and not to suffer him to go into any other place: and otherwise they could not, at least wayes, they would bring with them Sinsay, for that they would send him post vnto the uiceroy, for to declare vnto him all that had passed particularly. These sixe ships came verie nigh vnto that wherein was the generall aforesaid, at such time as our Spaniardes were with the generall, and they neuer could perceiue it, for that there were many in the baye, some going and some comming; but when that hee had discouered them, then he caused our people to be put vnder hatches because they should not be seene, and commanded those that were in the shippe to arme themselues for their defence if need required.

In the meane time that they made resistance with this ship, one of the sixe ships did borde that shippe wherein came Omoncon, pretending to take her, and beleeued to doo it with great ease. But it happened vnto them cleane contrarie, for that the souldiers that were within did defende their ship valiantly. Sinsay, with a very good will, would haue suffered the ship wherein his father came to haue carried away the other, if the souldiers of Omoncon would haue consented therunto. They did not only misse of their purpose, but also many of them were hurt in the attempting to enter the ship: the saide ship did fall aborde there whereas was their captaine Omoncon, who at that instant did call our Spaniardes in his shippe, out of the generalles shippe whereas they were; which was doone with such speede, that it was accomplished before any of the other ships could come vnto them, although they did procure it. Then did Omoncon arme himselfe to the warre, for to defend himselfe, his ship, and all that were therein, or to die there. The fryers and their companions, when they vnderstoode the cause of their strife and fighting, partly by suspition in that they had seene, as by that which Omoncon did sende them worde, did offer themselues vnto him, promising him to die with him if neede did so require, and requested him to appoint them what they should do, and they would accomplish it with a very good will. At this time all the ships were about that of Omoncon, who was not idle, but put foorth his artilerie for their defence, asking powder of the Spaniardes, for that they had little left: the generall did not depart from the shippe from the time that the Spaniardes went vnto him, neither did hee remooue out of his chayre, although all the rest that were in the ship were armed.

At this time the captayne of the sixe shippes of Chincheo did put himselfe in a boate and came towardes the shippe of Omoncon for to haue commoned with him; but he would not suffer them to come nigh, but shot at them, and caused them to depart against their willes, and called them all to naught from the poope of his shippe, with manie reprochfull woordes, saying that they came to steale the honour that hee with so great trauayle and perill had gotten. Then the generall, seeing that hee could not goe through with his purpose, hee determined to leaue him, and therewith to cast about with his shippes, and returned into the port of the baye from whence they came. This brought in his shippe a sonne of Sinsay, to giue occasion vnto his father for to come vnto him, and likewise his owne father, whome they did straightwayes put in prison, and his wife and mother: which is a thing commonly vsed in that countrie, the children to pay for their parentes, and to the contrarie, the parents for the children.

Sinsay, who feared the same, woulde not goe vnto his owne house till such time as he did carrie commandement from the uiceroy, for to deliuer out of prison those that were put there without desert: the which was granted by the uiceroy, with other fauours and great honour, as shall bee declared vnto you.

CHAP. XIII.

Omoncon doth disembarke himselfe with our Spaniardes in the port of Tansuso, and are verie well receiued by the justice, and made verie much of by the order of the Insuanto of that prouince.

Within a little while after that the captayne of the sixe shippes departed for Chincheo, Omoncon and his companie ariued at the port of Tansuso,[1] hard by, vpon Wednesday, in the euening, being the fift day of July. This Tansuso is a gallant and fresh towne, of foure thousand householders, and hath continually a thousand souldiers in garrison; and compassed about with a great and strong wall; and the gates fortified with plates of yron; the foundations of all the houses are of lime and stone, and the walles of lime and yearth, and some of bricke: their houses within very fairely wrought, with great courts, their streetes faire and brode, all paued. Before that Omoncon did come vnto an anker, they sawe all the souldiers and the people of the towne were gathered together vpon the rockes that were ioyning vnto the port, all armed readie vnto the battaile, amongst whom there was a principall captaine, and three more of his companions, that were sent him by the gouernor of Chincheo, whom they do call in their language Insuanto, who had vnderstanding of the comming of Omoncon and his companie by the ship (aforesaid) he sent them thither before, that in his name should entertain them and cherish them all that was possible. When the ship entred into the port, Omoncon did salute the towne with certain peeces of artilery, and discharged all his argubushes sixe times about,

[1] Ganhai.

and therewithal tooke in their saile and let anker fall. Then straightwaies the captaine whom the Insuanto had sent came abord the ship, who had expresse commission not to leaue the company of our people after that they were disembarked till such time as they came whereas he was, but to beare them companie, and to prouide them of all thinges necessarie: the which he did accomplish.

All these captaines and ministers of the king doo weare certaine ensignes for to be knowen from the common people, who are not permitted to weare any such; and they can not goe abroad in publike without the same, neyther will they if they might, for that by them they are obeyed and reuerenced, as well in the streetes as in any other place where they come: all such generally be called Loytias, which is as much to say in our language (gentlemen): the particular ensignes which they doo vse, bee broade wastes or girdles, embossed after diuerse manners; some of golde and siluer, some of the shell of a Turtuga or turtell, and of a sweete wood, and other some of iuerie; the higher estates hath them embrodered with pearles and precious stones, and their bunnets with two long eares, and their buskins made of satten and vnshorne ueluet, as we haue declared more at large in the first three bookes. *Ensignes to knowe the iustices.*

Then after, so soone as they were come to an anker in the port, the iustice did send them a license in writing for to come foorth of the shippe, as a thing necessarie, for that without it the waiters or guardes of the water side will not suffer them to put foote a land. This licence was written vpon a borde whited, and firmed by the iustice, whose charge it is to giue the licence. Then when they came a shoore, there were the souldiers that were appointed by the Insuanto in a readinesse to beare them companie, and did direct and leade them vnto the kinges houses of the sayde citie: the like hath euerie citie almost throughout all the kingdome, and there they did lodge them. These houses *The first landing of the fryers.*

are very great, and very wel wrought and gallant, with faire courtes belowe, and galleries aboue : they had in them stanges[1] or pondes of water, full of fish of sundrie sortes.

The Insuanto had giuen order vnto the iustice of Tansuso, wherein he had ordained what hee should giue them to eate, and all other things that should be done particularly by it selfe, without lacking of any thing, and appointed the captaine, that hee with his souldiers should not depart from them not a iot, but alwayes to beare them company whethersoeuer they went, and not to depart till he had farther order from him : in accomplishing whereof they remayned with them that night in the kings house. The iustice of the citie when that he had lodged them, went himselfe in person to the waters side, and caused all their stuffe to be vnladen out of the ship, and caused it to be carried with great care and diligence vnto the fryers whereas they were.

The people of the citie did presse very much to see these strangers, so that with the press, as also with the great heate, they were marueilously afflicted : which being perceiued by the iustice, he gaue order that they might bee eased of that trouble, and caused sergeants to keepe the doore, and their yeomen to make resistance against the people. Yet, notwithstanding, though they did not trouble them so much, they ranged about the house and clymed vpon the walles to procure to see them, as a rare thing, for that they came from countries so farre off, and apparelled verie different from that they do vse or otherwise haue seene. So when that the night was come, the iustice of the citie did make them a banket according vnto the fashion of the countrie : and it was in this manner following.

They were carried into a hall that was verye curiously wrought, wherein were many torches and waxe candles light, and in the middest therof was set for euerie one of the guests a table by himselfe, as is the vse and fashion of

The vse of their bankets.

[1] Evidently from Etang, *Fr.*, a pond.

that countrie (which more at large shalbe declared), euerie table had his couering of damaske or satten very well made, the tables were gallantly painted, without any table clothes, neither do they vse any, for they haue no neede of them, for that they do eate all their victualles with two little stickes made of golde and siluer, and of a marueilous odoriferous woode, and of the length of little forkes as they doo vse in Italy; with the which they doo feede themselues so clenly, that although their victuals be neuer so small, yet do they let nothing fall, neither foule their hands nor faces: they were set downe at these tables in verie good order and in gallant chayres, in such sort that although they were euerie one at his table by himselfe, yet they might see and talke one with an other; they were serued with diuerse sortes of cates, and very well dressed both of flesh and fish, as gamons of bacon, capons, geese, whole hennes, and peeces of beefe, and at the last many little baskets full of sweete meates made of sugar and marchpanes, all wrought very curiously. They gaue them wine of an indifferent colour and taste, made of the palme tree (whereof there is no other vsed in all that countrie), our Spaniardes did vse it, as that which was made of grapes. All the time that the supper indured, there was in the hall great store of musicke of diuers instruments, whereon they played with great consort, some one time and some another. The instruments which they commonly do vse are hoybuckes,[1] cornets, trompets, lutes, such as be vsed in Spaine, although in the fashion ther is some difference. There was at this banket (which indured a great while), the captaine that was ordained for their garde, and the captaine Omoncon and Sinsay. When supper was done, they were carried into very faire chambers, wheras were faire beddes, where they slept and eased themselues.

The next day following, in the morning, was brought vnto them their ordinarie victualles, and that in abundance, as

Wine of a palme tree.

---

[1] Hautboys?

well of flesh as of fish, fruits and wine, to be dressed vnto their owne content, and according vnto their manner: they would take nothing for the same, for so they were commanded by the Insuantes. This was brought vnto them euerie day so long as they were there, and in the way when as they went vnto Chincheo. The same day ariued a captaine of fortie ships in the same port, and as soone as hee was a shore, hee went straightwayes vnto the pallace for to see the strangers: who being aduertised of his comming, came foorth and receiued him at the pallace gate, where as was vsed betwixt them great courtesie. The captaine came with great maiestie, with his guarde of souldiers and mase bearers before him, with great musicke of hoybuckes, trumpets and drommes, and two whiffelers[1] or typp staues that made roome, putting the people aside: also there came with him two executors of iustice, or hangmen, hauing each of them in their handes a set made of canes, which is an instrument wherewith they doo whippe and punish offenders, and is so cruell that who soeuer doth receiue sixtie strokes with the same, although he be a verie stout man and strong hearted, yet it will kill him, for that hee is not able to abide it. They doo beate them vppon the thighes and calues of the legges, causing the offender or patient to lye downe vppon his breast or stomacke, and commande their heades and legges to be holden. The iudges, captaines, and loytias haue ordinarily these officers before them, for to beate such as will not goe out of the way when as they doo passe the streetes, and such as will not alight from their horse, or come out of their close chayres when they doo meete with them.

When this captayne came vnto the pallace gate whereas the father fryers and their companions did receiue him, he was brought on the shoulders of eight men verie richly apparelled, and he in a chayre wrought of iuorie and golde,

---

[1] One who plays on a whiffle or fife.

who stayed not till they came into the inner chamber, whereas he did a light from the chayre, and went straight vnder a cloth of estate, that was there ordinarily for the same purpose, and a table before him : there hee sate downe, and straightwaies arose vp, and standing he did receiue the strange guests, who did curtesie vnto him according vnto their fashion, which is to ioyne their handes together, and to stoope with them and their heads downe to the grounde : he gratified them againe with bowing his heade a little, and that with great grauitie. Within a little while after, he spake vnto them with great maiestie, bidding them welcome into his kingdome, being glad of their comming, saying that himselfe was come to see and cherish them, for that they should receiue no discontent, as y*e* proofe shal shew. These speeches being finished, there was brought foorth certain peeces of blacke silke of twelue vares[1] long a peece. And his officers did put on the fryers shoulders each of them two, which was for either shoulder one, and was brought about their bodies and girt therewith ; and the like was done in order vnto the Spanish souldiers, and vnto Omoncon and Sinsay, and to their interpreter. But vnto Omoncon and Sinsay was giuen vnto either of them a branch or nosegay made of siluer, which was set vpon their heads, which is accustomable honor that is done vnto such as haue done some great enterprise, or such like.

After that this ceremonie was done, they played vpon the instrumentes afore sayde, which came with the captayne. In the meane time of their musicke, there was brought foorth great store of conserues, marchpanes, and thinges made of sugar, and excellent good wine ; and so being on foot standing, hee caused them to eate, and he himselfe from the chayre whereas he sate did giue them to drinke euerie one in order, without rising vp, which is a ceremonie and token of great fauour and of loue.

[1] Yards, from Vara, *Span.*

This being done, hee arose from the chayre vnder the cloth of state, and went and sate downe in that which was brought on mens backes, and with declining of his head a little he departed out of the hall and out of the house, and went vnto his owne house, whereas by the counsell of Omoncon and Sinsay within an houre after they shoulde goe and visite him, the which they did: hee receiued them marueilously well and with great courtesie, who maruelled at his great maiestie and authoritie, for that Omoncon and Sinsay, when they did talke with him, were vpon their knees, and so did al the rest: yet that which they did see afterwardes done vnto the Insuanto and viceroy was much more.

He gaue them againe in his owne house a gallant banket, of diuerse sortes of conserues and fruits, and excellent wine of the palme tree, and did talke and reason with them in good sort, and was more familiar than at his first visitation, demanding of them many thinges in particular, and beholding their apparayle and garmentes, with showe of great content and reioycing.

CHAP. XIV.

The Spaniardes depart from Tansuso to visite the governour of Chincheo, who awaited their comming: where they sawe notable thinges by the way.

After that the fathers with their companions had remayned two dayes in the port of Tansuso, whereas they were marueilously well entertayned and feasted at the commaundement giuen by the Insuanto, as you haue heard, the third day they departed in the morning towardes Chincheo, whether they were commaunded to be carried with great speede and good intertainement.

At their going foorth of the towne they were accompanied with a great number of souldiers, both hargubushes and pikes, and before them a great noyse of trompets, drommes, and hoybuckes, till such time as they came vnto the riuers side, whereas was a brygandine prouided and made readie in all pointes to carrie them vp the riuer : all the streetes alongest whereas they went, there followed them so much people that it was innumerable, and all to see them. So when they were embarked, and which was done with great speede to auoyd the presse of the people, there came vnto them the captaine of the fortie ships, of whom wee made mention in the chapter past, with three brygandines, one wherein he was himselfe, and was marueilously well trimmed, and in the other two were souldiers that did beare him companie. As soone as he came vnto them, hee straight wayes entred into the brygandine whereas the religious men were with three Spaniardes, and brought with him great store of conserues, and made them a gallant banket, the which did indure so long as he was with them, which was the space of rowing two long leagues, in which time their pleasure was such that they thought it but a quarter of a league. From thence he departed from them and returned, but left many thinges behinde him for their comfort in their iourney, and made great offers, with an outwarde showe that it was a griefe vnto him to depart from out of their companie.

All alongest the ryuers whereas they went was seated with villages, verie gallant and fresh, both on the one side and on the other. Some of them did content our people verie much, who asked the names howe they were called, and the captaynes answered them and sayde, that those were villages that did not deserue the honour of a name ; but when you doo come there whereas the king is, you shall see cities that it shall be a woorthie thing to knowe their names ; the which townes haue three and foure thousande souldiers, such as in Europe are esteemed for reasonable cities.

At the end of the two leagues, there whereas the captaine did leaue the companie of our Spaniardes in the riuer, they came vnto a great baye, whereas was at an anker a fleete of more than a hundreth and fifte shippes, men of warre, whose generall was this captaine whom we haue spoken of, that did beare the fryers and the rest companie. At such time as the fleete did discouer them they began to salute them, as well with great peeces of artillerie as with hargubushes and other kinde of pastimes, which commonly they do vse at such times: and that is doone by the commandement of their generall.

At such times as they had made an ende of shooting and other pastimes, then did he take his leaue of them with the ceremonie aforesaide, and went out of the brygandine whereas the fryers were and went into his owne, which carryed him vnto the admiral, wherein he imbarked himself. Our Spaniardes, after his departure, did trauaile vp the riuer more than three leagues, hauing continually, both on the one side and on the other, verie many and faire townes, and full of people. In the ende of the three leagues they went a lande halfe a league from the towne of Tangoa,[1] whereas straightwayes all such things as they carried with them were taken vpon mens backs, and carried it vnto the towne before them, whereas they were tarrying their comming, for to giue them great entertaynment. At their going a shore, they founde prepared for the two religious men little chayres to carrie them vppon mens backes, and for the souldiers and the rest of their companions was ordayned horse. The fathers did refuse to be carried, and would haue gone a foot, for that the way was but short and pleasant, full of greene trees; and, againe, for humilitie, refusing to be carried in so rich chaires, and vppon mens backes of so good a vocation as they seemed to be. But Omoncon and the other captaine would not consent thereunto, saying, that it was the order giuen by the Insuanto, and that they could not by any

[1] Tong-gan.

meanes breake, but performe in all points, or else to be cruelly punished for the same—I meane such captaines as had the charge for to garde and beare them companie—and that no excuse could serue them; and, againe, that it was conuenient so to be done, for y^t from that time the Chinos should respect them and vnderstande that they were principal persons, for y^t they were carried vpon mens backes as they do their loytias.

The fathers obeyed their reasons, and entred into the chayres, and were carried with eight men a peece, and the other their companions with foure men a peece, according vnto the order giuen by the gouernor. Those that carried the chaires, did it with so good a will, y^t there was striuing who should first lay hands to them. This towne of Tangoa hath three thousand souldiers, and is called in their language Coan: at the entring in, it hath many gardens and orchards, and a streete, where through they carried the Spaniards vnto their lodging, they affirmed it to be halfe a league long; and all the streete whereas they went it was full of bordes and stalles, where on was laide all kinde of merchandise, very curious, and things to be eaten, as fresh fish and salt fish of diuers sortes, and great abundance of foule and flesh of al sorts, fruits and greene herbs, in such quantitie that it was sufficient to serue such a citie as Siuell is. The presse of people was so much in the streets, that although there were many typstaues, and souldiers that did make way wheras they went, yet could they not passe but with great difficultie. So they were brought vnto the kings house, which was very great, marueilously wel wrought with stone and brick, and many halles, parlers, and chambers; but none aboue, but all belowe. So soone as they were afoote, there was brought from the captaine or iustice of the towne, whom they doo call Ticoan, a message, bidding them welcome, and therewith a present, which was great store of capons, hens, teales, ducks, geese, flesh of four or fiue sorts, fresh fish, wine, and fruits of diuers sorts, and of so great quantitie that it was sufficient for two hundreth men. All the which they would haue giuen for a little coole aire, by reason that it was than very hoat wether; and againe the great number of people y^t came thether to see them did augment it the more.

So in the euening the two Spanish souldiers went forth into the streets to walk abrode, and left the two fryers within their lodging, vnto whom afterwardes they did giue intelligence of all things that they had seene, which did cause great admiration: the wall of the towne was very brode, and wrought with lyme and stone, full of loope holes and watch towers. And as they passed through the streetes there came foorth of a house a very honest man as it seemed, who was very well apparelled, and stayed them, for that in the same house there were certaine dames, principall personages, that did see them a farre off, and not content therewith, they did request them with great curtesie for to enter into the house that they might the better see them: the which they did straightwaies accomplish, and entring in they were brought into a court, whereas was set chayres for them to sit downe, and the ladies were there a little from them beholding them with great honestie and grauitie. Then a little after they sent them a banket, with marchpanes and sweet meates made of sugar, which they did eate without any curiositie, and dronke after the same. The banket being done, they made signes and tokens vnto them that they receiued great content with their sight, and that they might depart when y^t their pleasure was; the which they did after y^t that they had made great curtesies, with thanke for their friendship receiued of both parts.

So after they had taken their leaue they went to see a house of pleasure y^t was hard by ye town wall, wrought vpon the water, with verie faire galleries and open lodges for to banket in, made of masons worke, and therein many tables finely painted, and round about it sesterns of water wherein was store of fish, and ioyning vnto them tables of very faire alabaster, all of one stone, and the least of them was of eight spannes long: and rounde about them were brookes of running water, that gaue a pleasant sounde in the meane time they were banketting, and nigh thereunto many gardynes full of all sortes of flowers. And a little from that place they sawe a bridge all of masons worke, and the stones verie well wrought and of a mightie biggnesse; they measured some of them that were twentie and two and twentie foote long and fiue foote brode, and seemed vnto them that it was a thing impossible to be layde there by mans handes. Of this bignesse, yea and bigger, they did see layde vppon manie other bridges, in the discourse of their voyage going to Chincheo and Aucheo. In this towne they tarried and rested themselues all that night, marueiling verie much at that which they had seen. The next day in the morning, when they were vp and readie, they found in the house all thinges in a readinesse and in verie good order for their departure, as well their little chayres[1] and horse, as for men to carrie their stuffe and apparell, which did not a little make them to marueile, how that euerie one of them with a waster[2] vpon their shoulders, did diuide their burden in two partes, sixe roues before and sixe roues behinde, and did trauaile with the same with so great ease and swiftnes that the horse could not indure with them. They went vnto the Ticoan his house, he who sent them the present ouer night, to giue him thankes for his courtesie, and to take their leaue of him. They found him with great maiestie, but yet gaue them

---

[1] A chariot. In "The Squyer of Low Degree," (see Ellis's "Specimens of Early English Poetry), occur the lines:

"To morrow ye shall on hunting fare,
And ride my daughter in a *chare*."

[2] A waster is more properly a cudgel: it is here evidently used for a pole.

great and good entertainment, and craued pardon at their hands, if that he did not giue them the entertainement and courtesie as they deserued. He did likewise put vpon each of them two peeces of silke, in the same order as the gouernour of Tansuso did. So when they had surrendred vnto him thankes, they tooke their leaue and departed from Chincheo, whereas was the Insuanto or gouernor, by whose order was showed vnto them all the courtesie as you haue hearde.

CHAP. XV.

The Spaniardes doo prosecute their iourney to Chincheo, and seeth many notable thinges by the way.

From this towne of Tangoa vnto Chincheo, is thirteene leagues, and so plaine way that it giueth great content to trauaile it. In all the waye, they could not see one spanne of ground but was tilled and occupied. The like they doo saye is of all the grounde that is in the whole kingdome: it is full of people, and the townes one so neere to another, that almost you can not iudge them to be maine townes, but one; for that there was but a quarter of a league distant one towne from another, and it was tolde vnto them, that in all the prouinces of the kingdome, it is populared in the same order. All their ground they till is watered, which is the occasion of the fruitefulnesse thereof, so that they doo gather fruite all the yeare long, and our Spaniardes did see in all places whereas they came, that they were gathering of rice, some newe sprung up, some with eares, and some rype. They doo plough and till their ground with kine, bufalos, and bulles, which are verie tame, and although they be great, yet be their hornes but of a spanne long, and turning backwards to the tayle, in such sort that they can not do any hurt or harme with them; they do gouerne them with a corde, that is made fast to a ring that is in their nose, and in like sort do they gouerne the bufanos.[1] They doo feede them commonly in the fieldes of rice, for that they have no other grasinges, and all the time that they are feeding, a boy doth ride on euerie one of them to disturbe them, that they doo no harme therein, but to eate the weedes and grasse that doo grow in the rice. In this prouince, and all the rest of the fifteene in that kingdome, they gather much wheate, and excellent good barley, peese, borona,[2] millo,[3] frysoles,[4] lantesas,[5] chiches,[6] and other kindes of graines and seedes, whereof is great abundance, and good cheape. But the chiefest thing that they do gather, and a victuall that is most vsed amongest them and the borderers there aboutes is rice.

All the hie waies are couered with the shadowe of verie faire orchardes, which do garnish it verie much, and they are planted in verie good order; and amongest them there are shoppes, whereas is solde all manner of fruites, to the comfort of all such as doo trauaile by the way, which is an infinite number, some on foote, some on horsebacke, and others in little chayres. Their waters by the hie waies are verie good and light, although the wether, at that time, was verie hoat, especially at noone time; yet was the water of their welles and fountaynes verie coole. The same day, when they had trauayled halfe way, they saw a farre off comming marching towardes them in verye good order, a squadron of souldiers, which, at the first, caused them to maruaile, and to be a fraide, till such time as they drewe nigher; it was tolde vnto them, that it was the Captayne of the Garde vnto the Insuanto, or Governour of Chincheo,

---

[1] Misspelt for buffaloes.
[2] A sort of grain, resembling maize or Indian corn.
[3] Millet.   [4] Kidney beans.   [5] Lentils.   [6] Dwarf peas.

who came by his order to receiue them, with foure hundred
souldiers, verie well armed with pickes and hargubushes, and
well apparelled. So soone as the captaine came vnto them,
he was mounted on a bay horse, but of small stature, as they,
for the most part, bee in all that prouince; hee alighted, and
came vnto the fathers and his companions (who likewise did
alight from their little chayres), and did salute the one the
other with great courtesie. And the captayne tolde them,
how that the gouernour did sende him with those souldiers
for to receive him, and to beare him companie, and howe
that hee was in the citie tarrying their comming, with great
desire to see them; and commaunded that, with all speede
possible, they should shorten the way.

The captaine came verie well apparelled, with a chayne of
golde about his necke; a man of a good audacitie and vnderstanding. Harde vnto his stirryp hee had a page that went
with him, and carried a great tira sol, made of silke, that did
shadowe him all over. The bunnett that this captaine did
weare, was like vnto them that before they had seene others
weare; hee had before him great musicke of trompets and
hoybuckes, whereon they played in great concorde. This
captaine, with his foure hundreth souldiers, did continually
garde them, till they came vnto the citie of Chincheo, and
never departed from them a iot; the which was done more
for pompe, and to showe their maiestie, then of necessitie;
for that although the people are infinite and without number,
yet do they weare no weapons, for that they are commanded
by the lawe of the countrie to the contrarie, vpon paine of
death, of what state or degree soever he be; but onely the
souldiers, such as are in euery towne for the garde thereof,
and the garrisons that the king hath continually readie to
come foorth, when that any occasion shall serue.

In this hie way continually, there went and came manye
packe horses, laden with marchandice and other thinges;
but the most parts of them were mules. The hie wayes are

marginalia: A thing to keepe away the sunne.

marginalia: The people of the coun- trie weare no weapons, but the souldiers.

verie brode, that twentie men may ride together on a ranke, and one not hinder an other, and are all paued with great stones, and they say that the wayes throughout all the other prouinces be in the same order, and was done by a king of that countrie, who spent vpon the same a great part of his treasure. And it seemeth to be true, for that our Spaniards trauelling in that countrie, ouer high and mightie mountaines, yet did they finde the waies plaine, in such sort as hath been told you.

CHAP. XVI.

Our Spaniardes arived at the citie of Chincheo, whereas they were received and lodged, and what they sawe in that citie.

Vpon a Saterday, being the eleuenth of July, came our Spaniards vnto the citie of Chincheo, four houres before it was night. This citie is of the common sorte in that kingdome, and may haue seuentie thousande householdes. It is of great traficke, and well prouided of all things, for that the sea is but two leagues from it: it hath a mightie riuer running alongest by it, downe into the sea, by which is brought by water and carried downe all kinde of marchandice. There is a bridge ouer the sayde riuer, which is supposed to bee the fayrest that is in all the worlde; it hath a drawe bridge to serue in time of warres, or for any other necessitie: the bridge is eight hundreth paces long, and all wrought with stones of two and twentie foote long, and five foote broade, a thing greatly to bee marueiled at. At the entrie thereof, there were manie armed souldiers readie to fight, who, when they came within hargubush-shoote, did salute them in verie good order. There was nigh vnto the sayde bridge, in the riuer, riding at an anker, more than a thou-

<small>Chincheo hath seuentie thousand housholds.</small>

A thousand ships in one riuer. sande shippes of all sortes, and so great a number of boates and barkes, that all the riuer was couered, and euerie one full of people, that had entred into them for to see the Castillas, for so they did call the Spaniardes in that countrie, for the streetes in the suburbes nor in the citie could not hold them, the number was so great; yet their streets are as broade as our ordinarie streetes in anye citie in all Spaine.

This citie is compassed with a strong wall, made of stone, and is seuen fadam hie, and foure fadam broade, and vpon the gates many towers, wherein is placed their artilerie, *They haue no vse of castles.* which is all their strength, for that they doo not vse in their kingdome strong castels as they doo in Europe. The houses of the citie are all built after one sorte and fashion, but faire, *Earth quaks in this countrey.* and not verie hie, by reason of the earth quakes, which are ordinarily in that countrey.

All the streetes (but especially that wherein they passed at their comming thether), haue, on the one side and on the other, sheddes, vnder the which are shoppes, full of riche *Rich marchandice.* marchandice, and of great value, and verie curious. They have, in equal distance the one from the other, many trium-*Triumphant arches.* phant arches, which doo set out the streetes verie much, and is vsed in euerie principall streete thoroughout all the kingdome, in the which they have excellent market-places, whereas is to bee bought all things that you will desire to be eaten, as well of fish as of fleshe, fruites, herbes, comfits, conserues, and all thinges so good cheape, that it is almost bought for nothing.

Their victualles are verie good, and of great substance; their hogges flesh, whereon they doo feede much, is so holsome and good as the mutton in Spaine. The fruites that wee did see, some were like vnto them we haue in Spaine and others neuer the like seene by vs afore, but of an excellent taste and sauour. But in especiall one kinde of fruite, which is bigger than a muske million, but of the same fashion, but of maruellous, excellent, and precious victuall, and pleasant to be eaten; a kinde of plummes, that is of a gallant taste, and neuer hurteth anie bodie, although they eate neuer so manie, a thing prooued by our Spaniardes manie times. The streete that they came in at was so full of people, that if a graine of wheate had beene throwne amongst them, it would scarce haue fallen to the grounde, and although they were carried in little chayres, vpon men's backes, and the captaine (of whom we speake of) before them making way, yet were they a great while before they could passe the streete, and be brought vnto a great house, which was a couent, wherein dwelt religious men of that countrie: thether they were brought and lodged, beeing verie wearie of the presse of people, that did trouble them verie much, with desire to take their ease.

CHAP. XVII.

The gouernor of Chincheo doth call the Spaniards before him, and sheweth vnto them the ceremonies that they must vse to have audience.

The same day that they came into the cittie (as aforesaide), was a good while before night, with more desire to take rest, and ease themselues of their iourney, and of the trauell they had in the streets, by reason of the great number of people that came to see them, then to make any visitation that night; but the Insuanto, or gouernor of the cittie, did send, and commanded that forthwith they shoulde go vnto his house, for that hee had great desire to see them, the which they did more for necessitie of the time, then for any good will. They went forth from their lodging on foote, whether it was for that the gouernor's house was neere hande, or else peradventure at his commandment, which they could not well understande, but did as the captaine that guarded them did commande. In the midst of the streete, wheras was no lesse number of people then in the other wherby they entred into the citie, they met with a loytia that came to entertain them with great maiestie, and had carried before him manie banners, mase bearers, and tipstaves, and others which carried settes or whips, which they did traile after them, made fast vnto long stickes, which were the executioners, the which doo go alwayes making of way, parting the people before the loytias, as you haue hearde. The maiestie and company wherewith he came was so great, that they verely did beleeue him to be the Insuanto: but being certified, they vnderstoode that it was one of his counsailers that came from the gouernor's home to his own house, which was in the same street whereas hee met with them. This counsailor was carried in a chaire of ivory, garnished with gold and with curtines of cloth of gold, and on them the king's arms, which are certaine serpents knotted togither (as hath beane tolde you). But when he came right against the Spaniards, without any staying, he made a signe with his head, and commanded that they should returne backe againe vnto his house, which was hard by; the captains did straightways obey his commandment, and returned with them. The counsailor entred into his house, which was verie faire; he had in it a faire court, and therein a gallant fountaine and a garden. After him entred the Spaniards all alone, the rest remained without in the street at the loytia's commandment. He entertained them with verie good words of semblance, and said in conclusion that they were welcome into that kingdome, with many other wordes of curtesie: vnto the which they answered with the same curtesie, with signes and by their interpreter that they carried with them. This loytia commaunded a banquet to bee brought foorth, and wine to drinke. He began first both to eate and drinke. Then hee commanded to call in the captaine, vnto whome was giuen the charge to beare them companie, and did chide with him verie sharpely and seuerely, because he did carrie them on foote (they coulde not vnderstande whether it were doone for a policie or of a trueth, although the effectes wherewith hee did chide seemed of a trueth); hee straightwayes commanded two rich chayres to bee brought foorth for to carrie the fathers, and to giue vnto their companions horses; the which being done he willed them to go and visite the gouernor, who did tary their comming, and that another time at more leasure he would see and visite them.

They followed their way all alongst the streete, which seemed vnto them to be more fairer then the other wherein they entered, and of more fairer houses and triumphant arkes; and also the shoppes that were on the one side and on the other, to bee better furnished with richer thinges then the others, in so ample sort, that what therewith, as also the great number of people which they sawe, they were so amased, that they were as people from themselues, thinking it to be a dreame. To conclude, after they had gone a good while in that streete, delighting their eies with newe thinges neuer seene of them before, they came into a great place whereas were many souldiers in good order with their hargabushes, pickes, and other armour in a redinesse, apparelled all in a liuerie of silke with their ancients displayed. At the end of this place was there a very faire and sumpteous pallace, the gate was wrought of mason's worke of stone, very great and full of figures or personages, and aboue it a great window with an iron grate al guilt; they were carried within the gates, the souldiers and the people, which were without number, remained without and coulde not be auoyded but with great difficultie. When they were within the first court, there came forth a man very well apparelled and of authoritie, and made signes with his hande vnto them that brought the Spaniards, that they should carrie them into a hal that was vpon the right hand, the which was straightwayes done. The hall was very great and faire, and at the end ther of there was an altar, whereon was many idols, and all did differ the one from the other in their fashion; the altar was rich and very curiously trimmed with burning lampes; the aultar cloth was of cloth of gold and the fruntlet of the same.

After a while that they had beene there whereas the idols were, there came a seruant from the gouernor, and said vnto them in his behalfe, that they should sende vnto him the interpreter, for that hee woulde talke with him, and tell him some things that they ought to obserue if they would haue any audience of him; they straightwayes commanded him to go. And the gouernor said vnto him that hee should aduise the fathers and the rest of his companions, that if they would talke and treate of such businesse as they came for, that it must be done with the same ceremonie and respect as the nobles of that prouince do vse to talke with him, which is vppon their knees (as afterwards they did see manie times vsed); if not that they shoulde depart vnto the house whereas they were lodged, and there to tarrie the order that shoulde bee sent from the vizroy of Aucheo. The Spaniards, when they hearde this message, there was amongst them diuers iudgementes and opinions, striuing amongst themselues a good while; but yet in conclusion, the religious fathers whome the gouernour of the ilandes had ordeined and sent as principalles in this matter, and whose iudgemente they shoulde followe, saide that they ought to accept the condition, seeing that by no other meanes they coulde not come vnto that they pretended, and not to leaue it off for matters of small importance, for that therein they make no offence vnto God, and it may bee a meane vnto the conuerting of that mightie kingdome, whome the divell maketh reckoning to bee his owne, and not nowe to leaue it off, but rather to procure all meanes that may be, as they had began to do;

and seeing that it is no offence vnto God, as aforesaide, neither sent as ambassadors from the king of Spaine, I doo not know to the contrarie, but that we may consent vnto the will of the Insuant, and in especiall being a thing so commonly vsed in that countrie. This opinion and iudgement was followed, although the souldiers that were with them were of a contrarie opinion. So they sent answere vnto the gouernor with the said interpreter, that they will observe their accustomed ceremonies and will do all that he will commande them according vnto the custome of the countrie: otherwise they could not be permitted to intreat of such things, wherefore they came thither from farre countries and with so great travell.

CHAP. XVIII.

The Spaniards haue a louing and fauorable audience of the gouernor of Chincheo, to whom they do giue the letters they brought from the Ilands Philippinas.

When that the Insuanto understood that the Spaniards woulde enter with the reuerence accustomed, and in such order as was declared vnto them, hee straightwaies commanded that they should come into the hall whereas he was, which was a thing to be seene, as well for the bignes as for the riches that was in it, the which I do let passe because I would not be tedious. The Spaniards were carried foorth out of that hall whereas they were first, and after that they had passed the court whereas they came in, they entred into another hall as bigge as the first, whereas were many souldiers with their weapons in their hands, in verie good order and richly apparelled, and next vnto them were many tipstaves and sergeants, with different ensignes or badges, all apparelled with long robes of silke, garded and embroidered with gold, and euery one of them had a helme on his heade, some of siluer and other some of tynne guilt ouer, which was a gallant thing to see; all had long haire and dyed yealow, which hong downe behind their eares vpon their backes; they were placed in very good order, and made a lane that the Spaniards might passe thorough: then they came into a gallerie, which was ioyning vnto a chamber where the gouernor was, and there they heard such a noise of instruments of diuerse sorts, which indured a good while, and was of so great melodie that it seemed vnto them that they neuer before heard the like, which caused vnto them great admiration to see so great maiestie amongst gentiles. When the musicke was ended they entered into the hall aforesaid, and had not gone many steps, when as they met with the counsailer that met with them in the streete aforesaid, and with him other two of his companions, all on foote and bare headed before the gouernor, and their ensignes of maiestie left off: which is generally vsed in all the kingdome, the inferior to make anie shewe when that hee is before his superior. Then they made signes vnto them for to kneele downe, for that the Insuanto was nigh at hande in a rich tower, vnder a canopie of great riches, and did represent so great maiestie as the king himselfe: he did entertaine them with tokens of great loue and humanitie, and tolde them by their interpreter that they were verie well welcome, and that he did greatly reioyce to see them, with many other words of great favour. This gouernor was a man of goodly person, well fauored, and of a merrie countenance, more then any that they had seene in all that countrie. He caused to be put upon the shoulders of the fathers and of the souldiers that were with him, euery one of them, two peeces of silke, which was crossed about them like skarfes, and likewise to either of them a branch of siluer: the like curtesie he did vnto the captaine Omoncon and vnto Sinsay, and

Great maiestie.

commanded to give vnto all their seruants euery one of them a mantle of cotton painted. This ceremonie is vsed in that kingdome vnto al captaines and other men that haue done some valiant exploit (as we haue tolde you before). This being doone, the fathers did giue vnto him the letters which they carryed from the gouernor and generall of the fielde, and a note of the present that was sent him, crauing pardon for that it was so smal, but time and oportunitie would not serue as then to sende vnto him a thing of greater price and valor; certifying him, that if the friendship which they pretended did go forwards, and come to be established, that then all things should be amended and amplified. He answered vnto their profers with words of great fauor, and made signes vnto them to arise and to go and take their rests there whereas they were lodged; the which they did, and founde all thinges in verie good order and well furnished, as well of beddes as all other necessaries, which was done by the commandement of the gouernour. Before they departed out of the pallace, the captaine of the guard did carrie them vnto his lodging, which was within the court, and there he made them a banquet with conserues, and fruits in abundance: the which being doone, hee and other gentlemen of the pallace did beare them companie vntill they came to their lodgings, which they greatly desired, for that they were wery of their iourney, and also with the trouble of the great presse of people that pressed on them in the streets and otherwise for to see them: the which captaine of the guard did appoint a company of souldiers for to gard them both night and day, the which was done more for maiesty then for necessitie or securitie of their persons. They had a steward appointed to prouide them and all their company of all thinges necessarie, and that in abundance, and not to take of them any thing, which was giuen by particular commandement by the gouernour.

ing the inuiting for the next day, the which was giuen them, and accomplished in this forme following.

The next day when they went vnto the pallace, which was at dinner time, they were caried into a hall that was below in the second court, whereas were many chaires of velvet and tables that were painted with their frontals before; they had no table clothes on them, for that they doo not vse any in that countrie, as hath beene told you in the first part of this historie, neither is it needfull for their manner of feeding. In the first chaires they caused the friers to sit downe, euery one at a table by himselfe, and each of them other sixe tables, placed in order, compassing rounde like a circle; then were the Spanish souldiers set in the same manner, and each of them had fiue tables, and next vnto them the captaine of the guard belonging vnto the gouernor, and two other captaines, and euerie one of them had three tables; for that it is the custome of that countrie to make a difference in the qualitie of the guests by the number of the tables. All these were placed in circle or compasse (as aforesaide) that they might see one another. In the midest betwixt them there was a round compasse whereas was represented a comedie with much pastime, and indured all the dinner time, and a good while after. There was also great store of verie good and excellent musicke, accompanied with gallant voyces, also iesters, with puppets and other thinges of great pastime, to drive the time away.

On the first table was set, to euery one of the guestes, little baskets wrought with golde and siluer wyre, full of sweete meates made of sugar, as marchpanes, castels, pitchers, pots, dishes, dogges, bulles, elephants, and other things verie curious, and all guilt: besides this there were many dishes full of flesh, as capons, hennes, geese, teales, gamons of bacon, peeces of beef, and other sortes of flesh wherewith all the tables were replenished, sauing that whereat they did sit to dine, which was replenished with victuals that was dressed (for all the other was rawe), and was of so great aboundance that there was at times more than fiftie dishes, and they were serued with great curiositie. They had wine of diuers sorts, and of that which they doo make in that countrie of the palme tree, but of so great excellencie, that they founde no lacke of that which was made of grapes. The dinner endured foure houres, and according vnto the aboundance and diuersitie they had in victuals, it might have indured eight houres, for it was in so good order that it might haue beene giuen vnto any prince in the world.

Their seruants and slaues that they brought with them at the same time, did dine in another hal nigh vnto the same, with so great abundance as their masters. When dinner was done, the gouernor commanded the people to come vnto him, with whom he did talke and comon with great friendship and good conuersation, and would not consent that they shoulde kneele downe, neither to bee bare headed. So after that hee had made vnto them tokens of friendshippe, and detained them a while in demaunding of many thinges, lastly he told them that there was an order come from the vizroy of Aucheo, that they shuld go thither with great speede, so that it did require that they shoulde depart the next day following, for the which they were veri glad and ioyfull, for that they had great desire the one to see the other; and againe with him they might treate and comon touching their comming into that countrie, and for what intent, and for all other things needful, for that he was a man fit for their purpose, and one wellbeloved of the king. So hee tooke his leaue of vs with great friendship and curtesie, who did surrender the same after our custome, putting of our cappes, and making reuerence, for the which hee made shewe that it greatly contented him.

At their going foorth out of the hall they found the captaine that did dine with them, and with him many other gentlemen that tarried their comming for to beare them company vnto their lodging; going before them many seruants, that did carie the raw meate that was vpon the other tables ouer and aboue that which they did eate on, the which was done for great maiestie, and a ceremony verie much vsed in that kingdom, so many times as they do make any banquet.

So when they came vnto their lodging they founde that the Insuanto had sent them a very good present, in the which was for euery one of them four peeces of silke, and counting chestes with other thinges, and certaine painted mantels for the seruants and slaues. So after they had taken their leaue of the captaines and gentlemen that did beare them companie home, they beganne with great ioy to put all thinges in order for their iourney the next day following.

CHAP. XXI.

The Spaniards departe from the citie of Chincheo, and commeth to that of Aucheo, whereas the vizroy did tarrie their comming.

The next day in the morning, before that the Spaniards were stirring, there was within the house all thinges necessary for their iourney, as well of little chaires as of horses and men for to carrie them and their stuffe, the which they did with so good a will (as aforesaid) that they did fall out and striue amongst themselues who should be the first that should receiue their burthen. So all things being in good order they departed, hauing in their companie the same captaine and souldiers, that vnto that time had beene their guard, vntil they came vnto the cittie of Aucheo whereas the vizroy was. This iourney was vnto them ioyfull, as well for to entreate of matters touching their comming, and to be resolued what they shuld do, as also to depart out of Chincheo whereas they passed much trouble, by reason of the great number of people that came for to see them, who neuer would be satisfied, and y^t was in such extremity that some dayes at tenne of the clocke in the night the streetes round about their lodging were full of people, and onely to see them, which caused great trouble and heate with their rumor and presse amongst them. This day, by reason they vnderstood that they should depart, the prease and multitude of the people was so great, that although they had tip staues before them to beate the people away and to make roome, yet was it almost night before they could get out of the citie, so that they were constrained to remaine in a towne there hard by all night, where as by the commandement of the gouernour they were verie well lodged, and their supper made readie in verie good order, as it was in seauen dayes together, till such time as they came vnto Aucheo, without taking for the same, or for anie other thing necessarie for their sustentation, anie price or value. There went continuallie before them a post with a prouision from the gouernour, written in a great borde wherein was declared who they were and from whence they came, and commanding that there should bee prouided for them all things necessarie in abundance, vppon the king's cost, which was the occasion that so much people came for to see them, that in the high waies they were many times disturbed; so with great trouble, the thirde day they came vnto a citie which was called Megoa,[1] which was sometimes the head gouernement, the which was of fortie thousand housholds, but a great part thereof was dispeopled; the occasion thereof they told vs (and was), that about thirtie yeares past the Iaponese, who brought for their guides three Chinos, who doo nowe dwell in Manilla and are become Christians, and came vpon that cittie (to reuenge themselues of an iniurie that was done vnto them), the which they put in execution with so great secrecie and policie, that they made themselues lords of the citie without any daunger or hurt vnto themselues; for that fiftie Iapones, men fit for that purpose, did apparell

[1] Hing-hoa.

themselues in Chinos apparell without being knowne, and came vnto a gate of the cittie, whereas the souldiers that had the charge thereof were voide of all suspition of any enimies that woulde come, which was the occasion that their armor and weapon was not all in a redinesse. And within a little while after that followed two thousand, that did disembarke themselues in a secreat and vnknowne place, and came in verie secret order because they would not be discouered, and did beset that gate of the cittie whereas their companions were which they sent before; who so soone as they saw them nigh at hande, drewe out their weapons the which they caried hid vnder their apparell, and set vpon the souldiers (that were voide of feare and vnarmed) with so great furie and force that they being amazed were easilie slaine, so that they were lords of the gate, whereas they left verie good guard, and followed their victorie and made themselues lordes of the cittie without any daunger vnto their persons, and did possesse the same certaine dayes, and did sacke the same in spite of them all, with great barme and losse vnto the inhabitants thereof, vntill such time as the vizroy of Aucheo did leuie an armie togither of three score and tenne thousande men, and went vpon them with courage for to be reuenged on the iniurie receiued with the death of all the Iapones; but they seeing that they coulde not defend themselues against so manie, in one night they left the cittie and went vnto their shippes, whereas they had left them in verie good order, and carried with them the spoile of the cittie, leauing it beaten downe and dispopulared the greater part thereof, in which sort the Spaniards founde it, and the iniurie receiued so fresh in their minds as though it had beene doone the day before.

In this citie they were lodged in the king's house, the which was of verie great and faire buildings; there was giuen them to dine and suppe in very good order, and with aboundance. So soon as they came thither, the friers remained in their lodgings, but Pedro Sarmiento and Miguel de Loarcha went to visite the gouernor, vsing the Spanish curtesie with him, and he receiued them with great ioy and curtesie. After they had taken their leaue and returned vnto their lodgings, the gouernor sent to visite them El Tyu, who is the auncientest of his counsaile, who was with them a good while verie friendly, and offered his seruice in all thinges that were needfull, and so departed to his house maruellously well accompanied.

The gouernor sent vnto the two souldiers that went to visite him, ech of them two peeces of silke.

At their departure from this cittie, trauelling towards Aucheo, they passed ouer a mightie great ryuer, by a bridge all made of stone, the goodliest and greateste that euer they had seene, whose greatness did cause wonderful admiration, so that they stayed and did measure it from one end to another, that it might be put amongst the wonders of that country, which they tooke a note of. They found that it was one thousand and three hundred foote long, and that the least stone wherewith it was built was of seuenteene foote, and many of two and twentie foote long and eight foote broad, and seemed vnto them a thing impossible to be brought thither by man's art, for that all round about so farre as they could see was plaine ground without any mountaines; by which they iudged them to be brought from farre. When they were passed that bridge, they trauelled al the rest of the day till night vpon a causie that was very broad and plaine, and on both sides many victualling houses, and the fieldes sowed with rice, wheate, and other seeds; and so full of people as in the streetes of a good towne or cittie.

So when they came into the suburbes of the citie of Aucheo, they founde order and commandement from the vizroy what should be done, as more at large shalbe declared vnto you in the chapter following.

CHAP. XXII.

The entrie of the Spaniards into the cittie of Aucheo, and how the vizroy did entertaine and receiue them.

After they had travelled more then halfe a league in the suburbs of the cittie of Aucheo, they met with a post that came from the vizroy, who brought order that they should remaine in a house that was appointed for them in the said suburbs, and there to be lodged for that night, for that it was late and they could not come vnto the house appointed in the cittie for them, or else peraduenture to giue content vnto many that had great desire to see those strangers, for that they must passe thorough the cittie, and better to bee seene in the day then in the night. So soone as they were alighted, there came a gentleman to visite them, sent from the vizroy to bidde them welcome, and to know howe they did with their iourney, and also to see that they were well prouided for that night of all things necessarie, and that in aboundance. After all the which being done, he told them that the viceroy did verie much reioyce of their comming; and for that it was late, and the cittie farre off, it was his pleasure that they shoulde bee lodged that night in the suburbes vntill the next day, then will he giue order that they may enter into the cittie with the authoritie conuenient vnto their persons. After this gentleman came other captaines to visite them, and brought with them great store of conserues, wine, and fruit; which is a common custome amongst them when that they go in the like visitation, and it is carried by their seruants in little baskets very curiously wrought, or else in barrels made of earth all guilt. Within two houres after their comming thither, there came another messenger from the vizroy, with many men laden with capons, hens, geese, teales, gamons of bacon, and conserues of diuers sorts, and of great abundance, sufficient for one hundreth men to sup that night and for their dinner the next day.

The next day in the morning very early, there came much people vnto their lodging, sent by the vizroy, and brought with them two rich chaires for to carrie the fathers in, and the curtines tied up that they might the better be seene, and for their companions verie good horses, sadled after the fashion which they doo vse. They forthwith made haste for to depart, and although they made great speed, yet were they a good houre and a halfe before they coulde come vnto the gates of the citie, and seemed vnto them that they had trauelled two leagues in the suburbes; the which was so well peopled, so faire houses, and many shoppes full of merchandise, that if it had not beene told them, they would not haue beleeued it to be the suburbes but the cittie it selfe.

Before they came vnto the gates, they passed a mightie riuer three times, ouer bridges that were great and verie faire, and the riuer so deepe that great shippes came vp the same, but their mastes stooping downe to passe vnder the bridges. This cittie is the richest and the best prouided that is in all the kingdome; it is the heade cittie of all the prouince, verie rich and fertill, and manie townes belonging vnto it, and but eight leagues from the sea, and hath mightie riuers wherein great shippes come vp to it as aforesaide. At the enterie of the citie they founde many gentlemen that were there at the gate tarrying their comming, who after they had saluted the one the other after their fashions, without anie staying they trauelled forwards on, thorough a great and broad street that went directlie vnto the vizroy his pallace; vpon both sides of the streete, from the gate forwards, was placed one by another full of souldiers with their officers and ancient, euerie one with his weapon in his hands, as pickes, hargabuses, swords and target, all apparelled in one liuerie of silke, and a bunch of fethers vppon their crestes. They all stoode still and kept their places, and would not consent that any should crosse the way in the streete, whereas they went accompanied with the gentlemen.

They had no leasure to tell the souldiers; but they sawe that from the gate vntil they came vnto the vizroye's pallace on both sides, which was a good way, to be full of them, and all richly apparelled and of one colour. The people that were at the windowes and in the streete, betwixt the houses and the soldiers, were so great a number that it seemed to bee doomes day, and that all the people in the worlde were there ioyned together in that streete.

So when they came vnto the pallace, which was two houres after day, the gentlemen that were their guides did cause the Spaniardes to enter into a roome which was hard by, till such time as the gate was open, for that it is open but once a day, and so continue no longer time then the audience endureth, which is done by the uiceroy once euerie day, and that is but a small time. But first before he doth enter into audience, there is shot off foure peeces of artilerie, with a great noyse of trompettes, drommes, and waites; and there is no day that passeth without audience, as our people did see by experience so long as they were there, and were likewise informed of others. The houre being come, and the ceremony doone as aforesaide, the gates were opened, and there was in the court many souldiers apparelled in the same liuerie that those were of in the streete.

From the middest amongst them came forth a gentleman, who was, as it was told them, the captaine of the garde of the viceroy, who came with great grauitie and authoritie towards the place whereas our people were, and after they had saluted the one the other, he made signes vnto them that they should go towardes the gates of the pallace. When they were within the first court, the which was great and wrought with mightie pillers, there was a great number of souldiers, and many sergeants that entred into an other great covrt, and mounted vp a paire of stayres that was on the one side, whereas all the people were with great silence, sauing the captaine of the garde, who went with our people till they came to the gates of the hall whereas was the viceroy, at which gate he staied with his head discouered, and made signes vnto ours that they should doo the like, and to tarrie there till such time as hee had aduised the viceroy of their comming, and he to command them to enter.

CHAP. XXIII.

The Spaniardes haue audience of the viceroy of Aucheo, and are visited of some of the principall officers, who declare vnto them certaine thinges of that citie.

Then straightwayes came foorth of the hall a man apparelled in a long robe, of good personage, and asked of the Spaniards if they would speake with the viceroy, and they answered, yea: then asked he again from whom they came and by whom they were sent; they answered y^t they were sent by the gouernor of Philippinas, who was seruant vnto the mightiest king in all Christendome. When he had this answere he returned againe into the hall, and within a little while after he came forth and bad them come in, but gaue them to vnderstand that in entring into the hall wheras the viceroy was y^t they should kneele downe, and· talke with him in that order till he commanded to the contrarie; if they would vse this ceremony that then they should come in, if not that they shold returne back againe. They who were certified thereof by the gouernor of Chincheo did not stand therein, but saide y^t they would observe the order giuen vnto them. Therewith he went in, who seemed to be the master of ceremonies, making a signe that they should follow after him and doo that which he willed them to do.

At the entring in at the doore they stayed a little, and then kneeled downe right oueragainst there whereas the uiceroye sate in a chaire verie high like vnto a throne, with a table before him, and was in so darke a place that almost they coulde not see his face verie well. On the one side of him there were some like vnto heraldes of armes, with sceptres in their handes, and on the other side two men of a gallant comlinesse armed with corselets made of skales of golde downe to the cafe of their legges, with bowes in their handes of golde, and quiuers at their backes of the same. Both the one and the other were vpon their knees. There was vpon the table before him paper and all thinges necessarie to write, which is an ordinarie vse amongest them at all times when there is anye publike audience, and on the one side of the borde a lion made of blacke woode, which was (as after they vnderstoode) the armes of that prouince. So straightwayes he made signes unto them to drawe neare, which they did, and kneeled downe a little from the table which was whereas the master of ceremonies did will them. In this sort they beganne to talke with him by their interpreter, and tolde them the occasion of their comming into that citie and kingdome, and from whom and vnto whome they were sent. But hee made signes vnto them that they should arise, the which they did with a verye good will, and did perseuer in their intent. But the uiceroye did cut them off before they coulde make an ende, and asked if they had brought any letter from their king vnto the king his lorde, whome they would goe to see and talke with? but when they answered no, hee straightwayes took his leaue of them, saying that they were welcome, and that they should depart vnto their lodginges and to take their ease, for that afterwardes they should haue occasion to declare their mindes vnto him, and hee would giue them their answere, for that the king was farre of, and it requireth a long time to come whereas he is, but he would write vnto him, and according vnto his commandement he would make them answere. And therwith he tooke the letter, and the memoriall of the present, and commanded in his presence to put about the neckes of the friers, in manner of a scarfe, to eyther of them sixe peeces of silke, and vnto the souldiers their companions, and vnto Omoncon and Sinsay, each of them foure peeces, and to euerye one of their seruantes two a peece, and to giue vnto the two fryers and the souldiers, Omoncon and Sinsay, euerie one of them two branches of siluer, which is a thing vsed in that countrie vnto them that haue doone some woorthie deede, as hath beene tolde you before.

So with the silke about their neckes, and with the branches in their hands, they returned out of the hall and downe the staires the way they came, and so through the court into the streetes, from whence they saw them shut the court gate with so great a noyse as when they did open it. From thence, at the request of Omoncon and Sinsay, they went vnto the house of Totoc, who is the captaine generall of all the men of warre, and vnto the house of Cagnitoc, who is the chiefe standard bearer: their houses were nigh the one the other, very faire and great. They found them with as great maiestie as the viceroy, and in the same order, with a table before them, and had on ech side of them armed souldiers kneeling on their knees. Yet did they not vse our men with the curtesie that the viceroy vsed, to cause them to stand vp, which was the occasion that straightwayes they made a showe that they would depart and be gone, complayning of Omoncon and Sinsay for that they did carrie them thether, and tolde them with anger that the gouernour of Manilla did intreate them in a different sort, who was there resident for the mightiest prince in all the worlde, and they but easie marchants; neither was their going thether to be equalled vnto the benefite that they came thether for. This discontent the which they receiued, was the occasion that they would not go to make any more visitations, although the sayde Omoncon and Sinsay, for their owne interest, would haue carried them to the houses of other officers and gentlemen of the court. But they made signes vnto those that were their guides to direct their way vnto their lodgings, for that they would goe to eate somewhat and to take their ease, the which was ordayned in a great house of the kinges, there whereas ordinarily the iudges doo sit to heare matters of iustice.

So at their comming thether they founde all their stuffe in good order, and their dinner marueilous well prouided, and the whole house hanged and trimmed as though it had beene for the kings owne person, with many wayting men and souldiers, those which did gard them both day and night, and hanging at the doore two tables or bordes (commanded by the viceroy), wheron was written who they were that were there lodged, and from whence they came, and wherefore, and that none whosoeuer should be so hardie as to offer them any wrong or disturbance, vpon paine to be for the same offence seuerely punished. In this house they were more in quiet than in anie other place whereas they had been, neyther did the people giue them so much trouble, by reason of the great care which the iudges had in putting order for the same, by the commandement of the viceroy; yet was it the greatest towne and most populed of all that prouince (although in other prouinces there be that be much bigger), and is affirmed that the citie of Taybin or Suntiem (there whereas the king and his court is resident) hath three hundreth thousande housholds, and yet there is a bigger citie in the kingdome, called Lanchin, which requireth three dayes to go from one gate to an other, and is in compasse more then seuentie leagues, the which is not far distant from Canton, that which the Portingalles hath great notice of.

A citie of three hundred thousand housholds.

A citie bigger then the other, and requireth three daies to go from one gate to an other.

But of certaine there is very much spoken of the mighti-nesse of this citie, and I my selfe haue heard reported and affirmed to bee of a trueth, by men of authoritie that haue beene in the citie of Canton, religious fryers of the order of Iesus or Iesuites, to whom ought to be giuen credite.

Seuentie leagues compasse.

This citie of Aucheo hath a verie faire and strong wall made of stone, which is fiue fadam high and foure fadam brode, the which was measured many times by our people, for that they had a gate out of their lodging that did open to the same. This wall is all couered ouer with tiles to defende the rayne water fro hurting of it, which could not to the contrarie but receiue damage, for that there is no lyme vsed in the whole wall. They haue not one castle in all this citie, neyther is there any vsed in all that kingdome; for all their force and strength is in their gates, the which be made very strong, with a double wall within verie broade, betwixt the which are continually many souldiers, such as do keepe watch and ward both day and night.

The wall of the citie is fiue fadam high and foure broad.

Upon these gates they haue much ordinance, but verie ill wrought (I meane such as were seene by our men); yet they do say that in other places they haue excellent good and verie curiously wrought. The whole wall is full of bartilmentes, and thereon written the names of such souldiers as are bound to repayre thether in the time of necessitie. At euerie hundreth paces they haue lodginges, the which are very huge and great: there whereas in the time of necessitie doo remaine and dwell their captaynes, so long as their troubles doo indure. All the wall is fortified with two great mots or ditches, the one within and the other without, the which they doo fill at all times when they please by sluces, which they haue from the riuer for the same purpose, and doo serue of water almost all the houses in the citie, whereas they haue their stanges for the most part full of fish. This mightie citie is situated in a great plaine, and compassed round about with mightie rockes and mountaines, which is

The citie double mooted.

the occasion that it is not so healthfull; and the inhabitants saye, that it is by reason of the mountaines, and many times it is ouerflowen in the winter by spring tides from the riuer. And in that yeare that this doth happen, it doth destroy and ruinate a great part of the city, as it was at that time when our people did see it, for y^t in the winter before they were troubled with these great tides, which did them much harme.

Now to returne to our purpose, you shall vnderstand that in the kinges house aforesaide, our people remained all the time that they were in this citie, wheras they were made much of, and visited by the principall of the same, but in especiall of the viceroy, who the verie same day did send to inuite them for the next day following, who made vnto them a famous banket, as you shall vnderstand in this chapter following.

CHAP. XXIV.

The viceroy doth banket our people in his owne house two daies, one after the other.

The next day after that our people came into the citie, the uiceroy did sende to inuite them to dinner to his owne house, whereas he made them a great banket in the forme following. At their comming vnto the pallace there came foorth a great number of gentlemen, seruantes vnto the viceroy, to bid them welcome, with great store of musicke and tokens of mirth. Being entred into the first court, they brought them into a mightie hall that was marueilously well trimmed, wherein was a great number of tables, set in such order as they were in the banket that was made them by the gouernour of Chincheo (as hath beene tolde you), although in the number and furniture did far excell the other. But before they did sit down, there came vnto them two captaines, principall men, vnto whom the viceroy had committed the charge of the banket, to doo all things in his name, for that it is a custome in that kingdome, that noble men must not be present in their bankets they make. So the charge was giuen vnto them to make them be mery, and to bid his guests welcome. When they came vnto them they vsed great curtesie, and passed away the time in gallant discourses, till it was time to go to dinner, and that they began to bring in their victuals. Then before they did sit downe, *A strange ceremonie.* the captaines did take ech of them a cup in his hande, in maner of a sorlue,[1] as they do vse, and being full of wine they went together whereas they might discouer the heauen, and offered it vnto the sunne and vnto the saints of heauen, adding thereunto many words of prayers: but principally they did request that the comming of their newe guestes might be profitable vnto them all, and that the friendship which they did pretende to establish, might be for good both vnto the one and to the other. This their oration and prayer being done, they did spill out the wine, making a great courtesie; then were they straightwayes filled againe, and making reuerence vnto their guestes euerie one by himselfe, they set the cuppes downe vpon the tables whereas the fathers should dine, whereas they were set euerie one by himselfe. This being doone, the first seruice was set vppon the bordes, and the captaines were set at other tables, which were not so many in number, nor so well furnished nor dressed as the other: the dinner was famous and of manie diuersities of meates, exceeding verie much that which was made them by the gouernor of Aucheo.

The time which the banket indured (which was verie late) there was great store of musicke of diuers instrumentes, as of vials, gitterns, and rebuckes, and with them many iesters,

[1] We have not met with this word elsewhere, the Spanish word is *salva*, occasionally, and probably here, used for *salvilla*, a saucer.

88   A DISCOURSE OF THE

did make them merry at their dinner. The which being done, the saide captaines did beare their guests companie out of the pallace, whereas they did anew inuite them to dinner for the next day in the same hall : they obeying their request did come, wheras was made vnto them a banket more famous than the first.

This day at the banket was present the Totoc, hee whome they visited the first day, came in his owne house, and founde with so great maiestie. Likewise there dyned with them the captaynes that were at the first banket. In this seconde banket they had, as the day before, verie much musicke, and a comedie that indured long, with manie pretie and merrie iestes : there was also a tombler, who did his feates verie artificially, as well in vauting in the ayre as vppon a staffe that two men did hold on their shoulders. Before the comedie did beginne, was tolde them by their interpreter the signification thereof, that the better they might content themselues in the conceiuing, whose argument was, that in times past, there was in that countrie manie mightie and valiant men. But amongest them all, there was in particular three brethren that bid exceede all the rest that euer were in mightinesse and valiantnesse. The one of them was a whiteman, the other was ruddish or hie coloured, and the third blacke. The ruddish being more ingenious, and of better industrie, did procure to make his white brother king, the which iudgement was agreeable vnto the rest. Then they altogether did take away the kingdome from him that did at that time raigne, who was called Laupicono, an effeminate man and verie vicious. This they did represent verie gallantly, with garmentes verie meete for those personages.

The banket and play beeing finished, according as they did the day before, the captaynes did beare them companie till they were out of the pallace, and from thence they went vnto their lodgings, with their ordinarie companie appointed

[margin: Comedies vsed amongest them. Tomblers. The argument of their comedie.]

by the viceroy, which was that captaine that we haue spoken of, with his souldiers, who neither night nor day dooth not depart from their garde.

CHAP. XXV.

The Spaniards do carie their present vnto the viceroy, who, hauing receiued it at the hands of Omoncon, doth seale it and sende it vnto the king : our men bee forbidden to goe foorth of their houses to see any thing in the citie : and it doth intreat of other particular things.

The same night our men did common amongst themselues, to see if it were good presently to giue order to put in vre the thing they came for : seeing that they might treat therof with the uiceroy, he being a man that shewed vnto them so much fauour and good will. So in conclusion they were all resolued, that straightwayes the next daye in the morning, shoulde goe vnto him Michaell de Loarcha and Peter Sarmiento, and carrie vnto him the present which they brought, and to haue with them to beare them company Omoncon and Sinsay ; and being presented, to request that hee would appoint a day when they might goe and talke with him about principall matters.

This accorde they put in execution according vnto their determination, and the two souldiers went and carried the present as it was agreed. So they came vnto the pallace, and hauing tarried till such time as they opened the gates of the audience (which was with the ceremony spoken of in the 22. chapter), it was tolde vnto the viceroy that the Castillos were there and had brought a present, who incontinent saide that as then he could not talke with them ; but that the captaine Omoncon and Sinsay should enter in with the present, and that they should returne vnto their lodginges, for that he had a care to call them when that opportunitie did serue, to intreat of all things to their pleasure. They did as they were commaunded, and those who carried the present in, did afterwarde giue our people to vnderstand all that had passed with them; saying that in opening the present, there was a note thereof taken before a notarie, and straightwayes commanded to bee put in againe, where it was taken out before the sayde notarie and other witnesses; the which being done he sealed it vp, and sent it vnto the citie of Taybin vnto the king and his counsell, and therewith that which the gouernour of Chincheo did sende him, as shall be tolde you: for that they haue a rigorous lawe in that kingdome, that dooth prohibite all such as haue any office of gouernement to receiue any present, of what qualitie so euer it be, without lycence of the king or of his counsell, vpon paine to be depriued of bearing anie office all the dayes of their liues, and to bee banished and condemned to weare red bonnets (as wee haue declared the effect thereof).

This is conformable vnto that which the gouernor of Chincheo did, in the presence of our people, at such time as they went to take their leaue of him for to goe vnto Aucheo, which was, that in their presence they commanded to take foorth all that they brought him in present; and shewing it vnto them peece by peece, he asked if it were that which they had brought, and they aunswered that it was the same (although it was with troubled mindes), beleeuing that it was to checke them because it was so small in respect of their mightinesse: he asked them if there lacked any thing? they answered, No: then straightwayes he commanded to put it againe where as it was taken out in their presence, and before a notarie and witnesses: the which being doone, was mailed and sealed and so sent vnto the viceroy of Aucheo in their companie, and saide that hee could not receiue it without the licence aforesaid.

So our souldiers seeing that they could not be suffered to

enter in with the present, they tooke it for a great discourtesie and disfauour, and therewith departed vnto their lodging, to giue the fathers to vnderstande thereof, who liked not well thereof; but yet they concluded amongest themselues to suffer for a while, and to commit vnto God the direction thereof, as it best may be for his holy seruice.

The next day following, the viceroy did send to visite them, and to aske of them a sword, a hargubush, and a flaske; for that he would cause others to be made by them; the which they did send, and afterwards vnderstood that they had counterfeited the same, although not in so perfect manner.

Then after a time, our people seeing that their beeing in that citie seemed to be long and like to be longer, they did procure to driue away the time in the best manner they could, and went abroad into the citie and did buy eyther of them that which they thought best. Whereof they found great abundance, and of so small price that they bought it almost for nothing. *All things good cheape.*

They bought many bookes that did intreat of diuerse matters, which they brought with them to the ilands (as appeareth more at large in the chapter for the same).

The next day they went to see the gates of the citie, and all such curious thinges as were to be seene so farre as they could learne or vnderstande, which were many. But amongst them all they sawe a sumptuous temple of their idolles, in whose chiefe chappell they counted one hundred and eleuen idols, besides a great number more that were in other particular chappels; all were of carued worke, verie well proportioned and gilted, but in especiall three of them that were placed in the middest of all the rest, the one had three heads proceeding out of one bodie, the one looking on the other in full face. The second was the forme of a woman, with a childe in her armes; the third, of a man apparelled after the forme and fashion that the Christians *111 idols in one chappell.*

doo paint the Apostles. Of all the rest, some had foure armes, and some had sixe, and other eight, and other some marueilous deformed monsters. Before them they had burning lamps, and many sweete parfumes and smelles, but in especiall before the three aboue specified.

But when that the viceroy did vnderstande that our people did go viewing the citie gates and temples (and perceiueth that they that gaue him the notice did suspect it that it was to some ill intent), therewith he straightwayes commanded that they should not goe foorth out of their lodging without his licence: and likewise commanded the captaine that was their garde not to consent thereunto as he had done, and likewise that none should carrie them any thing for to sell, for he that did it should be punished with whipping. Yet notwithstanding, they had euerie day verie sufficient necessaries for their personages, in such ample wise that there did alwayes remaine, and not lacke.

In this closenesse and keeping in they suffered many dayes with much sadnesse, and oppressed with melancholick humors, to see that their purpose wherefore they went thether seemed to be long, and euerie day was worse and worse. Yet notwithstanding they did passe it ouer in the best wise they could, in committing it with heartie zeale vnto God, for whose honor and glorie they did attempt that voyage, and prayed vnto him for to mooue their hearts to consent that the religious fathers might remeine in that countrie for to learne the language (as they had begun many daies before), by which meanes their soules might be saued, and clearely deliuered from the tyrannie of the diuell, who of truth had them in possession. So after many dayes that they had remained in that close estate as aforesaide, they determined for to goe and talke with the viceroy, and to bee fully resolued either to tarry or returne from whence they came. They straightwayes did put it in vre, and what ensued thereof you shall vnderstande in the chapter following.

CHAP. XXVI.

The Spaniardes talke with the viceroy, and not being suffered, they do write to him a letter, and he doth answere it by word of mouth, with other particular matters.

It hath been declared vnto you, that the same day y^t the Spaniardes did talke with the viceroy, he asked them if they had brought any letter for their king, they answered, No: he told them that he would write vnto the court, and hauing answere, they should be fully satisfied of their pretence and demaund.

But they seeing that his answere was long a comming, and great delaye made therein, and that they had them as halfe prisoners, they determined to go and speake with the viceroy to be fully satisfied of his determinate will and pretence, and to haue some order eyther to goe vnto the court, or to remaine in that citie, or else to returne vnto the ilands, and there to tarrie the time till it pleased God to open a gate in that kingdome, wherein might enter his holy gospell.

With this then pretended purpose, they did perswade with their captaine to permit them so much libertie as for to go and speake with the viceroy, who for that hee bare them loue and good will did consent therevnto. So they went, but when they came thether they that kept the gates would not consent y^t they should enter, which was the occasion that they returned vnto their lodgings verie sad and sorrowfull, and almost without any hope to bring their matter to passe, for the which they went thether; for that it seemed vnto them, although they did plainely declare vnto them their pretence, yet did they worke in such order for to cause them to depart. In this order they remained in the citie certaine daies, and for to conclude either to stay there or depart the kingdome they were resolute; and determined to write a letter vnto the viceroy, and therein to giue him to vnderstand particularly that their comming thether into yᵉ countrie was to intreat that betwixt them and the Castillos there should be peace and friendship, and being concluded that their souldiers should with that newes depart vnto the islandes from whence they came, to giue the gouernor to vnderstand therof, and they to remaine in that countrie preaching yᵉ holy gospell. They could finde none that would write this letter for them, although they would haue payed them very well for their paines. Till in the end, by great request and prayings, the captaine Omoncon did write it for them, and straightwaies departed vnto the citie of Ampin that was not farre off, making an excuse for to go and see the visitor of the prouince, whom they doo call Sadin: he would very faine haue carried with him two of our people, yᵗ he might haue seene them, but none would go with him. This iourney which Omoncon made, hee did it to put away the suspition they might conceiue that he did write the letter, if that peraduenture the viceroy would take it in ill part.

<small>People in great subiection.</small>

Their letter being written, they found great difficulty in the sending the same, for that there was none that would carie it, neyther would they consent that our men should enter into the pallace to deliuer it. But in conclusion, what with requestes and giftes, they perswaded their captayne of their gard to carrie it, who did deliuer the same vnto the viceroye, in name of the Castillos, saying that hee tooke it of them to bring it vnto him, for that they did certifie him that it was a thing that did import verie much. Hauing read the letter, hee answered that he would giue the king to vnderstande thereof, as he saide at the first time. And in that touching the fryers remayning in that countrie to preach, at that time he could make them no answere, for that in such matters it was first requisite to haue the good will of the royall counsell. Yet would hee make answere vnto the letter they brought from the gouernour of Manilla, and that they might depart, and returne againe at such time as they brought Limahon, prisoner or dead; the which being done, then shall the friendshippe be concluded which they doo pretende, and to remaine and preach at their will. With this answere they remained without all hope to remayne there, and did incontinent prepare themselues for to depart from Manilla, and bought manie bookes to carie with them, wherein was comprehended all the secrets of that kingdome; by reason whereof they might giue large notice vnto the royall maiestie of King Phillip. The which being vnderstoode by the viceroy, who had set spies to watch their doings, did sende them worde that they should not trouble themselues in the buying of bookes, for that hee would giue them freely all such bookes as they would desire to haue: the which afterwardes he did not accomplish: whether it was for forgetfulnesse or other occasion, as wee haue more at large declared vnto you, we know not: yet did the uiceroy send and demanded to see some of those bookes that the fryers had bought; who after that he had seene them, did returne them againe, and requested of them some writing of their owne handes, who did accomplish his request, and sent them written in Spanish and in their own language, the Lords Prayer, the Aue Maria, and the Ten Commandements, who according vnto the relation of him that did carrie the same, saide, that after hee had reade it, he made showes that he receiued great content therewith, and said that all which was there written was good.

In the time that they stayed in this citie, amongst all other things that they vnderstoode to driue away the time was one, it was giuen them to vnderstande that in one of the prisons, there was a Portingale prisoner, who was taken in a shippe of the Iapones with others of his nation, who were all dead in the prison, and none left aliue but he alone. Our people being verie desirous for to see him, and to learne

of him some secrets of that countrie, for that he had beene
there a great while, they did procure to talke with him,
asking licence of the supreme iudge and lieutenant vnto the
viceroy, who did not onely refuse to grant it them, but did
make diligent inquirie who they were that did giue them to
vnderstande thereof, for to punish them, which without all
doubt should be executed with sharpe and seuere punishment. Yet our people would neuer tell them of whom they
had it, although it was demanded of them diuerse times, and
with great intreatie. They had so great desire to know it,
that they did vse all meanes possible as it appeared in the
boldnesse of their demandes.

CHAP. XXVII.

*There came newes vnto Aucheo that there was a rouer vpon the coast of
Chincheo, which did much harme, and had sacked a towne. The
viceroy doth suspect him to be Limahon, and how that our people,
with Omoncon and Sinsay, had not declared vnto him the truth.*

The Spaniards remained in the citie of Aucheo twentie
days, in the order as hath been told you, without any hope
that the religious fathers should remaine in that countrie for to
preach the holy gospell, which was the principall occasion of
their going into that kingdome. Upon a suddaine there
came newes vnto the citie that the rouer Limahon was vpon
the coast of Chincheo, vsing his olde accustomed cruelties,
and how that he had spoiled and robbed a towne vpon the
sea coast. This newes was throughout all the citie, and appeared to be true, touching the effect of the dead: yet false
touching the person, for that the rouer was called Taocay,
an enimie and contrarie vnto Limahon, but a friend vnto
Vintoquian, of whom we haue spoken of. But thereupon

the viceroy and all them of the citie were conformable in the suspition that they had receiued, which was, that our people were come into that kingdome vpon some euill pretence, and to see the secrets thereof, to some euil end, which was the occasion y[t] from that time forwards they shewed them not so good countenance as they did before.

These newes was not so soone come, but straightwayes the viceroy did send for Omoncon (who was then returned from his visiting) and Sinsay, vnto whom he had done courtesie, and giuen them the title of loytias and captaynes, and he did reprehende them verie sharpely for that they had brought ouer people thether, and sayde that they had tolde him a lye in saying that Limahon was besieged in such sort that hee coulde not escape, neither had the Castillos burnt his shippes, and howe that all was but a made matter amongest themselues, and howe that the captaines which they brought, and sayde that they had taken from Limahon, they had robbed from other places, with other wordes in the same order, and said that the Spaniardes were spyes that came to discouer the secretes and strength of the kingdome, and how that they had brought them thether by force of giftes that they had giuen them.

They answered him with great humilitie in saying that in all that which they had sayd they did speake the trueth, and that it should appeare at such time as the newes of the rouer should be better knowen, the which, if it shall appeare to be contrary, they were there readie for to suffer whatsoeuer punishment y[t] shold be giuen them. The viceroy being somewhat satisfied with this their iustification, bad them to depart, remitting all things vnto time for the true declaration thereof. Then Omoncon and Sinsay came straightwayes to giue y[e] Spaniards to vnderstand of all that had passed with the viceroy, and what they vnderstoode of him, which caused in them so great feare, y[t] for the time which it endured (which was till such time as they vnderstoode the truth as

Suspition of euill.

aforesaide) they paied very well for their feasts and bankets the which they had made them. All this happened in the time that Omoncon and Sinsay were at variance, and spake many iniurious words the one of ye other, discouering their intents and deuises, whereby it plainely appeared that in al y^t which they had tolde vnto the viceroy, they lied, but in especiall Omoncon. Sinsay did dissemble, for hee sayde and tolde vnto all people, that by his order and industrie our peo- ·ple did fire the shippes of Lymahon, and beseiged him, with other speeches in the like sort; yet twentie dayes before his comming thether, all was ended and doone, as appeared. The occasion of their enimitie and falling out, was for that the viceroy had giuen vnto Omoncon a title and charge of more honor then vnto Sinsay, hauing made betwixt them a consort that the reward or dignitie should be equally deuided betwixt them, and that the one should speake of the other the best they could, because the viceroy should do them friendship. This condition and consort (as appeareth) was euill performed, by Omoncon being addicted vnto selfe loue, and seemed vnto him that Sinsay did not deserue so much as he did, for that hee was a base man, and of the sea, and he of the more nobilitie, and had the office of a captaine. All this which I haue said, was the occasion y^t the truth came to light betwixt them, and to cause the viceroye to suspect, that as they lyed in this, they might also fable in the burning of the ships and besieging of Limahon.

CHAP. XXVIII.

The gouernours of the prouince do assemble together, to intreat of the Spaniardes business, and are resolved that they should returne vnto the ilandes. They do see many curious thinges before their departure.

With this griefe and care remained the Spaniards certaine daies, kept close in their lodgings, and were not visited so often as they were when they first came thether, which did augment verie much their feare, till such time as they vnderstoode that the viceroy, eyther of his owne good will or else by some particular order from the king and his counsell, had called together all the gouernours of that prouince of Aucheo to intreat of matters touching Limahon, as also in particular why and wherefore the Spaniardes came thether, and to resolue themselues wholly in all things requisite for the same. So when that they were all come together, which was in a short time, and amongst them the gouernor of Chincheo, who by an other name was called Insuanto, they had particular meetings together with the uiceroye, in the which they were all agreed to haue a generall meeting, whereunto should bee called the Castillos, and to demande of them in publike audience the cause of their comming (although notwithstanding they had giuen to vnderstand thereof vnto the Insuanto and vizroy), and being hearde, to giue them their answere according as they had determined: for the which vppon a day appointed they met all togither (but not the vizroy) in the house of the Cagontoc, and commanded to come before them the Castillas, who did accomplish their request with a great good will, for that they vnderstoode that they were called to entreat of their matter, either to tarry or depart. So when they came thither, they were commanded to enter into a mighty hall, whereas they were all set in verie rich chaires, with great grauitie and maiestie. The Insuanto seemed to bee the chiefest among them, but whether it was for that hee was the principallest next vnto the vizroy (or as it was tolde them), for that it was he that sent Omoncon in the chase of the rouer Limahon, they knew not; but so soone as they were entred into the hall, they were commanded to drawe nigh there whereas they were all placed, without bidding them to sit downe, neither did they vse any particular circumstances or curtesie.

The Insuanto tooke vpon him the charge, and demanded of the Spaniards (by meanes of the interpreter) what was the occasion of their comming into that country, and to declare their pretence, for that they would giue vnto them the resolute will of the vizroy, at whose commandment they were called and there assembled togither. The Spaniards answered vnto their request, and said that their comming thither was to treat with them peace and friendship, by the order of the gouernor of ye Philippinas, who had his authority from the king of Spaine, with a particular charge euer since the said islands were discouered, who in all thinges that possible hath beene, haue shewed themselues, not onely in words but in deedes, as vnto this day the gouernor dooth accomplish the same, in ransoming all such Chinos as they can finde, or come vnto their powers, and send them home free into their countrie with giftes, and not in this only, but in other matters, which is not vnknowne vnto them: and more, that which lastly had happened in the destruction of the fleete, and the besieging of the rouer Limahon, with which newes they came thither to intreate and conclude betweene them and the Castillias a perpetuall friendship: this was the principall occasion of their comming, the which if they coulde bring it to passe (as a thing that did accomplish both the one and the other), they would with ye same newes send word with the souldiers (who came with them for the same effect) vnto the gouernor of Manilla, who sent vs thither for that he might send the good successe thereof to the king of Spaine, and there to remaine in such place as they woulde appoint them to studie the learning of the language, and to preach and declare to them ye holy gospell, which was the right way vnto the salvation of their soule. Unto all the which they gaue attentiue eare, although with little desire to see the experience, as appeared; for that the chiefest matter in effect they did let passe, and asked of them in what order they left the rouer Limahon, and whether hee might escape or not, and other questions touching the same matter, which endured a good while without touching of anie other matter in effect. The Spaniards answered as they thought, and supposed that at that time it could not be, but that he was either taken prisoner or slaine.

Then did the Insuanto conclude his speech in saying vnto them, that they should returne vnto their owne country to the ilands; and at such time as they did bring Limahon, they woulde conclude all things touching the friendship they requested, as also for the preaching of the gospell.

So with this last resolution they tooke their leaue and went vnto their lodging, with pretence not to speake more of that matter, for that they sawe it booted out: after they had giuen their censure: and againe, as they vnderstood it was by speciall order from the king and his counsaile; and therewith they beganne to put all thinges in good for their departure, the which they greatly desired, for that they saw little fruite to proceede of their great labour and trauell, as also to see themselues cleare of that manner of prison in the which they were, not to go forth of their lodgings without express licence.

So from that day forwards they did procure with all haste for to depart, and gaue the vizroy to vnderstande thereof; who answered them and saide, that they should comfort themselues and receiue ioy and pleasure, and that he would dispatch them so soone as the visitor of that prouince was come to Aucheo, which would be within tenne dayes, for that hee had written vnto him that he should not dispatch them vntil his comming, for that he would see them.

From that day forwards hee commaunded that sometimes they should let them go forth abrode to recreate themselues, and that they should shew vnto them some particular pleasure or friendship. So one of them was carried to see the mustering of their men of warre, which they haue in a common custome throughout all the kingdome to doo at the first day of the newe moone, and is sure a thing to be seene: and they doo it in the field which is ioyning vnto the wals of the citie, in this manner following.

<small>The vse of their mustering.</small>

There were ioyned togither litle more or less then 20 thousand souldiers, pickemen and hargabus shot, who were so expert, that at the sounde of the drum or trumpet, they straightwayes put themselues in battle aray, and at another sound in a squadron, and at another the shot doo deuide themselues from the rest, and discharge their peeces with very gallant and good order, and with a trice put themselues againe into their places or standings: this being doone, the picke men came foorth and gaue the assalt altogether with so good order and consort, that it seemed vnto the Spaniards that they did excel al the warlike orders vsed in all the world: and if it were so that their stomacks and hardinesse were equall vnto their dexteritie and number of people, it were an easie thing for them to conquer the dominion of all the world. If it so chance that any souldier should lacke in his office, and not repaire to his place appointed, he is straightwayes punished very cruelly, which is the occasion that euerie one of them hath a care vnto his charge.

<small>Souldiers are punished.</small>

<small>Their mustering is one throughout the whole kingdome.</small>

This their muster endured foure houres, and it was certified vnto the Spaniards that the same day and houre it is done in all cities and townes throughout all the whole kingdome, although they are without suspection of enimies.

Fiue and twentie dayes after that the Insuanto had giuen

the resolute answere vnto the Spaniards, came the visitor thither: and the whole citie went forth to receiue him, who entred in with so great maiestie, that if they had not knowne who hee was, they could not haue beene perswaded but that he had beene the king.

So the next day following the Spaniards went to visite him, for dueties sake, as also for that he had a desire to see them. They found him in his lodging, where he began to make visitation of the cittie.

In their courtes were an infinite number of people, which came thither with petitions and complaintes, but in the halles within, there was none but his seruants and sergeants. When that any came for to present his petition, the porter that was at the entrie made a great noise, in manner of an o. est.,[1] for that it was a good way from the place whereas the visitor did sit; then commeth forth straight wayes one of his pages, and taketh the petition and carrieth it vnto him. At this time it was told him how that the Castillas were there: hee commaunded that they should enter, and talked with them a few words, but with great curtesie, and all was touching the imprisonment of Limahon, without making any mention of their departure or tarrying. So after a while that he had beholded them and their apparel, hee tooke his leaue of them, saying, that by reason of the great businesse he had in that visitation, he could not shewe them any curtesie, neither to vnderstande of them what their request and desire was; but gaue them great thankes for their curtesie shewed, in that they woulde come to visite him. Hee was set in the same visitation after the same manner and order as they founde the gouernor of Chincheo, and the vizroy, with a table before him, with paper, ynke, and other thinges readie to write, the which, according as it was giuen them

[1] These words, "in manner of an o. est," are supplied by the translator, and would seem to be intended for the crier's exclamation of "Oyez."

to vnderstand, is a common vse in all ye kingdome, vsed with all iudges, whether it be for sentence of death, or other matters of iustice, as hath beene told you many times before.

Three dayes after the visitor was come thither, the Insuanto departed for his owne house, with order that with all speede possible he should ordaine shippes wherin the Castillias should returne vnto the Philippinas.

Likewise the same day, all those that were there assembled by the order of the vizroy departed vnto their owne houses. And the Spaniards were commanded for to stay vntill the full of the moone, which should bee the twentieth of August, and that day they shoulde take their leaue of them: for on that day amongst them it is holden for good to beginne any thing whatsoeuer. Wherein they do vse great superstition, and doo make many banquets, as vppon new yeares day, as hath beene tolde diffusedly.

<small>Superstition.</small>

The day before ye departure of ye Spaniards, there came some in behalfe of the vizroy to inuite them, and made them banquet in the order and fashion as at first: although this (for that it was at their departure) was more sumptuous, wherein was represented a comedie which was very excellent and good, whose argument was first declared vnto them as followeth.

There was a young man newly married, and there chanced difference betwixt him and his wife; hee determined to go vnto certaine warres, the which was ordained in a countrie not farre from that whereas he dwelled: whose acts and deeds was therein so valorous, that the king did shewe him great fauour, and being fully certified of his worthinesse, he sent him for chief captaine of the most importunate enterprises that might bee offered, who did accomplish his charge with conclusion thereof with great content and satisfaction to the king and his counsailers: for the which he made him his captaine generall, and in his absence did commit vnto his charge his whole campe, with the same authoritie that he had himselfe.

The warres being doone, and hee hauing a desire to returne vnto his owne countrie and house, there was giuen vnto him three cart loads of golde, and many iewels of an inestimable price, with the which hee entered into his owne countrie with great honour and riches, wheras they receiued him with great honour.

All the which they did represent so naturally, and with so good apparell and personages, that it seemed a thing to passe in act. There was not in this banket the vizroy, but those captaines which were there the first time: and another captaine, vnto whome was giuen the charge to bring the Spaniards vnto Manilla, who was called Chantalay, a principall captaine of that prouince.

So when the banquet was ended, they were carried with great company from the hall whereas the banquet was made, vnto the house of the Cogontoc, who was the kings tresuror and dwelt there hard by, of whom they were maruellously wel receiued, with louing words and great curtesie : in saying that he hoped very shortly to see them againe, at such time as they shall returne with Limahon, and that as then their friendship should be fully concluded, and would intreat with them in particular of other matters. This being doone, he gaue vnto them a present for to carrie vnto the gouernor of Manilla, in recompence of that which was sent vnto the vizroy: the present was fortie peeces of silke and twentie peeces of burato,[1] a litter chaire and guilt, and two quitasoles of silke,[2] and a horse. Likewise he sent the like present vnto the generall of the fielde, and to either of them a letter in particular: these things were put in chestes, which were very faire and guilt. Besides this, hee gaue other fortie peeces of silke of all colours, for to bee parted

[1] A light kind of silk stuff used for veils by the ladies in Spain.
[2] Parasols.

amongest the captaines and other officers that were at the siege of Limahon, with three hundred blacke mantles, and as many quitasoles, to be parted amongst the souldiers. Besides all these, hee gaue vnto the friers ech of them eight peeces of silke, and vnto the souldiers their companions foure peeces of ech of them, and to euery one his horse and a quitasol of silke; their horse were verie good to trauell by the way. This being done the Cogontoc tooke his leaue of them, and willed them to go and take leaue and licence of the vizroy and the visitor, that they might depart, for that all thinges were in a redinesse for their voyage: the which commandement they did straightwayes accomplish, being very well content and satisfied of the great fauours and curtesies the which they receiued, both of the one and the other: likewise of the Totoc, who is captaine generall, whome they also did visite and tooke their leaue. These visitations and leaue taking being doone, they returned vnto their lodging with great desire for to take their ease, whereas they remained til the next day following, wherin they departed vnto the port of Tansuso, after they had remained in Aucheo seuen and forty daies.

To keepe away the sun.

CHAP. XXIX.

The Spaniards departe from Aucheo, and come vnto Chincheo, wheras the Insuanto was: he commanded them to depart vnto the port of Tansuso, whither he went himself for to dispatch them: at whose departure he sheweth great fauor and maketh them great feastes.

The Spaniards departed from the citie of Aucheo vpon a Tewsday, being the 23 of August, in the sight of all the people of the citie, who came foorth to see them with so great presse and thronge, as they did when they first came thither into the countrie : they were al carried in litter chayres, yea their verie slaues, for that it was so commaunded by the vizroy; the friers were carried by eight men a peece, and the souldiers by foure men a peece, and all their seruants and slaues were caried by two men a peece. Looke so many men as was to carrie them, there went so many more to help them when they waxed weary, besides foure and twentie that carried their stuffe. There went alwayes before them a harbinger for to prouide their lodgings, and with him went a paimaster, whose charge was to ordain and prouide men for to cary their litter chaires, and to giue them for their trauell that which is accustomed, and to pay all costs and charges spent by the Spaniard. After that they departed from Aucheo they made of two daies iourney one, which was the occasion that they came to Chincheo in foure daies. At their entring into the citie they found a seruant of the Insuanto, with order and commandement that they shuld proceed forwards on their iourney, and not to stay in the citie, but to go vnto the port of Tansuso, whither he wil come the next day following. They obayed his commandement, and made so much haste that in two dayes they came vnto the village of Tangoa, wheras they had bin before, and particular mention made thereof. In the same village they were lodged, wel entertained, and had great good cheere : from thence they went in one day to Tansuso, which was the first port wheras they did disembarke themselues, when as they came from the ilands vnto that firme land : the iustice of the town did lodge them in the same house whereas they were first lodged, and did prouide for them of all things necessary and needfull, and that in aboundance, til the comming of the Insuanto, which was within foure dayes after; for that he could not come any sooner (although his desire was) for that it was very foule weather.

The next day after his comming thither, which was the

thirde of September, he sent and commanded the Spaniards that they should embarke themselues, for that it was that day the coniunction of the moone (although at that time the ships were not fully in a redines). They obayed his commandement, and the Insuanto himself went to the water side, in whose presence came thither certain religious men of their maner, and after their fashion they made sacrifice with certain orations and praiers, in the which they craued of the heauens to giue good and faire weather, and a sure voyage and fauorable seas vnto al those that saile in those shippes.

This ceremony being done (which is a thing very much vsed in that countrie) the Spaniards went vnto the Insuanto, who was there with great company and maiestie : hee entertained them very friendly and with cheerful wordes, making an outward shew that hee bare them great loue, and that their departure was vnto him a great griefe. Then hee requested them to giue him a remembrance of such thinges as was necessarie and needful for their prouision for the sea, for that hee woulde giue order for the prouiding of the same ; the which he did, and was with so great aboundance, that they had for the voyage and remained a great deale to spare. Hee then commaunded to bee brought thither cates to eat, and drink, and gaue it them with his owne hands, as well the one as the other ; hee himselfe did eate and drinke with them, which is the greatest fauour that can be shewed amongst them.

The banquet being ended, he commaunded them in his presence to go abord their shippes, because that was a luckie day, and also to accomplish that which the vizroy had commaunded, which was that they should not depart from thence vntil they had first seene them imbarked. The Spaniards obeyed the commandement, and tooke their leaue of the Insuanto with great curtesie and reuerence, and with outward shewes that they remained indebted for the great curtesie and good will that they had receiued: and therewith they departed to the waters side, towards the boat which was tarrying for them.

As they passed by the religious men (that before we spake of) they saw a great table set, and vppon it a whole oxe with his throte cut, and hard by the same a hogge and a goate, and other thinges to bee eaten: the which they had ordained for to make sacrifice, which they do vse in the like affaires. *Strange sacrifices.*

They being imbarked in the boate, they were carried aborde the Admirall, which was the shippe appointed for them to go in: then presently they beganne to stirre the shippe from one place vnto another, with certain boates and cables which they had there readie for the same purpose. The shippe did not so soone begin to moue, but the religious men a shore did beginne their sacrifice, the which did indure vntill night, ending their feastes and triumphes in putting forth of the cittie and vppon their gates, many cressets and lights. The souldiers shot off all their hargabushes, and the ships that were in the port shot off all their artilerie, and on the shore a great noise of droms and bels: all the which being ended and done, the Spaniards went a shore againe vnto their lodging; but first the Insuanto was departed vnto his owne house, with all the company that hee brought with him.

The next day the sayd Insuanto did inuite them vnto a banket, which was as famous as any which had bene made them vnto that time. He was at the banquet himselfe, and the captaine generall of all that prouince. There was aboundance of meates, and many pretie deuises to passe away the time, which made the banquet to indure more then foure houres; the which being done, there was brought forth the present which the Insuanto did sende vnto the gouernor of Manilla, in returne of that which was sent to him. The present was fourteene peeces of silke for the gouernor of Manilla, and tenne peeces for the generall of the field: hee also commanded to be giuen vnto the friers each of them foure peeces, and vnto their seruants and slaues certaine painted mantels, and therewith he tooke his leaue of them very friendly, and gaue vnto them letters, the which hee had wrote vnto the gouernor, and vnto the general of the field, answere vnto those the which they had wrote vnto him, and said that all things necessarie for their departure was in a redinesse, with victuals for ten monethes put a bord their ships, so that when as winde and wether did serue they might depart. Also that if in their voyage it should so fall out, that any of the Chinos that went in their shippes shoulde do vnto them any euill, either abrode or at the ilands, that the gouernor therof should punish them at his pleasure, and how that the vizroy will thinke well thereof: in conclusion he saide vnto them, that hee hoped to see them there againe verie shortly, and to returne againe with Limahon, and then hee woulde supplie the wantes which now they lacked. The Spaniards did kisse his hands, and said, that they had receiued in curtesie more then they deserued, and that in all thinges there did abound and not lacke, that they remained greatly indebted vnto him for their friendship, and would giue their king notice thereof, that whensoeuer occasion shoulde bee offered, to repay them with the like: and therewith the Insuanto departed to his owne house, leauing in the companie of the Spaniards fiue captaines, those which should go with them in their company to sea, and also Omoncon and Sinsay, who were that day in the banquet, with the habite and ensigne of loytias, for that the day before it was giuen vnto them by the Insuanto.

Upon Wednesday, which was the fourteenth of September, the wind came faire, wherewith they hoised vp their sailes and went to sea; at their departure there was at the waters side the Insuanto and the iustice of Chincheo to see them saile, the which Insuanto had conceiued so great loue and friendship of the Castillas, that when he sawe them depart he shedde great aboundance of teares, as was affirmed by diuers Chinos that saw it; to which the Spaniards gaue credit vnto, for that they knew him to be a maruellous louing person, and humaine, of a good condition, and of a gallant personage, and did exceede all other that they had seene in all the time of their being in that prouince.

CHAP. XXX.

The Spaniardes departe from the port of Tansuso towardes the Ilandes Philippinas, and euery day they doo harbor themselues in ilands by the way; declaring what they saw in them.

Being departed out of the port as aforesaide, the Spaniards deuided themselues into two shippes, to wit, the two friers and Michael de Loarcha, Omoncon and three other captaines in one shipp. And Peter Sarmiento, Nicholas de Quenca, and Iohn de Triana, Sinsay, and all their souldiers, in another ship, with eight other ships of warre, which went with them for their safegard: they sailed forwards, directing their course towards a small iland that was not farre off, with determination there to take water for their ships, for that it had in it many riuers of very sweete water. Within a smal space they ariued there, and it had a very faire and sure port, wherein might ride in securitie a great nauy of ships. All Thursday they were there recreating and sporting themselues, for that it was a pleasant ilande, and full of fresh riuers. Uppon Friday, being the sixteenth of September, the day being somewhat spent, they made saile and tooke port foure leagues from that place, in another ilande called Laulo, for to put themselues in a newe course different and contrary vnto that which they brought when as they came vnto that kingdome, for that the Chinos had by experience prooued, that in those monethes the windes were more fauourable then in other monethes, and for the most part north and northeast windes. Al that night they remained in that iland, and the next day following they sailed vnto another iland which was called Chautubo, not farre distant from that of Laulo. This ilande was full of little townes, one of them was called Gautin, which had fiue sortes of towers made of lime and stone, verie thicke and strongly wrought: they were all foure square, and sixe fatham high, and were made of purpose for to receiue into them al the people of those little townes, to defend themselues from rouers and theues that daylie come on that coast. These fortes were made with battlements, as we do vse, with space betwixt them: and for that the forme and fashion of their building did like them verie well, they were desirous to see if that within them there were anie curious matter to bee seene; wherewith they bent their artilerie towards them, and went a shore. But when they which had the garde and keeping off did see their comming, they did shut the gates, and woulde not consent that they shoulde satisfie their desire, for any intreating or promises that they could make.

They verie much noted, that although this ilande were rocke and sandie, yet was it tilled and sowed full of rice, wheate, and other seedes and graine. There was in it great

Mine¹ kine and horse. store of kine and horse, and they vnderstoode that they were gouerned, not by one particular man, to whom they were subject, neither by any other amongst themselues, nor of China, but in common: yet notwithstanding they liued in great peace and quietnesse, for that euerie one did content himselfe with his owne. Uppon Sunday, in the afternoone, they departed from this ilande, and sailed their course all that night, and the next morning they ariued at another iland called Corchu, which was twentie leagues from the port of Tansuso, from whence they departed. The Span-

[1] Query misspelt for *maine*, from the old French word *maint*,—many.

iards seeing what leasure they tooke in this their voyage, they requested the captaines to commaunde the marriners that they shoulde not enter into so many portes or harbors, for that they had no certaintie of the weather, and not to detract the time, but to take opportunitie before that contrarie weather do come: for to saile in that order it seemed more for recreation then to achiue or obtaine a voyage. The captaines answered, and requested them to haue patience, for that in making their iournies as they did, they doo accomplish and follow the order set downe by the vizroy and Insuanto, who did expressely commaunde them with great charge for to direct their nauigation by those ilands with great deliberation and consideration, because they might in safetie and health ariue at Manilla.

The same day the north winde beganne to blowe verie strongly: in such sort, that they thought it not good to go forth of that harbor (as well for that aforesaid, to be commanded to the contrarie), as also for that the Chinos are very fearefull of the sea, and men that are not accustomed to ingulfe themselues too farre, neither to passe anie stormes. *The Chinos are fearefull of the sea.*

Neere vnto this iland there was another somewhat bigger, which is called Aucon, wholly dispeopled and without anie dwellers, yet a better countrie and more profitable for to sowe and reape then that of Corchu. The Spaniards being at an anker there, vnderstood by the Chinos that in times past it was very well inhabited, vnto the which ariued a great fleete belonging to the king of China, and by a great storme were all cast away vpon the same: the which losse and destruction being vnderstood by another general that had the guard of that cost, suspecting that the dwellers thereof had done that slaughter, he came to the shore and slew many of the inhabitants, and caried all the rest in their ships vnto the firme lande, who afterwards would neuer returne thither againe, although they gaue them licence after that they vnderstoode the truth of that successe: so that vnto that time it remained dispeopled and full of wilde swine, of the broode that remained there at such time as they were slaine and caried away as you haue heard.

This iland and the rest adioyning thereunto (which are very many) haue very excellent and sure ports and hauens, with great store of fish. These ilands[1] endured vntill they came vnto a little gulfe, which is fiue and fortie leagues ouer, and is sailed in one day, and at the ende thereof is the port of Cabite, which before we haue spoken off, and is neere vnto Manilla.

So when that winde and weather serued their turne, they departed from the ilande of Aucon, and sailed til they came vnto another ilande called Plon, whereas they vnderstoode by a shippe that was there a fishing, howe that the rouer Limahon was escaped, wheras he was besieged at Pagansinan: the manner and forme of the policie hee vsed therein shalbe tolde you in the chapter following.

CHAP. XXXI.

They haue newes how that the rouer Limahon was escaped, and howe that he was in an ilande there hard by: some gaue iudgement to go and set vpon him, but they resolued themselues to the contrarie, and follow the voyage to Manilla.

Being at an anker in the iland of Plon, tarrying for a wind to followe their voyage, with great desire to come thither whereas they might vnderstande what had happened vnto Limahon, at the same time entred into the saide harbor a shippe with fishermen; they beleeuing that hee had beene one of the ilands,[2] they went vnto him and asked of whence

[1] The names of the various islands mentioned in this chapter are not now recognizable.
[2] Islanders.

they were, and from whence they came, and what newes they coulde say of Limahon (who was knowne vnto them all, either by some harme that they had receiued, or else by report of others that had receiued hurt). These fishermen gaue them particular and whole relation, by the which they vnderstoode that Limahon was fledde and not perceiued by the Spaniards: he escaped in certaine barkes, the which he caused to be made very secretlie within his forte, of such timber and bords as remained of his shippes that were burnt, the which was brought in by night by his souldiers, on that side of the fort which was next vnto the riuer, and were not discouered by the Castillas, which were put there with all care and diligence to keepe the mouth, that no succour might come in to helpe them. And towards the land there whereas he might escape, they were without all suspection (they were so strong), and did not mistrust that any such thing shoulde bee put in vre, as afterwards did fal out, the which was executed with so great policie and craft, that when they came to vnderstande it, the rouer was cleane gone and in sauegard, caulking his barkes at the iland of Tocaotican, the better for to escape and saue himselfe, and they saide that it was but eight dayes past that hee fledde.

With this newes they all receiued great alteration, but in especiall Omoncon and Sinsay, who returned vnto the Spaniards and saide, that the escaping of the rouer is not without some misterie, and that it coulde not bee done without the will and knowledge of the Spaniards, and that the rouer had giuen vnto the generall of the fielde some great gifts for to let him go, for that otherwise it were a thing impossible for him to escape, being besieged as hee was, although the Spaniards had slept: the Spaniards did giue their discharge in such prouable maner, that the captaines of China were satisfied of the false opinion they had receiued, as afterwards they were fully perswaded when they came to the cittie of Manilla, and heard the generall of the fielde and other captaines and souldiers that were at the siege. This iland of Tocaotican whereas the rouer was mending and caulking of his barkes, was distant from the iland of Plon, whereas the Spaniards were, onely twelue leagues, and being by sea it seemed to be lesse, for that very plainely you might see the one ilande from the other. The which with the great cholor that Omoncon and Sinsay had for the escaping of the rouer, as also with the feare they receiued in that which might happen vnto them by reason hereof at their returne vnto China, which at the least might bee to take away (to their great shame) the titles of loytias, which was giuen them in that respect, did cause their stomakes and mindes to rise, and to seeke occasion to go and fight with him, for that it seemed vnto them they should get victorie with great ease, for that hee was vnprouided and wearied with the long time of his siege. Being in this determination there came vnto them the captaine that was appointed generall ouer them, and saide that the vizroy of Aucheo and the gouernor of Chincheo had sent them onely to carrie those Spaniards vnto Manilla, and to bring with him aliue or deade the rouer Limahon, if they woulde giue him vnto them, and that hee woulde not digresse from this order by no manner of meanes, neither could they, if that they were so disposed, for that the shippes were pestered with the horses : and againe, their people they had brought with them, was more for to saile and gouerne their shippes then for the fight. Moreouer the fight would be verie dangerous, for that it was euident that the rouer and his companions would rather be al slaine then to yeelde themselues in any respect, and for to put such an enterprise in effect, it were requisite to haue both ships and men, and not to go so vnprouided and pestred as they were. All which reasons being considered, they were all conformable vnto the opinion of the generall, and determined that so soone as winde and weather did serue, to set saile and to passe the gulfe for to go vnto Manilla, whither as they were bound, and not to come vnto the ilande of Tocaotican whereas the rouer was.

So after they had remained three weekes in that harbour detained with a mightie north winde, that neuer calmed night nor day in all that time, the eleuenth day of October, two houres before day, they set saile and went to sea. By reason of this great wind, there was not one shippe of all those that were in the port of Plon coulde go foorth to giue any notice vnto the rouer of the going of the Spaniards, neither of the captaines of China. Sixteene leagues from the port, sailing towards the south, they discouered a mightie iland, verie high land, which was called Tangarruan, and was of three score leagues about, all inhabited with people like vnto those of the Ilands Philippinas: they passed hard by it in the night, with a stiffe norwest winde, which was the occasion that the shippe wherein the friers went was constrained to go to sea; and the other nine, which were in their companie for their safegarde, shrowded themselues hard vnder the iland; by reason whereof they were so farre separated the one from the other, that in the morning they coulde not see them. They were in great danger, because that night there was a great storme of winde, in the which they lost the rudder of their shippe, and almost without any hope to escape the fury thereof.

Being in this extremitie, they commended themselues with contrite hearts vnto almightie God, and put their shippe before the sea, vntill such time as they had supplied their rudder, the which they did, although with great trauell and labour: then straightwayes it was the will of God that this contrary wind was somewhat calmed and his furie abated, and a prosperous wind fauoured them, so that vppon Sunday, in the morning, being the seuenteenth day of October, they discouered the iland of Manilla, of them greatly desired, yet could they not reach vnto it vntill Saint Simon and Judes day: by reason that they returned backe vnto the riuer of Pagansinan to seeke the other nine shippes, for that it was concluded amongst them, that if it should so fall out, they to be separated in any storme, that they should come vnto that riuer, and to meete togither as they did.

So they departed from thence vnto the port of Buliano, and not entring therin, the captaine Omoncon did set a man on shore, one that could speake the language of that iland, and gaue him charge to informe himselfe of all that had happened with the rouer Limahon, for at that time he could not beleeue that which had beene told him. Untill such time as he returned, the shippes being without at the sea, did play vnder fore sailes, who did declare vnto them the verie same thing, the which was tolde them at the ilande of Plon, without faultring any point : the which caused Omoncon and Sinsay to receiue much more griefe then they did when they heard the first newes, for as then they were doubtfull of the truth. The Spanyards as then suspected that they would haue returned vnto the firme land, and not haue gone vnto Manilla, but to haue left them there all alone vpon that iland. But it fell not out as they suspected : for although that Omoncon and Sinsay did make an outward shew to doo it, and sayde that they would sende the Spaniards in a shippe, for that as then they were out of all danger, and in sight of Manilla : yet was the generall of a contrarie opinion, and sayd, that for no manner of occasion that might happen, hee would not differ one point from the order which was giuen vnto him ; and therewith they sayled towards the iland that they so long desired to see, and came thither the twentie eight day of October, as aforesaid.

So that from the port of Tansuso, which is the first part of China till they came vnto the iland of Manilla, they were fiue and fortie dayes, and is not in all full two hundred leagues, which may bee made with reasonable wether in tenne dayes at the most.

<small>From the Philippinas to the China is two hundred leagues.</small>

CHAP. XXXII.

The captaines Chinos ariued with the Spaniardes at the citie of Manilla; the gouernor and those of the citie doo receiue them with great ioy and triumphes, and after they had remained there certaine dayes, they returned vnto the firme land, being instructed and satisfied of many things touching our holy Catholike faith, with great desire to receiue the same.

After that it was knowen vnto the gouernor of the citie of Manilla and vnto the generall of the fielde, as also vnto the rest of the captaines and souldiers, of the ariuall of the Spaniardes, whom they with great care desired to heare of; as well for the particular loue they beare vnto them, as also for to vnderstand and heare the newes from that mightie kingdome of China, to be declared by witnesses of so great faith and credite, they altogether went foorth to receiue them with great ioye and pleasure, and likewise all such captaynes and souldiers as came in their companie.

They were straightwaies conueighed vnto their lodginges to rest themselues of their long iourney which they had by sea, for it was requisite and needefull: for the which afterwardes there was great feastes and bankets, which was made by the gouernor, the generall of the field, and other particular persons, vnto the Chinos, in recompence of that which was done vnto the Spaniards in their countrie.

All which feastes did giue them little content when as they did remember the flying and escape of the rouer; but in especiall Omoncon and Sinsay, who continually and euery moment did call vpon the generall of their fleete to make haste and to shorten the time that they might depart from the firme land, where giuing notice vnto the gouernor of Chincheo of the estate of Limahon, he might giue order that before he had reedified and repayred himselfe they might take him (which is a thing most desired in all that kingdome). The generall was verie glad and reioyced of their good intertainment, and answered vnto Omoncon and Sinsay, saying that by reason of the great storme and foule weather past, their ships had great neede of reparation, and likewise the mariners to ease themselues, the which being done he would with all his heart depart.

The generall of the fielde was verie sorrowfull and much greeued for that the rouer Limahon was so escaped, and the more when he vnderstoode that he was suspected that hee did consent vnto his departure: for which occasion, if that the captaynes had not beene verie much wearied with the long siege, and euill weather which happened in that time, without all doubt he would haue followed him, and neuer to haue left him till he had taken or slaine him.

Although they were fully perswaded that Limahon was so terrified with the great perill and danger in the which he was, and againe with so small number of people, that rather hee would desire to put himselfe in securitie then to offende or doo any harme, neyther to put himselfe in any place whereas hee might receiue damage of any of them to whom hee had doone so open wrong (who were so much desirous to be reuenged), who for to preuent all that might happen (as after we vnderstoode), hauing made readie his barkes and boates which he ordayned in his fort, and put in them victualles for their iourney, he departed with his small number of people vnto an ilande farre off and vnknowen, there whereas he vnderstoode that none would goe to seeke him, and there hee remayned a time whereas he fell sicke of a melancholike infirmitie, which grewe by an imagination that hee had to remember in what state he was at that time, and howe he had seene himselfe at other times feared throughout al the kingdome of China, which was an imagination sufficient for to bring him to his ende: his companions were dispersed abroad, so that we neuer heard more of them.

Now returning to our purpose, after that the China

captaines had recreated them selues with the feastes and sportes that was made vnto them, and taken recreation many dayes, and tarryed, hoping that the weather would proue fayrer to prepare themselues to depart. In the same time they did intreat of many thinges in particular touching Christian religion, whereof with great care they did informe themselues of our religious men, and tolde them some secret things that were vnknowen vnto them of their countrie, for that they were strangers.

So when as time and weather did serue, they did take their leaue, with many signes and tokens of griefe for to depart and leaue the conuersation of so good companions, and did promise vnto them to procure all that was possible that the friendshippe begunne betwixt them and the Chinos should continue and perseuer, for that it was a thing that did content them all.

Their generall himself did take this particular charge vnto himselfe, with a determinate purpose for to declare in effect to the gouernour of Aucheo (whose private seruant he was) the good meaning of the Castillos; and what principall people they were, and the ceremonies they vsed, with the which hee was marueilously in love. Likewise hee would giue him to vnderstande of the flying of the rouer Limahon, how and in what manner and order it was, and how that the generall of the field and the other captaines were in no fault thereof. This he would do, in respect that if it should so fall out that Omoncon and Sinsay, for their owne credite, should declare any thing against the Spaniardes that was not true, that they might not be beleeued.

Besides all this he tolde the gouernour certaine things in secret, how they might with great ease purchase the friendship they pretended. And amongest them all, one was, that hee should make a supplication vnto the Catholike king in requesting him to write a letter vnto their king, and sende him embassador, and such as shoulde giue vnto them the light of the Catholike and Christian faith, with the which diligence there was no doubt that not onely the friend-shippe betwixt the kinges and their subiectes shoulde bee established, but also the king and all his kingdome would receiue the Catholike faith, for that there are manye ceremonies vsed amongest them which doo much resemble those of our Christian religion; and againe in their liuing morally, they doo obserue in manie thinges the Tenne Commandementes of Gods lawe, of the which in particular he did informe himselfe: so that the greatest difficultie was in the entring in of the preaching of the holy gospell, and beeing by this meanes ouer come, in a short time all the whole kingdome would turne Christians. And considering that in their worshipping, as they doo worship all thinges in the seconde essence, with great facilitie they would change their adoration and giue it vnto the first, as most worthie, and vnto whom it is their duties. The generall did adde more thereunto, and saide that he was so much affectioned vnto the faith of the Christians, that if it were not that he should be banished and loose his countrie, house and landes, without all doubt he would haue beene baptised: the which he could not doo without loosing of all, for that they haue a law in their countrie, the which is obserued and kept inuiolably, by the which it is forbidden that none whatsoeuer can receiue any strange religion differing from theirs vpon paine of death, without the consent of the king and his counsell.

Marginal note: The Papists and the Infidels ceremonies much alike.

This law was made to take away nouelties, and to liue all in one vniformitie of religion, with one manner of rites and ceremonies.

This only was the occasion that certaine marchants of China, being affectioned vnto the law of the gospell, were baptised at the Philippinas, and there do dwell at this day in the citie of Manilla amongest the Spaniardes, and are become verie good Christians.

So with these offers, and with promises to be great friendes vnto the Spaniardes, the generall departed from Manilla to goe vnto the firme lande, and with him the other captaynes Omoncon and Sinsay, with great hope that verie shortly they should be all of one faith. So the one tooke their leaue of the other with reasons of great affection and tokens of great loue, signifying that in any thing that should be offered they should finde them friendly.

They being departed, the Spaniardes remayned verie carefull in praying vnto the diuine maiestie, desiring of Him to direct all thinges in this their request, that it might be to his holy seruice, and also to inspire the Catholike maiestie of King Phillip their lorde for to sende his embassador vnto the king of China, offering his friendship, and to admonish him to receiue the faith of Christ, the which according vnto the report of the Austen fryers that entred into that countrie (of whom we haue made mention manie times in this booke with their companions), and also the generall of China tolde them that there was no other means but only that for to bring their purpose to effect.

This counsell with all the speede possible they put in vre, and sent vnto his maiestie one of purpose, and in the name of all them of those ilandes to request him, and to declare how much it did import. They sent vnto him this relation, with manie particular persons, for to mooue his most Christian minde for to sende an embassador, as in effect hee did, in that sort as hath beene tolde you in the last chapter of the thirde booke of this historie, whereas it is declared in particular, and in what estate it doth remaine vnto this day. God for his mercies sake direct all thinges, that it may be to his seruice and glorie, and the saluation of so many soules.

THE END OF THE FIRST BOOKE OF THE SECOND PART.

THE SECOND BOOKE

OF THE

SECOND PART

OF THE

HISTORIE

OF THE

MIGHTIE KINGDOME OF CHINA,

IN THE WHICH IS CONTAINED THE VOYAGE THAT WAS INTO THAT KINGDOME IN THE
YEAR 1576, BY THE FATHERS FRYER PETER DE ALFARO, COSTODIO IN THE
ILANDES PHILIPPINAS, OF THE ORDER OF SAINT FRANCIS, OF THE
PROUINCE OF S. JOSEPH, AND OTHER THREE RELIGIOUS MEN
OF THE SAME ORDER, AND THEIR MIRACULOUS ENTRING
INTO THAT KINGDOME, AND WHAT HAPPENED VNTO
THEM FOR THE SPACE OF SEUEN MONTHES THAT
THEY THERE REMAINED, AND WHAT THEY
DID SEE AND VNDERSTAND OF: ALL
THE WHICH ARE NOTABLE
AND VERIE RARE.

———

CHAP. I.

The fryers of Saint Francis came vnto the Ilandes Philippinas, and procured to passe vnto the firme lande of the kingdome of China, with zeale to preach the holy gospell.

THE day of the visitation of our Ladie, in the yeare 1578, there came out of Spaine to the citie of Manilla, in the Ilandes Philippinas, the father Fryer Peter de Alfaro, who went for Costodio of that prouince, and fourteene more other religious persons of the same order in his companie, and were sent by the king of Spaine and his royall counsel of the Indias, for to be ayders and helpers of the Austen fryers, who vntill that time had beene there alone in those ilandes, occupied in the conuerting of the people in that countrie, and were the first ministers of the gospell, preaching the same with great zeale, vnto the profite of their soules : of the which people those fryers had baptised (when the others ariued) more then one hundred thousande, and the rest prepared and cathecised to receive the like. Because that at the first occasion that might be giuen, they might enter into the kingdome of China to preach the holy gospell. The which Fryers, when that they had been there the space of one yeare occupying themselues in the same exercise in preaching and conuerting the people of that countrie, in the same time they were giuen to vnderstande by the relation of the selfe same Austen fryers, as also by many marchants of China which came vnto them with marchandice, of things to be wondred at of that mightie kingdome, and of the infinite number of soules which the diuell had deceiued and brought vnto his seruice with false idolatrie. The which being by them well vnderstood, they did burne with great zeale and desire of their saluation, and to goe and preach the gospell, although it were to put their persons in whatsoeuer hazarde or danger.

So with this their great desire, they did many and diuerse times communicate with the gouernor that was there at that time for his maiestie, who was called the Doctor Francisco de Sandi, desiring his fauour and licence for to goe vnto China in the companie of certaine marchants of that countrie, that were at that present in the port with their ships, offering themselues to get their good will, although it were to offer themselues to be slaues or otherwise whatsoeuer. And seeing that at all such times when as they did intreat of that matter, they found him but luke warme, and that he did (as it were) but to detract the time, and feed them with hope: then they calling to minde that the chiefest intent and cause of their comming out of Spayne, was to enter into that kingdome, caused a newe desire to grow in them, what with the contractation they had with the sayde Chinos, as well in conuersation as in talke, and finding them to be a people of great abilitie and discretion, and of verie good iudgements, the which did greatly content their desire, they did perswade themselues that it was an easie matter to make them to vnderstande the things appertaining vnto God. So that they determined to put other remedies in practise, because that which they required with the good will of the gouernor, seemed to be a large and long matter. So it happened that vpon a time intreating of this matter, and hauing requested of God with great instance for to direct them the readie way which was best for his seruice, and for the profite of those soules, there came to the Ilandes Philippinas a Chino, who, according as they did vnderstand, was one of the priests and religious men of that kingdome (of the which priestes there are a great number in euerie towne): this priest went diuerse times vnto the monasterie of the Fryers, and did common with them of the creation of the worlde and other things, which did open the way that they might declare vnto him thinges appertayning vnto God, vnto the which he did hearken with great good will. And after that hee had declared vnto them in particular the mightinesse and secretes of this mightie kingdome of China (whose conuersion they so greatly desired), he very inquisitiuely asked of them matters touching the Christian faith, of whome within a fewe dayes after he desired to be baptised, for that he would be a Christian, being instructed before in many matters touching our Catholike faith.

Our religious men did accomplish his desire, the which was an incredible ioy vnto all the dwellers of the citie, and a content vnto himselfe.

So after that he was made a Christian hee remayned in the monasterie amongest the other, but yet would he neuer eate any other thing but colde herbes: and he seeing that all the religious men did arise vp at midnight to mattens and discipline themselues, spending the greatest part of the night in prayer before the holy sacrament, hee did not faile one point, but did imitate them in all their dooings, with outwarde showes of a verie good will. All the which did incyte the Fryer Costodio and all the rest of his companions to put in execution their great desire they had, according as it hath beene tolde you. Whereupon he went once againe vnto the gouernour to intreat him by faire meanes that which before they had comoned with him of, and that he would procure some order or meanes, that those religious men might go to the kingdome of China to preach the lawe of God, offering himselfe to be one of them, with protestation that if he would not giue them leaue, they would procure to go without it, with that authoritie the which hee had of God and of his superiors, for to teach and instruct these poore infidels their neighbors: and this should be done with the first opportunitie they might finde or haue.

The Spaniards rise at their midnight mattens and whip themselues.

But neither this, nor yet the example of that good Chino, which was newe christened, was sufficient to perswade the gouernor to consent vnto their request; but perseuering in his first opinion, he answered and said, that it was too timely, and that the friendship which they had with the Chinos as yet was very small, and how that the fathers of S. Austen had manie times attempted the entrie into that kingdome, and yet neuer could obtaine their desire. And howe that the Chinos that did carrie them did deceiue them, and left them in certaine ilands, till such time as they heard farther newes of the rouer Limahon, and of the returne of the captaine Omoncon, who did carrie them with the good newes of the straight siege in the which they had the rouer: and yet for all that they commanded them to returne from Aucheo, without giuing them anie licence to remaine in the countrie to preach the holy gospell; and nowe to attempt the same, was but to giue occasion vnto the Chinos euerie day to mocke and make a iest of the Spaniardes, and willed them to staye till such time as it were the will of God to giue way vnto the same, which could not be long.

This Fryer Costodio vnderstanding the answere of the gouernour, perseuering still in his first opinion, and did not goe about to seeke any meanes to accomplish their desire for the entring into the firme lande, hee straightwayes beganne secretly to procure by all meanes possible to attempt and accomplish that iourney, although it were without the order and consent of the gouernour (when that it might not be doone otherwise), the which incontinent they beganne to put in vre, for that the Fryer Costodio and Fryer Steuen Ortiz (who was a religious man, that for the great desire he had did learne the China tongue, and at that time did speake it resonablie), they both together did giue to vnderstande of their desire and pretence vnto a deuout souldier of their religion, and one that they made great account of, who was called Iohn Dias Pardo, who often times had made manifest vnto them and saide, that he had a great desire to do some especiall seruice vnto God, although it were to hazarde his life in the same, who at that instant did accomplish his desire, and did promise them to beare them companie vnto the death.

So with this conformitie they went straightwayes altogether to speake with a captaine of China that was in the same port, in a shippe of his owne, who many times did repayre vnto their conuent, to aske of them thinges appertayning vnto God, and the heauens, with showe of a very good vnderstanding, who vnto their iudgement did consent and accept all with great pleasure and delight.

Unto this captayne they did giue to vnderstande the effect of all their desire, requesting him of his ayde and helpe in the prosecuting of the same. Who straightwayes did offer himselfe to accomplish their request and to carrie them vnto China, so as they woulde then giue him some thing for to bestowe amongest his marriners. The souldier Iohn Diaz Pardo did promise to giue them all that they would aske, and gaue them in earnest certayne ryalles of plate. And for that all thinges shoulde bee doone in good order, and in such sort that the gouernour nor any other shoulde haue any suspition or knowledge, it was ordayned amongest them that the captaine of China should with all speede dispatch himselfe and depart to the port of Bindoro, which is twentie leagues from the citie of Manilla, and there to tarrie for them, and to carrie in his companie the Chino that was new baptised as aforesaid.

The captaine made haste, dispatched himselfe, and departed vnto the port appointed, and within a fewe dayes after the father Costodio and his company, with the souldier his friend, did followe them. But when they came thether they found the captaine Chino in an other minde, in such sort that neyther gifts nor faire intreatie was sufficient to perswad him to performe that which he had promised in Manilla, but returned vnto them their earnest before receiued, affirming that for any thing in al the world he would not carrie them, for that he knewe very well, if hee should so doo, it would cost him his life and goods.

The newe baptised religious Chino seeing that, wept bitterly, with discontentment to see how the diuell had changed the minde of the captaine, for that in that kingdome the holie gospell should not be preached. The father Costodio did resolue himselue to returne vnto Manilla, and there to abide a better oportunitie, as in effect they did, whereas they remayned certaine dayes, till such time it happened as followeth.

Upon a day the gouernour sent and called vnto him the father Costodio, and requested of him that he would let him haue some Fryer for to sende vnto the riuer of Cagayan, whether not long before he had sent certaine Spaniards for to inhabite.

The Fryer Costodio promised him one, and that he should go with him in companie till he came to the prouince of Illocos whether he went, and that from thence he would dispatch him vnto the riuer of Cagayan, according vnto his worships commandement, requesting of him to haue in his companie, to keepe watch and warde in that iourney, the ensigne Francisco de Duennas, and Iohn Diaz Pardo the souldier, his friend as aforesaide, with pretence to depart from thence vnto China, as in effect they did, as shall be tolde you. The gouernor being very willing for to pleasure him, did grant his request. So with great speede he departed, and carried with him the foresaide souldiers, and for companion a religious man called frier Austin de Tordesillas (he who afterwards did put in memorie all thinges that passed with them in China), out of the which hath beene taken this small relation.[1] So when they came vnto the Illocos, they found fryer Iohn Baptista and fryer Sebastian, of S. Francis, of his owne order, occupied in the teaching and instructing the people of that prouince, which was the fourth day of Iune.

The next day following they called a counsell, where it was concluded that all those that were there present would venture themselues for to go vnto China, to conuert those gentiles, or else to die in the quarrell. And the better to bring their purpose to passe, they thought it good to speake vnto an other souldier that was there with them, called Pedro de Villa Roel, not telling vnto him their pretence, because they would not be discouered (but asked him in this manner) if he would beare him companie, and the other two souldiers, who altogether went about a business of great honour and seruice of God, and the benefite and sauing of

[1] The friar Augustin de Tordesillas was one of the founders of the province of St. Gregory in Luzon. His narrative seems never to have been printed elsewhere. See Sbaralea's *Supplement* to Waddington, and N. Antonio's *Bibliotheca Hispana Nova*.

manye soules; and that he would declare vnto them whether he would go or not, without asking whether nor from what place, for that as then they could not giue him to vnderstand, till time did serue. His answere was, that straightwaies he would beare them companie, and would neuer leaue them to death.

So foorthwith they altogether with singular ioy went to the ship wherin the father Costodio and his companion, with the other two souldiers, came in from Manilla to that place with a reasonable frigat, although with but fewe marriners, and they not verie expert. So being altogether in the shippe, with all such thinges as they could get together in that small time for their prouision in that iourney, they made all thinges in a readinesse to set sayle the same day, which was the twelfth day of the said moneth of Iune. So after they had sayde masse and commended themselues vnto God, requesting Him to direct their voyage that it might be to His glorie and seruice, they set sayle vppon a Fryday, in the morning, with intent to goe foorth of that port; but they could not by no meanes possible, for that the sea went verie loftie vpon the barre, and contending with the sea for to get foorth they were in great danger to haue beene cast away, which was the occasion that with great sorrow they returned into the port, whereas they remayned all day.

CHAP. II.

The fryers and their companions depart from the port of Illocos, after they had committed vnto God the direction of their voyage. They passe great daungers and troubles, and do ouercome them all with the confidence they haue in God, and came vnto the kingdome of China miraculously.

[Early in the morning of the following day (being the festival of St. Antony of Padua), they said mass and returned to the frigate to take their departure; but the sea was still so boisterous and rough that it took the ship on her broadside, and she leaked very much, until at length it pleased God that she drove on the shore, where, striking on the sand several times, it was a most evident miracle that she did not go to pieces, and that all in her were not drowned. It was their firm belief that God had done this through the intercession of the blessed St. Anthony, whose day it was, and to whom they had with sincere devotion commended themselves. They then put back from the river which they had left, and this they accomplished, but with great exertion and danger, insomuch that the Father Stephen Ortiz became so terrified, that no persuasion could induce him to continue the voyage which they had started upon: He replied that he would not further tempt God, since the signs which they had seen were sufficient to show that it was not His holy will that they should prosecute that journey at that time, the which proved a trouble and stumblingblock to all the rest. The Father Costodio concealed his vexation and put a good face on the matter, telling them all to keep up their courage, for that great difficulties attended every good work at the commencement, but that these easily yielded to perseverance and patience, as experience had often shown. In this manner he talked with them until the day of the Trinity, when, after the priests had said mass and confessed the laymen, and administered the sacrament to them, they all returned with good will to go on board, except the abovementioned Father Ortiz, who remained at home in his old obstinacy, and with him the Chinese who had been baptized, the latter having fallen very ill, which caused great grief to all.][1]

So the next day, after they had committed themselues to God with great deuotion, they embarked themselues and made sayle, and by the will of God they went out of the

[1] The commencement of the chapter, here inserted between brackets, is not given in Parke's translation.

harbour, although with great danger; and they carryed with them an other barke a sterne their ship, in the which they did determine for to set a lande such Indians as they carried with them from the Esquipazon,[1] to helpe them out of the harbour: the which they did not for feare they should be drowned. So when they were out of that riuer, they sayled towards the little iland that was but one league from that place, and there they put the Indians a shore, and with them a young man, a Spaniard, that they brought from Manilla to serue them. So those which should go on that voyage remayned there the same night, who were the frier Costodio; frier Peter de Alfaro, borne in Siuel; frier Iohn Baptista, borne in Pesaro in Italy; fryer Sebastian de San Francisco, of the citie of Boecia;[2] and frier Augustin de Tordesillas, of the same towne whereof he hath his name; all these foure were priestes of the masse.

The fryer Costodio would with a very good will haue carried more of them, but he durst not for two causes; the one for that hee would not haue beene discouered, and the other (which was the principal occasion), because he would not leaue that prouince of the Illocos without such as shold instruct them, whereas were many baptized: for which respect he left some behind him, which afterwarde hee would have beene very glad that they had beene in his companie. There were three Spaniards souldiers that did beare them companie, the one was called the ancient Francisco de Duennas, of Velez Malaga—the other John Diaz Pardo, of Saint Lucas de Barameda, the third Pedro de Villa Roel of the citie of Mexico. Besides these they had a boy of China who could speak the Spanish tongue, and was one of them that were taken at the siege of Limahon the rouer, and other foure Indians of Manilla.

[1] This word (thus given by Parke with a capital letter) means the equipment or rigging of a vessel, evidently put for the vessel itself.

[2] Misspelt for Baeza, in the province of Jaen, in Andalusia.

They departed from this little islande upon a Munday, the first quarter in the morning which was the fifteene day of the said moneth of June, and sayled that way so nigh as they could gesse to be the way vnto China, without pilot or any other certaintie, more than that which God did shewe and put into their minds with their great desire, which seemed vnto them to comprehende and bring it to passe. This day the winde was contrarie and against them, which was the occasions that they sayled but little. Towardes the evening, the winde changed and blewe at the north (the which winde vppon that coast is very dangerous), which made them greatly afrayde; yet was that feare driven away by an other feare much greater than that, which was that they should be discovered, and that they should be pursued by the commandemente of the governour of Manilla, for which occasion whereas they should have throwed themselves under the land, they wrought contrary and cast about vnto the sea in great danger to have beene cast away; but it was the will of God that when as night came, the winde did calme (which commonly falleth out to the contrary), but the sea remayned very rough and loftie, that they thought verily to have beene drowned with the furie thereof, for it tossed the frigetta in such sort, that it seemed a whole legion of diuels had taken holde on both sides of the shippe, forcing the one against the other that it rowled in such sort that many times the halfe decke was in the water, so that the mariners could not stand upon their feete, but were driven to sustaine themselves by the ropes and cables. But the religious men trusting in God, whose zeale had caused them this great trouble, did pray and desire him with many tears, that hee would deliver them out of the same daunger, and not to give place vnto the diuell for to disturbe them of their voyage and enterprise. *They were in great perill.*

These their orations and prayers did so much prevaile, with certaine coniurations which they made against the diuels, (who they thought they did see visibly), that after *The Fryers vsed certaine coniurations for that S. Antonie was asleepe.*

midnight the north winde ceased and began to blowe at the north east, with the which the sea began to waxe calme ; so that they might make their way to be east north east, for that they had intelligence that that course was the shortest cut to the firme land. This winde which was so favourable vnto them, did increase so much in two hours that the sea waxed loftie and caused them to forget the sorrowe past, and constrained them (for that the shippe was but small) to cut their mast ouer borde, and to put themselves vnto the courtesie of the sea with little hope to escape the danger. But our Lorde whose zeale did moove them to attempt that iourney, did direct their voyage in such sort, that the next day following it came to be calme in such sort that they might set up a newe mast, in the place of that which was cut ouer borde in the storme, and therewith to nauigate forwardes with their begunne voyage. So upon the Fryday following at the break of the day they sawe lande, and thinking that it had beene the firme land of China they gave thanks unto God, and rejoiced, in such sort that they had cleane forgotten the troubles of the stormes and foule weather passed, so they made towards it and came thither about noone, but when they were a shore, they found that it was but a small island and situated foure leagues from the firme land; and for that it was so nigh, a farre off it seemed to be all one thing. But when they came unto this ilande they did discover many ships which were so many in number that it seemed all the sea to be covered with them. The friers, with the great desire they had for to knowe in what port they were, they comanded to gouerne their ship towards whereas they were, who when they saw them, and could not know them by the strangenes of their ship and sailes, they did fly from them all that ever they could. The which our men perceiving and could not imagine the cause thereof, they were very much agrieued and sorrowful, and the more for that they could not learne nor vnderstand where they were. But seeing nigh vnto them to the lewarde three ships, they made towards them, and when they were somewhat nigh they put themselves as the others did. In this sort they spent all the rest of the day in going from one port to an other vnto those ships, for to informe themselves where they were; but all this diligence prevailed them nothing at all till it was almost sunne set. They entred with their frigat into a gut vnder the shore, whereas fell from a high rocke which was more than one hundredth fatham by estimation, a stream of water which was as bigge as the bodies of two men together.

In this gut there was three other ships, and they came to an anker in the middest amongest them, the which beeing done they asked of them what countrie that was, but they answered nothing, nor made any semblance, but looked the one upon the other; and in beholding of the Spaniards they gave great laughters. In this gut they remained all that night, almost amased to see how those people were, as though they were enchanted; and they without any light of their desire, which was to knowe where they were. So the next day folowing (which was Saterday), very early in the morning they set sayle, and went amongst a great sort of islandes, always bearing vnto them, which they thought to be the firme lande, being greatly amarueiled to see the infinite number of shippes both great and small that they sawe; some were a fishing, and some under sayle, and other some ryding at an anker. The same day about noon there happened unto them a strange and miraculous thing, and it was, that passing through a straight that was but a quarter of a league of bredth, which was betwixt the firme lande and a small islande, in the which was continually four score ships of warre set there for watch and warde; they passed through the thickest of them and were never seene, for if they hadde, without all doubt they had sonke them or slain them. Their order and commission is so straight given them by their generalles of the sea, in the which they are commanded, that whatsoever kinde of people of strange nations that they do meete upon the coast, for to kill them or sinke them, except they do bring licence from some governor of such cities as be upon the coast; for that such as doo meane to have traficke doo sende to demand the same, leaving their ships a great way at sea.

This lawe for to watch and warde was made and ordayned (as they do say), in respect of the Japones who did enter into certain of their portes, dissembling themselues to be Chinos; being apparelled as they were, and speaking their language, they did vnto them great and strange hurtes and damages, as is declared in the booke before this. So when they were passed this straight, they sayled almost sixe leagues forwardes into a verie fayre and great bay, following other shippes that went before them; for that it seemed that they would enter into some port, and there they might informe themselues where they were, which was the thing that they most desired. When they had sayled about two leagues in this bay, they overtook one of the three shippes, and asked of the people that were within her (by the intrepreter they had with them), whether they sayled, and what lande that was which they sawe before them.

Then the principall that was in that ship, did put himself into his boat the which hee had at sterne, and came vnto the ship where the Spaniards were, the better to vnderstande what they did demand; for they before by reason that they were somewhat farre off the one from the other, could not vnderstande the Spaniards demand but by signes. So when that he vnderstoode their request, he answered them that it was the country of China, and how that he came laden with salt from the citie of Chincheo, and went to make sale thereof vnto the citie of Canton, which was so nigh hand that they might ariue there before night. But when that he was entred into the Spanish ship and saw the friers and the rest that were in their companie, and saw that their apparell and speech was strange vnto him, he asked of them what they were and from whence they came, and whether they went? (and when that he vnderstood that they were Castillos, and of the islands Philippinas, and came from the said islands and were bound vnto China, with intent to preach the holy gospell), he asked them whose licence they had to conduct them vnto the firme lande? But when he vnderstood that they had none, hee asked them howe they passed and escaped the fleete of ships that was in the straight aforesayde? The Spaniards answered, that they found no impediment nor let. So he being greatlie amazed as well of the one as of the other, entered into his owne boate, and with great furie departed from their shippe and went into his owne; but at his departure the Spaniards did request him that he would conduct them vnto the citie, who gave them to vnderstande by signes that he woulde, although he feared the rigorous punishment that in that kingdom is executed vppon all such as doo bring into the same any man of a strange nation (as hath been tolde you in the first part of this historie.) So hee fearing that if hee shoulde enter with him into the port, the fault would be imputed unto him, therefore at such time as hee came within halfe a league of the riuer's mouth, he cast about his shippe and sailed to sea, and went so farre that in a short time the Spaniards had lost the sight of them; who when they saw that they had no guide, they followed the course of another shippe that they had discovered before the other did cast about to sea, for which occasion the other two ships that we spake off before were departed. So a little before the sunne set, they discouered the mouth and entrie of a great and mightie brode riuer, out of the which came two great streames or armes, and in them many ships entering in and going forth; and considering how they had the winde which serued them well they entered into the same. But when they had sailed forwards a quarter of a league, they discouered so great a multitude of barkes that it seemed vnto them a grove, or some inhabited place, and as we drew nigh vnto them, they not knowing our shippe, all began to flie and run away with so great noise, as though they should haue beene all set on fire or smoke in that place. The Spaniards seeing that they were the occasion of this feare amongst them, they withdrew themselves into the middest of the riuer, whereas they strooke saile and came to an anker, and there they did ride all that night, and it was in such a place that none of al the other barks and boats came nigh them by a great way.

The next day following, which was Sunday, the one-and-twentieth day of June, they weighed anker, and went vnder their foresaile vp that arme of the riuer, the which within a little while they had sailed did ioine with the other arme aforesaide, and was in that place of so great widenesse that it seemed to bee a sea; there sailed in and out many shippes, barkes, and boates, of whom the Spaniards demaunded how farre the port was off from that place, but they answered nothing at all, but with great laughter and wonder to see the Spaniards and their kind of attyre, they departed. But when they had sailed two leagues up the riuer, they discouered a high towre and very faire, vnder the which were at an anker a great number of shippes; thither they sailed right on. So when as they came right ouer against the towre, they saw on shore a great mighty crane, to discharge merchandize withal, whereat lay many ships; but when they came to the point, fearing that some ordinance would be shot at them, they strook all their sailes, according vnto the vse and custom in the ports of Spain. They, after a while that they had remained in that sort, and saw that neither the towre nor the ships did make any motion towards them, they turned and hoised up again their sailes and went wheras al the ships were, and when they came amongst them they let fall their anker; wheras they did ride, looking when they would come to demand of them anything.

CHAP. III.

The fryers and their companions came vnto the cittie of Canton, they went on shore, and praised God for that it had pleased Him to let them see their desire fulfilled. There comes a iustice to visite them, and hath with them great communication.

The Spaniards seeing that they were there at an anker a good while, and that there was none that came vnto them to demand any question, they hoisted out their boate, and went in it on shore, wheras they al kneeled downe upon their knees, and with great deuotion did say *Te Deum laudamus*, giuing thankes to God for that he had so myraculously brought them into the kingdome of China, of them so much desired, without any pilot or other humane industrie; the which being doone, they began to walke along by the crane aforesaid, nigh unto the which were certaine houses wheras were kept ropes and tackling belonging vnto the shippes; so they proceeded forwards with intent to seek the gates of the citie, the which after they had gone the space of foure hargabus shot, they found the gate, which was verie great and sumptuous of a strong and gallant edifice. The people of the country seeing them at their comming a shore how they did kneele downe, and how that their manner of attire was different from the people of the same, and not knowing from whence they did come, did cause in them great admiration, and to ioyne togither a great troope of people, and followed them with great desire to see the end of their enterprize.

This great multitude of people was the occasion that they entered in at the gates of the cittie without being discouered of the guards and posts that were put there for that purpose, neither were they disturbed of the entry by reason of the great throng of people and strangenesse of the matter. So after they had gone a while in the streete, the people increasing more and more to see them, they staied in the porch of a great house there, where as the iustices of the sea, or water bailies, do keepe their courts of audience; and in the meane time that they remained there, which was a pretty while, the guardes of the gate understood that amongst the presse and throng of the people, did enter certaine strangers, contrary to the precept given them vpon great penalties; they straightway, with great fear that their ouersight should be discouered, ran and laid hands vpon the Spaniards, and carried them backe againe and put them out of the gate of the citie, without doing any evil or harme vnto their persons, and willed them to stay there in that place till such time as they had given the gouernor of the cittie to vnderstand thereof, and he to send them licence that they may enter in againe. So after a good while that they had remained there wheras the guards had set them, there came vnto them a man who was a Chino, called Canguin, and could speake Portugal, who knowing them to be Christians by their faces and attire, did aske them in the Portugal toong, what they sought? the Spaniards answered him, that their comming into that kingdom was for to shew and declare to them the way to heaven, and to give them to vnderstand and know the true God, the creator of heaven and earth, and that they would very faine talke with the gouernor to entreat therof. This Chino by and by brought to them a man that could speak very good Portuges, who as after they did vnderstand, both he, his wife and children were christened; and although they were borne in China, yet did they dwel thre years with Portugals that were inhabited in Machao, which is twenty leagues from that cittie of Canton. This did demande the same question of them that the other did, and wherefore they came into that countrie? They answered him the same as they did the other; hee replied, and asked them who was the pilot that brought them thither? they answered, the will of God; they not knowing howe, nor from whence: but after they had sailed at the sea certaine dayes, they came vnto that place that according as it was given them to vnderstande, is the cittie of Canton, of the which they have heard declared many straunge thinges. The Chino asked how the guardes of the sea, and shippes that were in the straight aforesaid, did let them passe? they answered that they saw no guards nor any other that did trouble them their passage. This last answere did cause the christian Chino greatly to admire, who being moued with a good zeale, said vnto them, that they should returne againe vnto the shippe, and not to come forth untill such time as he had giuen aduice of their comming vnto the mandelines of the sea, which be certaine iudges appointed to giue aduice of all such matters to the governor, that he may command what is to be done therein.

So the Spaniards returned vnto the shippe, wheras they remained a good while, and passed great heate, for that it dooth exceede in that port. So after a while, they sawe come vnto a house which was neere vnto the gate of the cittie, a man of great authoritie, who was brought in a litter chaire, and much people came with him; he stayed at that house, and from thence sent to call vnto him the religious men and all the rest that came in their company; before them all came one that carried a table, all whited, and thereon was written certain great letters, with blacke ynke, the which (as after they understood) was the licence that the gouernor of the cittie gaue them for to come a shoore, without the which there is no stranger permitted. The fathers did straightwayes obey it, and came forth of their shippe with more companie than they desired, of such as came to see them, who were so many in number, that although the sergeants and officers of the iudge that sent for them, did beate them for to make way, yet was it a good while before they coulde come vnto the house wheras the iudge was, although the way was but short. So when they approched nigh, one of the sergeants bad them kneele down before the iudge, the which they did with great humilitie without any replication. Hee was set in a verie rich chaire with so great maiestie that they were greatly astonyed to see it, and the more when that they understood by the christian Chino that he was not the gouernor, neither of the supreme iudges; hee was apparelled in a robe of silke, close from aboue down to the foot, with the sleeues very wide, and a girdle imbossed, and on his head a bonnet full of brooches, such as bishops doo use on their mytres. Before him was set a table, whereon was paper and inke, and on the one side and on the other, two rankes of men, as though they were to guard him, yet without weapons. They had al of them in their hands, long canes of foure fingers brode, with the which (as after they did vnderstand), they do beat such as are offenders, vpon the calues of their legges, with great crueltie, as hath been told you in the first books of this historie. All these had vppon their heads a manner of helmet, made of blacke leather, and on them great plumes of pecocks' feathers, with brooches made of mettal, a thing vsed to be worne in that countrie of such as are executioners or ministers of iustice.

The iudge had the interpreter to aske them of what nation they were, and what they sought in that countrie, and who was their guide to bring them into that port: the which being vnderstood by the religious men, answered that they were Spaniards, and subject vnto the king Philip of Spaine, and came thether to preach the holy gospel, and to teach them to know the true God, creator of the heauen and earth, and to leaue off the worshiping of their idols (who haue no more power of themselues, then that which is giuen them by him that doth make them): the which worship is knowne and receiued by his holie law, and declared by the mouth of his only begotton Sonne, and confirmed with diuine tokens from heauen, in whose guarde doth consist the saluation of all soules. And to the last, touching who was

Marke the Friers confession of images.

their guide vnto that kingdome: they answered, That it was
God, vnto whose will all creature are subiect, as vnto the
true creator : all the which (as afterward it did appeare) the
interpreter did not truely interpret of the interpretation of
the Spaniards : vnderstanding, that if hee should truely interpret what they saide, the iudge would forthwith sende
them away, which would be the occasion that he shuld get
nothing of them. So that he made his interpretation as at
best seemed for his purpose, fearing (as after he did confesse) that if he shuld declare the truth of that which the
Spaniards had said, it would haue beene verie odious to the
iudge, and afterward both vnto them and to himselfe might
be the occasion of some great euill : but to conclude, he
answered and told the iudge that they were certaine religious men, who liued in common a sharpe and asper life,
much after the manner of those of that kingdome : and that
going from the Iland of Luzon vnto the Ilands of the Illocos,
in a great storme and tempest that chanced them, the ship
wherin they were was cast away, and al their people cast
away, sauing they, who escaped by vsing great diligence,
and put themselues in that small ship, which came in company with another greater shippe, without pilot or mariner,
for that they were almost all drowned ; and setting saile in
the best manner they could or knewe, being holpen and
constrained by necessity, they let their ship saile, and go
whither as fortune did cary them. So after many dangers
and stormes at the sea, according to the will of the heauens
they came vnto this port, whose name as yet they knew not.
The iudge asked them where they had that Chino that
they brought in their company for an interpreter. They
answered that he was in Luzon, and captiue vnto a Spaniard : they tooke him and set him free, and hee vnderstanding that they were bound vnto the firme land of China,
which was his naturall countrie, he requested them to carrie
him thither ; the which they did with a very good will, for

that they had neede of him to vtter their desire, if neede did so require. All the which the other interpreter fearing, that if he should tel vnto the iudge how that he was captiue vnto the Christians, hee would bee offended, and therefore hee did falsifie the same and saide, that comming vnto an iland to take in fresh water, they found the boy there, where he was captiue eight yeares before, and came thither forced with a great storme, in the which was drowned a merchants shippe that was bound to Luzon, and he alone escaped by swimming; and so hee came aborde the shippe in the which were the fathers, not knowing whither they went. All these vntruthes he did inuent for to dissemble and go forwards with his knavish pretence, and would not declare the true intent of the friers: the which he had decreed with himselfe how to doo before the iudge did sende to call them. Moreouer, the iudge did aske them what they brought in their small shippe; they answered that they brought nothing but one chest and two little fardels of bookes, and an ornament for to say masse. This did the interpreter declare truely vnto the iudge, for that experience might be made thereof. So the iudge forthwith commanded that it should be brought before him, the which being done, he caused it to be vndone, and he perused euery thing by it selfe, the which being strange vnto him, for that he neuer saw the like, he made signes vnto them that he receiued great contentment in the seeing of them, but specially of the images they brought: but that which did best please him was an ara or sopra-altar, of a blacke stone, the which did shine so bright that they might see themselues therein, as well as in a glasse. These friers did bring the same with them out of the kingdom of Mexico, whereas you haue great aboundance, but specially in the prouince of Mechuacan. So after that hee had seene all, and sawe that it was drie, without any signe or token that it had beene in the sea, hee called to remembrance the wordes of the interpreter in the name of the fathers, touching the storme wherein their shippe was cast away, and howe that they escaped by swimming, and put themselues in that small shippe in the which they came : and considering of the same, it seemed vnto him that they did fable in that which they had saide: so that he did replie and asked if it were true that which they had before declared, and howe it shoulde bee that their bookes and other things were not wet at the sea, which was an euident token and plainely to be vnderstood that they had fabled and told lies, and so he belieued they did in all the rest. The interpreter, fearing least by that argument his falshod would be discouered, he fel in talke a while with the friers, asking and answering things very different to that which the iudge had commanded him. Then he with a strange and sharpe boldnes answered to the difficulty proponed by the iudge, and said, That as all merchants at such time as their shippes are readie to sinke and to be lost, they doo procure first to saue such thinges as are of most estimation, forgetting all the rest: euen so these religious men did procure with great care and diligence to saue those books and that ornament, which is all their treasure, and yet for all their diligences done they lost a great number mo. All these fables and lies, after many dayes, the religious fathers came to haue the knowledge of.

The iudge did aske them if they brought any armor or weapons in their shippe? they answered that they were no men to bring them, neither according vnto their profession, they could not wear nor use them, for that they were religious, and professed other matters contrary vnto the vse of armor or weapon, promising and auowing vnto God perpetual povertie and chastitie, and vnto their superior prelates obedience all the dayes of their liues. The iudge returned and asked them if they had any monie, and where withall they did eate and apparell themselues, and bought those bookes and ornaments? they answered, that all that which they had was giuen them by secular christians for God's sake whome they did serue, for that they should pray for them, and for the saluation of their soules.

The iudge, when he heard this, was greatly astonied, for that the interpreter did declare the truth, and made signes that he recieued griefe and had pittie on them, although he gaue not full credite to that which he heard, but said that he would go aborde their shippe, to see if they did say the truth, in not bringing anie armor or weapon, neither siluer nor merchandize. This did hee straightwayes put in ure, and commaunded them that brought him in the litter chaire vpon their shoulders to go thitherward. All those people did beare him companie, as also a great number that were there ioyned togither to heare the examination of those strangers, and also the Spaniards he commanded to go next vnto him.

So that when he was in their shippe, set in his chaire, his ministers began to search the shippe in all places, both aboue and below, and could finde nothing but a little rice, which was left of that which they brought with them: they gaue the iudge to vnderstand thereof, who looking vpon the Spaniards, said that all they that were in the shippe might heare him. These do speak the truth, and they doo seeme vnto me to bee good people, and without any superstition, and without all doubte they doo come and will be after the manner of our religious men, according as is to be seene in the vniformitie of their apparell, as also in their heads and beardes. Then he beganne to demaunde of them certaine thinges, more of curiositie then of suspection; who answered him, casting up their eies vnto heauen, (for that their talke was thereof), and they saw that the iudge did greatly reioyce and had pleasure therein, for that it seemed that they had the heauens for their God, as they haue, by reason they did so much looke upwards. After this the iudge came foorth of the shippe, but the religious men remained behind at his commandment with his companions; and likewise hee commaunded certaine of those officers that came with him, to remaine about their ship at the water's side, for their guard, more for that none should doo to them any harme, then for any euil suspition they had of them.

Al that day that the Spaniards were in their ship the countrie men came downe to the water side to see them, and that in so great number that they did woonder to see them; and on the other side they were greatly reioyced to see so many soules there ioyned togither, hoping that when it should bee the will and pleasure of God to giue them oportunitie, to baptise them all.

The next day following, in the morning, they sawe another mandelin or judge, comming towards their shippe, accompanied with much people, and with little less maiestie than the other had, who entered into their shippe and commaunded to search both aboue and belowe, to see whether they brought any armour, weapon, or any other kinde of merchandize; and seeing that they could finde nothing else but their bookes and their ornament aforesaide, he commaunded it to be brought before him, who did peruse the same peece by peece with great admiration, and shewed great contentment that hee received to see their bookes and images, although that which did most content him was to see the ara of blacke stone, as was said before. Then hee commanded one of the fathers for to reade in one of the said bookes, and for to write, the which was done before him with so great facilitie, that the judge receiued great contentment to see it. Then hee asked them if that with the said letters they could write any other language that were different vnto theirs. The fathers answered yea, that they coulde write any language; and for a plainer proofe they wrote on a piece of paper, certaine reasons in the iudges language, the which did cause him greatly to maruell, and said (turning his face to some of them that came with him), these men are not barbarous, nor of any euill condition, so farre as I can see.

With this he departed out of their shippe, and went to giue the gouernour (who sent him), to vnderstand of that he had seene and coulde vnderstande of the Spaniards in this his visitation, who straightwayes did sende them a licence vpon a table, that they shoulde come on shore, and be suffered to enter into the cittie freely at their will.

CHAP. IV.

The Spaniards go forth of their ship, and go into the citie unto the christened Chinos house, and are carried before another superior judge in common audience, and manie other passe with them.

So soone as they had their licence, they went forth of their ship and entred in at the gate of the cittie, although with great trouble by reason of the great number of people that came to see them, as a thing neuer seen before. Then they went to the christened Chinos house (hee that serued for their interpreter), who made very much of them, and giuing them to vnderstand that hee had made a true report of all that they had commanded him, and did offer himselfe to do so much with the justices, that he would procure to get licence of the gouernor for them to remain in the countrie, and to giue them a house wherein to remaine and dwel; and did admonish them that at that time they should not deale for to make the Chinos christians, vntil such time as they were better knowne, and coulde speake the language, and then should they doo it with a great deale more ease. All these promises, with the falsifying of that the Spaniards spake before to the iudges, was to content the friers (as in discourse of time they did vnderstande), and onely to get monie from them, for that it seemed vnto him that it could not be but that they shoulde have good stoore, for that they came from a rich countrie whereas it was; and againe to come about businesse of so great importance, about the which they shoulde remaine there a long time (as aforesaide), as they afterwarde did more at large vnderstande. If that interpreter had declared in fidelitie all that which they had spoken, without al doubt they woulde not have suffered them to have come on shoare, else have put them in some prison for that they came on land without licence; and to have shewed them the most fauour they woulde haue caused them to returne from whence they came; whereas the guardes of the straight (of whom we have spoken of before), woulde either in secrete or publike sinke them at the sea, for that they were all greatly in hatred against them; the reason was that the Aytao, who is (as is declared in the first booke of this historie), the president of the counsell of warre, had vnderstanding howe that they passed thorough the fleete and were not seene, which was a thing that they all wondred at.

This Aytao did forthwith make secret information of the same, and found it to be true, whereuppon hee did iudge the captaines to perpetuall prison where they were well whipped, and did secrest[1] all their goods; for the which all their kinsfolkes and the rest of the guards had great indignation against the Spaniards, and would with great ease have beene reuenged on them, but that they did feare the punishment that should bee doone on them after that it should be knowne. In the which they doo execute their iustice in this kingdom more then in any place in all the world.

In the house of this christened Chino they dined that day, as they did many more afterwarde, but every night they returned to their fregat to bed, for that they durst not leave their things alone, neither to lie out of their shippe, for that one of the iudges had so commanded.

[1] Sequester.

CHAP. V.

The Spaniards are called before a iudge, who doth examine them, and offer them great favour; he dooth write vnto the visroy, giuing credit vnto the persons who sendeth commission vnto a iudge called Aytao, for to examine their cause. The chiefe captaine of Machao dooth accuse them in saying that they were spies, and doth intreate of other strange matters.

Vpon Saint John baptist day they were called before a iudge, who (as after this did vnderstand), was a superiour vnto the other past; but when they came whereas he was in place of audience, his ministers did straight wayes commande them to kneele downe at such time as they came in sight of the iudge, which was vnto the religious men no small torment. He demanded of them the same that the others did, and they answered in briefe, that they came to preach the holy gospell, and requested him to giue them licence to execute the same, and to remain in that cittie of Canton for to learne the China tongue, whereby they might giue them to vnderstande and knowe the trueth of the heauen. The interpreter did falsifie their wordes as hee had doone vnto the other iudges, and said no more but for so much that fortune and foul weather had driuen them into that port, they would liue amongst them, although it were to serue them as slaves; for that if they woulde returne vnto the ilande of Luzon, or by another name called Manilla, they could not for that they knewe not the way, neither had they anie pilot to conduct them.

The iudge had pittie on them, and commanded that such thinges as they had in their shippe should be brought on land, for that he woulde see them; amongst the which, the thing which caused him most to maruell at was when hee sawe the images, and ara (or alter stone), of blacke jasper stone (of the which we have made large mention.) Hee requested of the Spaniards that they woulde giue them two images, which when they had given them they made shew to esteeme greatly of the present, for that they were things that they have not amongst them. He talked with them very friendly, and caused them to arise from the ground whereas they did kneele, and to shewe them the more fauour he caused to be giuen them to drinke, in his presence, a certaine beurage which they do vse made of certaine hearbs, and vse it for a comfortable thing for the heart, and is commonly vsed amongst them although they are not dry, and amongst the Chinos is a shew of particular fauour.

This iudge did more vnderstande the intent of the Spaniards than any of the other past, for their interpreter had tolde unto him that they woulde remaine in the countrie for to cure sicke persons and to bury the dead, the which they could do excellent well. When the iudge heard these wordes hee gaue with his hande a great stroke vppon the table that was before him, and said with showes of great wonder unto other inferior judges that were with him: Oh! what good people are these as it seemeth; it would be vnto mee a great ioy, if that I coulde of mine owne authoritie accomplish that which they do desire, but our lawes do forbid the same and that with great rigour. All this did their interpreter tel them afterward. At this time there entred into the place of audience whereas they were, a man of China, one of the common sort, al imbrewed with blood, crying out and making a great noise without any consort, who prostrating himselfe upon the ground did complaine of other Chinos with whom he had fallen out, and was beaten and buffeted in cruell sort. The iudge when he saw him, did straight wayes command his officers to bring the offenders before him, the which was done with a trice, and they returned with the plaintife, bringing three other Chinos bound together by the armes, and as it seemed they were men of base sort. The

The Chinos most vpright in all their iudgements and in execution of iustice.

judge incontinent made information wholly of all that passed, and condemned them without writing any letter, in twenty sotes[1] or strokes a peece. The officers forthwith took them with so great cruelty as though they had bin diuels, and threwe them vpon the ground with their bellies downwards to execute the sentence giuen by the iudge; and when they had pulled off their hose, they began to whippe them vpon the calues of their legges with a sot made of canes, in manner as hath beene told you before. The religious people who were present all this while, and taking pity on these condemned men fell downe at the feet of the iudge, and by signes and tokens did craue of him for the love of God, that his sentence might not be executed, who straightwayes commanded the executioners to cease, condiscending vnto the petition of the friers, and did pardon the offenders fifteene sottes or strokes of the twentie, wherein they were condemned.

The iudge did very much woonder at the pouertie of these religious men, and at the sharpe and asper apparell that they weare: but the chiefest thing that they did maruell at, was when that he vnderstoode howe they had passed the fleete of ships that were put in the straight for to defende and keepe the coast, and were neuer seene, which seemed vnto him a thing impossible, except it were by permission of the heauen.

So when this examination and talke was finished, he commanded them to returne unto their shippe, promising them for to write vnto the vizroy (who was thirtie leagues from that place), and to giue him to vnderstand that they were men without any suspicion, and that he might wel giue them licence for to come to his presence: vpon which relation hee woulde commaunde what shoulde bee doone, either to tarrie or to go vnto him.

Within few dayes after they vnderstood that the iudge had

[1] The translator seems to have made this word himself from the Spanish, "azote", a scourge.

accomplished his promise, for that the vizroy had committed the matter vnto another iudge called Aytao, whose office is for to examine and inquire the causes of strangers: the wordes of the commission were as followeth.

"I am written vnto from Canton, howe that there are come thither certaine men apparelled very sharpe and asper, after the fashion of our religious men in the wildernesse, who bringe no weapons, neither any other thing that might seeme to pretend any euill intent: and for that they are thy charge, examine them with care and diligence, and prouide to doo therein that which shall be most requisite and conuenient: giuing vs to vnderstand the large and true relation of that which shall happen." *The vizroies commission.*

The verie same day of Saint Iohn, the Spaniards being verie merry and vnmindfull of any thing, for that they had all that day receiued the Sacrament: there came vnto them abord their shippe or frigat the interpreters, and did euidently declare their euill purpose and intent, (saying) that it was apparent what they had done for them, and in what perill they did euery day put themselues in for their matters, and that it was reason that they shoulde pay them for the same, and if not, they would not helpe them any more, neither interpret or take paines in their businesse: certifying them that if they did faile to satisfie them, that they should not finde any that would doo it with so great good will and diligence (as they should finde by experience); and how that they had beene put in prison if they had not beene, for entring into that kingdome without licence; and for that they enterpreted for them with great curtesie and fauour, they had also been commaunded to returne back againe from whence they came, which by their meanes was the cause that the iudges did entreat them so friendly as they did. The father Costodio when he vnderstoode their intente, and did evidently see that it was wholly grounded vppon gaine; considering also the vrgent necessitie that they had of them, and not satisfying them, it was difficult to find any for to help them in that their necessitie, of two euils he chose the best, and deliuered vnto them a pawne for their contentemente, one of the two challices they brought with them, giuing them great charge to vse and keep it as a sacred thing and dedicated for to consecrate the blood of Christ. The principall interpreter did take it with great content, and presently gaue it a newe master, in selling it vnto a gold smith for as much as it was woorth, who did melt it, and made things thereof according to his trade: yet they not being content therewith, and that it seemed vnto them that those fathers could not but bring with them much riches, they inquired of the China boy whom they brought to bee their interpreter, with faire words to know if they had any golde or siluer, or pretious stones, or any other thing of valure; but when they vnderstoode that they brought none of those things but onely their bookes and some other ornaments to say masse, they straightwayes imagined in their mindes, and that with great care and diligence, to procure some way to get from them the other challice which they had seen; and the better to put it in execution, they repeated againe vnto the friers that which before hath been told you, augmenting thereunto many wordes and reasons, affirming that they had spent vpon them in giuing them to eate twelue taes[1] more then the challice which they had giuen them did weigh or amount to, which was twelue ducats of Spaine; hauing before giuen them to vnderstand at such time as they did eate they did it of almes and for God's sake, and with so great content, that many times it happened when they saw the Spaniards would not eate any dainty thing, but woulde feed and content themselues with base victuals, he would say vnto them they shoulde eate without any grief or care, that when it should so fall out that

A sacred thing no doubt of it.

---

[1] Tael, Tale, or Taes, is the Portuguese word for Leang, the Chinese word for ounce, usually ounce of silver, and about one-third more than an ounce avoirdupois.

his subtance did fail him, hee woulde then pawne one of his sonnes to buy victuals.

The father Costodio plainly seeing and vnderstanding that their intent and purpose was wholly grounded for to get from him the other challice, he answered that he had not for to giue them, and how that he had giuen the other challice in pawn of that which they had spent in victuals, and for their trauell that they had taken for them. The interpreter did replie, saying, that if they had nothing, that they shoulde seeke it, seeing that they ought it for their victuals which they had eaten; and it was the vse of that countrie, that when any man did owe any thing, and hath not for to pay the same, for to sell their children, or else to become slaues vnto their creditor; they demanded the other challice that remained, for that the other which they had giuen them did weigh but sixteene taes, which was but a small matter in respect of their desert, onely for their trauel in their enterpretations. This frier Costodio did pacifie them in the best maner hee coulde, promising to pay both the one and the other, hauing oportunitie for the same, and that they woulde procure it with as great care as was possible, and requesting him for to keepe the challice, that he had given him in pawne, in great veneration, for that hee did esteeme it much more for the consecration and dedication vnto the deuine Colto,[1] then for the value of that it wayed, and more, promised him upon his worde to write vnto the Portugals that were in Machao, signifying unto them their necessitie and to demande their almes and charity, and looke whatsoever they did send them, being little or much, should be giuen him. Then the interpreter, who had his eyes fixed vppon gaine, saide, that they shoulde forthwith write, and that hee woulde giue him a messenger for to carrie the letter, and to bring answere of the same, as he had doone the like not many dayes before. The father Costodio did

[1] Worship.

write vnto the bishoppe that was in Machao, giuing him to vnderstande of his comming and of his companions vnto the cittie of Canton, and howe that his comming thither was onelie to procure for to preach the holy gospel, and for to conuert and turne to God those blinde idolaters. The which letter being receiued by the bishop, he made answere, praysing their intent and purpose, animating them with godly wordes of exhortation, and therewith did sende and demand the copie of such authoritie as they brought from the holy father touching that the which they pretended. This hee did for that all the sayde countrie vnto the lande of Iapon was committed vnto him by the holy father.

Unto this letter, the father Costodio answered, that hauing oportunitie, he woulde obey his commandement, and shew vnto him the facultie he brought, and also woulde him selfe in person go thether for to kisse his handes, and to satisfie all the inhabitants of that towne, for that it was giuen him to understande that they reported euill of them, and sayde that they were vacabondes and lost men, and not true religious men, neither sacerdotes nor priests; and how that they had requested certaine Chinos, which at that time came vnto Machao, that at their returne againe vnto Canton they should tell the iudges and aduertise them with good aduisement, how that there were certaine Castillos come into their cittie, whom they did certainely know not to be of their nation, but of an other, and subiects vnto a different and strange king, whom they did beleeue to come thether for some ill intent and purpose in counterfeit attire, and came for spyes from the Castillos of Luzon, and that they did beleeue that after them did come some armie to do hurt in some part of that countrie, and that they should prevent it in time, for that if so be that any thing should happen, the fault should not be imputed vnto them.

All this the Portingales did (as afterwards they did plainely vnderstande) for feare that the Castillos should take from them their contractation and gaine which they had in that city; by which occasion their intente did so proceede forward, that they did certifie the Chinos, that the chiefe captaine of Machao, who was put there by the king of Portingale, had presented a petition vnto a citie that was ioyning to Canton, aduertising the iudges of that before spoken of, and protesting that if any harme or damage should come to that country in admitting the Castillos, that it should not be imputed vnto them.

But the iudge vnderstanding their euill intent, and that their accusations were more vppon malice and enuie then of any trueth, he answered vnto the same, that he was particularly informed of those religious persons, against whom they did complaine, how that they were men of whom they needed not to feare, and without any suspition; as it did plainely appeare when they did visite their ship, wherein they came, where they found nothing, but onely a fewe bookes and some other thinges which did more signifie deuotion than to make any warre. This iudge (notwithstanding the answere he made), for that afterwards the chiefe captaine should not raise vp some inuention, tooke the originall petition, and sent it with great securitie vnto the viceroy of the prouince of Aucheo, that he might see and peruse it; who when that he had easily perceiued it, and vnderstood the intent of him that presented the same, and the innocencie of them that were therein complained of, he sent and commanded the gouernor of Canton for to giue them good intertainment, and not to permit any harme or hurt to be done vnto them, and that he should send them vnto the city of Aucheo, for that he would see them, for that it was tolde him that they seemed to be holy men, and although that they had their apparell in the same forme, of the Austin friers, (whome he had seene), yet their garments were of an other colour and more asper.

The chief captaine seeing that his intent fell not out well with the iudges of China, he commanded to be proclaymed publicke in Machao that none should write vnto them, nor communicate with them vpon paine of banishment, and to pay two thousande ducats. All this was not sufficient for to coole the mindes of some deuout persons of the religion of the glorious Saint Francis, but were rather incyted to offer their fauour and helpe seeing they had neede thereof; but in particular the bishop did helpe tham alwaies with his almes, and also an honorable priest called Andres Cotino, who making small account of the proclamation did write vnto them diverse times, although secretly, and sent their letters with almes and many exhortations to proceed forward with their holy zeale and intent. Besides this they sent vnto them a Spaniard called Pedro Quintero, who had dwelt there many years amongest the Portingals, and hauing oportunitie they sent him many times with comfortable things and letters, but not signed, for if happily they should be met with all, they might denie them to be theirs.

Now returning to our purpose, the interpreter, with desire to be payed of that which hee saide he had spent and laide out, did bring the messenger that he promised them to go vnto Machao to carrie their letters vnto such religious men as they knewe ; in the which he craued their almes and helpe for to pay their interpreter, and praying them for the love of God to sende them likewise so much as should redeeme their challice (who at this time knew not how it was solde and broken).

This messenger went with all diligence and secrecie, and returned with the like, and brought with him that which they sent for and other iunkets of great content, the which came in very good season, for that one of the sayde friers, called frier Sebastian, of S. Francis, was very sick of a strong ague, whereof in few daies after he died, very wel and with a strange desire to suffer martyrdome for God's sake. When this messenger came, there was come thither the Aytao who is iudge of the strangers, and was without the citie, vnto whom was committed the examination of the Spaniards, who after that he had concluded other matters, commanded them to be brought afore him with great love and gentlenesse, for so the viceroy of Aucheo had commanded him.

CHAP. VI.

The Spaniards seing themselues in great necessitie, hauing not to maintaine themselues, they go into the streets to ask almes: the gouernor vnderstanding thereof commandeth to giue them a stipend out of the king's treasure: the interpreter goeth forwardes with his couetousness and deceit: they be carried before the iudges of the citie, with whom they do intreat of diuers matters: they do aduise the viceroy of al, who commandeth to send them to Aucheo.

Because they would not see themselues in the like danger with the interpreter, as that which was past, they would not go any more to eate at his house, but rather to giue an example vnto those of the citie, they went foorth every day by two and two to aske almes; and although they were infidels, yet they gaue them with great contentment and ioie, because it was a rare thing in that kingdome to see them begge in the streetes, by reason, as hath been tolde you, that they haue no poore folk, neither are they permitted, if there be any, to aske in the streetes nor in their temples. When that the gouernor vnderstoode thereof, and how that they did it for pure necessitie, and had no other waies to maintaine themselues, hee commanded to be giuen them euerie day, a certaine stipend vpon the kinges cost, the which was with so great abundance, that mainteining the souldiers that came with them, and all the rest, yet had they to spare, for that their stipende was giuen them in money, which was sixe mayesses[1] of siluer, whereof they had to spare, for that all thinges in that countrie is so good cheape, as hath been told you in many places.

Their interpreter, seeing the good newes that was brought from Machao for the Spaniardes, by a bill that a certayne deuout man had sent him in secret, whereupon would be giuen vnto him all that was needeful, with protestation to pay all that should be giuen vnto them although it should amount vnto a great summe (with the which hee wrote a letter vnto the Fryer Costodio of great comfort, in strengthening him and all the rest to perseuer in their intent which God had put in their mindes for the saluation of those soules), the Interpreter (I say) beganne to imagine, that for to profite himselfe it was conuenient for to delate and detract the departure of the Spaniardes, and did exact vpon them euery day, in the buying of their uictuals, the halfe of the money that was giuen them.

So vpon a day he came verie much out of order, and fayned that the aytao had commanded that they should forthwith depart out of the kingdome; but yet notwithstanding he would present a petition in their name, saying, that for as much as time did not serue them to nauigate, neither was their shippe in plight for to make their iourney, that it would please them to get them a house whereas they might remaine three or four monethes, in the which time they might prouide them of all thinges necessarie for their voyage; and possible it may so fall out that in this time, they seeing their manner of liuing to bee good, and to shew good examples, they may let them to remaine in the countrie liberally and to learne the language, and then beginne to preach and declare the right way vnto heauen. All this he

---

[1] Mace or mayes is the Portuguese word for Tsien, the tenth of an ounce. These words mayes, tayes (see page 156), belong to the same class as mandarin, bonze, joss-house, etc., all of which have been invented by the Portuguese.

spake with great dissimulation for to profite himselfe, for he knewe verie well that the aytao had willed him to tell them, that they could not remaine in that countrie with the pretence they had; for that there was a lawe ordained to the contrarie, without expresse licence from the king, the which will last of all be granted vnto the Spaniardes or Portingals, for that there is a prophesie amongest them, spoken by the mouth of the diuell, and esteemed amongest them for a very truth, for that other thinges which he spake when that was spoken hath beene verified, in the which he doth pronounce that a time shall come, that they shall be subiect vnto a nation whose men shall haue great beardes and long noses, and sharpe broade eyes (as we would say cats eyes), in the which they do differ from them. For it is a great maruaile to finde a man amongst them with more then twentie heares in his beard, little more or lesse, flat noses, and their eyes very little, so that when they will mocke a man, or doo him any iniurie by word, they will call him "cats eyes". *A prophesie.*

Now for that the desire of the Spaniardes was nothing else but to remaine in that countrie, for to bring to effect their good zeale, they did gratifie the interpreter for the great fauour hee shewed them, and did earnestly entreat him for to present the petition, thinking thereby their desire should be vnderstood, and Gods cause iustified, so that they first would enter into them by the way of preaching. He presented the petition when that all the iudges were together, who had great pitie and compassion ouer the Spaniardes, and willed that they should come before them, for that they would see and vnderstande the roote and foundation of their will. They obeyed their commandement with great ioy, and when they were come into the hall, one of the iudges, who was superior ouer all the rest, and a man of great authoritie, did aske of them by way of the interpreter, what was their pretence in that they did aske a house to dwell in, the Frier Costodio did answere, that he did desire it for to learne the language well, by which meanes they might the better learne them to know the true God, and to set them in the true way to goe and glorie with him, because it was his office and his profession.

The interpreter tolde all this truely, the which fewe times before he had done, as hath beene tolde you. Then the iudge, in name of all the rest, sayde, that in that their demand they could not grant, neyther had they any such authoritie to giue licence.

This being spoken, the interpreter replyed, without tarrying to heare what the Spaniardes would say, and said, that at least wayes they would giue them licence to remaine there till such time as the Portingals did come thether for to lade their marchandice, which would be within few daies, with whom they would go, for that they were all of one law and faith. The iudge did againe aske them if that the Portingals and Spaniards were al one. The father Costodio answered, that in religion and lawes there was no difference, but the one were subiects to one king and the other to another, although they were kinsmen and that very nigh. This last petition seemed to the iudge to be more reasonable and iust than the first, and that they might grant it them with lesse difficultie, although he answered them and said, that he could not grant it vnto them, but he would write vnto the viceroy for to grant it them. For that the Portugals would bee there at the farthest within foure or fiue monethes, and that in the meane time he would giue them a prouision that they may go freely abroad, and none to hurt nor harme them.

So the next day following, which was the second of August, he did accomplish his word and promise, and sent vnto the viceroy their petition, and therewithall his iudgment and of all the rest that were there with him, what they thought touching that matter. The answere staid many daies after and came not, but in the ende there came a commandement from the viceroy vnto the gouernor of Canton, in the which hee willed that the Spaniards should be sent vnto Aucheo whereas he was, and that there should be carried with them all such thinges as they brought with them, which was their bookes and ornaments.

The iudge did straightwaies send and gaue them to vnderstande of this new order, because they should make themselues readie for to trauaile: the which they did with great ioy and diligence, as you shall vnderstand in the chapter following.

CHAP. VII.

The Spaniardes take their iourney towardes Aucheo, and declare what happened in the way thitherwarde.

The next day following, which was the sixteenth day of August, the Spaniards departed from Canton towards Aucheo to see the viceroy, with great hope and confidence that he would giue them licence for that which they pretended. But at their departure, they would have left there two Indians for to keepe their ship or frigat; but the iudges that were present said, that it was not needefull for them to haue any such care, for that they would take the care vppon them to see all thinges in good order. So presently they sent certaine writing in papers, and commaunded them to bee glewed vppon the hatches of their shippe, in such sort that they could not bee open but they must be perceiued. Then presently was brought for the Spaniardes foure barkes, verie gallant and wide, with verie fayre galleries and windowes; and beeing imbarked, they charged them verie much to make all haste possible to accomplish the commandement of the viceroy; and sent with them conuenient persons for to be their guides, and to giue them all thinges necessarie for their iourney. They traueiled continually in a mightie riuer against the current, in the which they did see many thinges woorthie to be noted for the space of foure daies that their iourney indured.

There was alongest the riuer side manie cities and townes verie great, which were so many in number that they could not make any memorie of them, by reason that they passed manie of them by night, to obserue the tides, and to auoid the heate, which was great vppon the water. Alongest the riuer side (whereas it was not inhabited) was full of corne fieldes, whereas they sawe them go to plough with many bufalos, much different vnto the vse of Spaine; for that one alonely buffe did drawe the plough, with one vpon his backe, who did gouerne and guide him with great ease whether hee would they should go, with a corde made fast to a ring at his nose, which serued in steede of a bridle.

They sawe also flockes of geese, in the which were more then twentie thousand; with whom they did weede, and tooke away the grasse which did growe amongst the rice and other graine and seedes, driuing them in the middest of their fieldes; and it seemed that they had the vse of reason, considering how they did separate and make a distinction betwixt the good seede and the bad, and the great care they had to feede and do no harme, neither to plucke vp the good plant, which was a thing that they wondred at aboue all the rest. All the countrie is verie populous, and the townes one so neere an other, that it may better be sayde to be all one towne and not manie, and might with more propertie be called the citie of China, and not the kingdome of China. In all the whole countrie there is not one foot of ground vnoccupied, by reason of the great abundance of people that there is; and they permit amongest them no idle people (as more at large it hath beene declared vnto you); and the countrie beeing fertile, is the occasion that they have all thinges in great abundance and at a lowe price.

Now to returne to their voyage, the which they made verie well and with great recreation, as well in the townes alongst the riuer side, as vpon the riuer, whereas they were cherished with great care: in the end of foure dayes, which was the twentieth day of August, they entred into the suburbes of the citie of Aucheo, but so late that they were constrayned to remaine there till the next day: whereas they found all thinges necessarie and in good order, aswell for their bedding as for their supper, to passe away the night. The next day, very early in the morning, he that was their conduct and guide, made great haste for to goe and see what the viceroy would command.

They trauailed through a great and long streete, which seemed vnto them to be more than a league, and thought that they had gone through the citie. So when they had passed that street they came vnto the gate of the citie, and there they vnderstoode that the rest which they had gone and passed was the suburbes. The mightinesse of this citie, and the great admiration they had, with the multitude of people, and a wonderfull great bridge the which they passed, with many other thinges of the which they made mention, we do let passe, for that it is declared vnto you more at large in the relation giuen by the Augustin friers, in the booke before this, at their entrie into the sayd citie.

So when they came to the pallace of the viceroy, he was not stirring, neither was the gate open, for as it hath beene tolde you, it is open but once a day. Their guide seeing that it would be somewhat long before that they would open it, he carried the Spaniardes into a court of an other house, which was ioyning vnto that of the viceroy.

In the meane while they were there, came all the iudges to sit in audience, but when they vnderstoode of the comming of the strangers, they commanded that they should be brought before them; who greatly marueiled at the aspernesse of their apparell, and not at any other thing, for that they had seene there before the Austin fryers. Straightwayes the gate of the pallace was open with great noyse of artilerie and musicall instruments, as trumpets, bagpipes, sackebuttes and hoybukes, with such a noyse that it seemed the whole citie would sincke. At the entrie in the first court, there were many souldiers armed, and had hargubushes and lances, and in a very good order. In an other court more within, which was very great, and railed round about with timber, painted blacke and blew, which a far off seemed to be yron, and was in height a mans stature; there they sawe also many other souldiers, placed in the same order, and in liuerie as the others were, but they seemed to be men of a gallanter disposition. When they came into this court, there was brought vnto them a commandement from the viceroy, in the which they were commanded to returne and come thether againe in the after noone, for that he could not speake with them before, by reason of certaine businesse he had with the lords of the counsell, which could not be deferred. With this answere they departed out of the pallace, and returned againe in the after noone, as they were commanded, and into the same court aforesaide, out of the which they were carried into a mightie great hall, very richly hanged and adorned; at the ende thereof was three doores, that in the middest was great, but the other two but small, the which did correspond vnto other three doores that were in an other hall more within, wherein was the viceroy, right over against the doore in the middest, in at the which there is none permitted to enter nor go foorth. Hee was set in a marueilous rich chayre wrought with iuorie and gold, vnder a canopie or cloth of state all of cloth of gold, and in the middest was embrodered the kings armes, which were (as we haue said) certaine serpents woond in a knot together. He had also before him a table whereon were two candles burning, for that it was somewhat late, and a standish with paper. Right before the viceroy the wall was verie white, whereon was painted a fearce dragon, who did throwe out fire at his mouth, nose, and eyes, a picture (as was giuen them to vnderstand) that all the iudges of that countrie commonly hath it painted before their tribunall seates whereas they sit in iustice, and is there to the intent to signifie vnto the iustice, the fearcenesse that he should haue sitting in that seat for to do iustice vprightly without feare or respect to any. The order they haue in giuing audience is with the ceremonies in all points as it hath beene shewed you in the relation of the fathers of S. Augustin. All people when they talke with the viceroy are kneeling on their knees, although they be iudges or loytias, as the fryers did see them many times.

This day, they seeing the Spaniardes remained looking alwaies, when they should be commanded to enter in, the viceroy gaue audience vnto the scriueners or notaries, to certifie himselfe if they did their offices well, and commanded fiftie of them at that present to be sotted or beaten for that they were found culpable in their detayning of matters, and others the like for that they had receiued giftes and bribes of their clyents, the which is prohibited and forbidden vnder greeueous penalties, for that the king doth giue vnto them all sufficient stipend for their maintenance, for that they should not incroch nor demand any thing of their clyentes. The sots or stripes which were giuen them were with great crueltie, and executed with certaine canes, and in that order as in other places it hath beene told you. The viceroyes gard were in number more than two thousand men, placed all on a ranke, all apparelled in one liuery of silke, and on their heads helmets of yron very bright and glystering, and euerie one his plume of feathers. These souldiers made a lane from the gate of the hall there whereas the viceroy was, vnto the principal gate of the pallace wheras they did first enter. Those which were in the hals and vpon the staires had swords girt vnto them, and they in the courtes had lances, and betwixt euery one of them a hargubusher. All this gard (as was giuen them to vnderstand) were Tartaros and not Chinos: but the reason wherefore they could not learne, although they did inquire it with diligence.

CHAP. VIII.

The Spaniards are brought before the viceroy: he asketh of them certaine questions, and doth remit them vnto the Timpintao his deputie, who receiueth them well, and giueth them good speeches.

At that present came forth a seruant of the viceroyes, a man of authoritie, and made signe vnto the Spaniards to enter into the hall, instructing them that at the first entry they should kneele downe on their knees: the which they did presently: from that place vnto the seat of the viceroy was more than a hundreth foot in length, yet did the viceroy himself make signes with his hand that one of the religious men should come nearer him, the which the father Costodio did, and kneeled downe againe when he drew nigh vnto the table that was before him. The viceroy did consider and beholde him a good while, and that with great grauitie and maiestie, and then asked him of whence he was, and what he came to seeke in that kingdome, into the which none might come vpon paine of death, without expresse licence of some of the iudges alongst the sea coast. The father Costodio answered, that he and the rest of his companions were Spaniards, and that they were come into that kingdome mooued with the zeale of God, for the saluation of their soules, and for to preach the holy gospell, and show them the way vnto heauen. Hauing declared the interpreter this (although they did not vnderstand whether he did vse fidelitie in the declaration or not, but rather, by that which the viceroy did forthwith demand, it is to be beleeued that he did it with falshood as he had done many times before; for that without replying vnto that which he had saide of the preaching of the gospel, he asked them what marchandice they brought with them: the said father answered, That they brought none, for that they were not men that did deale in any marchandice, but in declaring of things appertaining to heauen, and to direct their soules to that place. Hearing this answere (or that which the interpreter would imagine to be better for his purpose) the viceroy did bid them depart, and commanded them to returne againe the next day and to bring with them their images, and the other things wherof he was certified from Canton that were founde in their frigat, for that he would see it all. They did accomplish his commandement, and returned the next day in the morning, at such time as it was tolde them that the pallace gates would be opened: the which was done in the same maner and order as the day before, with the noyse of musicke and artillerie as aforesaid. So when that the viceroy was giuen to vnderstande how that the Castillos were come, he commanded that one of them with alonely the interpreter should enter there wheras he was, and to bring in such thinges as he had commanded to be brought, the which was presently accomplished. Hee straightwaies began to looke vpon the images euery one by it selfe, and the bookes: and made a stay betwixt euerie one to consider well thereof, and made a showe of great content he receiued in the sight of them. Although, aboue all the rest, the ara of black iaspar did most content him, and caused a marueilous strangenesse in the rest of the iudges that had seene it. All this while was the father Costodio vpon his knees, and the interpreter by him, and hee neuer asked of them any question, neyther did they say any thing. They that did bring those thinges vnto them for to see them, seemed to be principall and ancient men, who, when they gaue it him into his handes, they did it kneeling.

So after that he had seene them al at his pleasure, he commanded to put them againe in the place that they were taken out, and made signe vnto the father Costodio and to the interpreter that they should depart, and to carry with them al those things which they had brought. One of the ancient men that were with him, did go foorth with the Spaniards, and told them when they came into the second hall, that the viceroye did reioyce much to see them, and all those which they brought, and said that they should repaire vnto the Timpintao, who was his deputy, and he would dispatch al such matters as were asked of the viceroy by petition, following the same till it was concluded, and that he would consult with the viceroy, who would set down such orders as shold be obserued. They straightwaies did put in execution this order, and comming vnto the house of the deputie vnto the viceroy, the which was very great and faire, they found that he had a garde very little lesse than that of the viceroy, and almost with as much maiestie. So after they had remained in the court a good while, abiding his commandement (to whom it was giuen to vnderstand that the viceroy had sent them vnto him), he commanded them to ascend into the place wheras he was, which was into a hall very well dressed, in the which was almost al such things as they had seene in the hall of the viceroy, and he himselfe in the same manner sate in a rich chaire, with a table before him. He commanded to take out those things which they brought in their chestes, and did behold them with great consideration peece by peece, as the viceroy had done, and reioysing much to see the images, he did demande of them with curiositie the signification of some of them, but in especiall a crucifix, that after that he had considered with great attention, he asked what man was that which was vppon the crosse, and what those letters did signifie that were tituled ouer his head. But when the father Costodio had declared it vnto him, he beganne to laugh thereat, as though he had heard some foolish fable. Hee came and feeled the habites of our religious men, and made signes of great woonder to see the aspernesse thereof.

The father Costodio seeing his affabilitie, and as it seemed by outwarde showe that he did very much pitie them, he requested to helpe and fauour him with the viceroy, and that he would aske licence that they might remaine and dwell in that countrie, in any place where his pleasure was to appoint, for that they were men without any hurt, and would put all their care and diligence to do workes of charitie, and to procure that men might go to inioy the happie estate to the which they were borne.

The interpreter dealt here in his office with as great fidelitie as at other times, in saying that which the fathers did request of him, was that he should be a meanes vnto the viceroy that he would let them to remaine in that countrie two or three moneths, for that as then it was an ill time to nauigate the sea, and that without great danger of their liues they could not returne vnto the Ilands Philippinas. The iudge answered that they should not feare, but remaine with content, for that he would procure that there should be giuen them a house for those three or foure moneths, with a commandement that none whatsoeuer should do them any harme. The interpreter tolde them that the deputie to the viceroy was very glad that they would remaine in that countrie, for that they seemed vnto him men of good example and necessarie in their common weale, and that they might freely learne the language (as they sayd) for to shew and instruct them the way vnto heauen. The Spaniards hauing heard this, it made them very much to maruaile, and from that time forwards they had good hope to prosecute that which they did pretend. So with this and with great spirituall and corporal ioy they tooke their leaue of the iudge, and went vnto their lodging, wheras they gaue thanks vnto God for the good directing of their busines, and did pray vnto him to helpe them, that they might see a finall conclusion of their desire. All this falsenes that the interpreter did vse, was by the diuine permission (as afterwards they did gather), when that by himselfe they were put out of all doubt, and did declare what he did pretend by the way and order he tooke. For without all doubt, if that the iudges had plainely vnderstood that they would haue there remained, they would not haue suffered them to haue entred and seene the countrie. And the viceroy being aduertised thereof, would haue caused them to depart in that troublesome wether, whereas possibly they should haue beene all drowned, for that the moneths of July, August, and September in that countrie, are ordinarily full of stormes and tempestes.

CHAP. IX.

The Spaniards remained certaine daies in Aucheo: they go to visite the beautie of that citie, but in especiall the captaine generall of the sea, who was so affectioned vnto the ara of blacke stone they brought, that hee did with all care and diligence procure it of gift.

All the time that they remained in Aucheo, they did occupie themselues in visiting of the principals of the court, amongst whom he that did most reioice to see them was the captaine generall of the men of war of that prouince, who after that he had intreated them very friendly and louingly, he desired them that they would returne the next day to uisite him, and to bring with them the ara of blacke stone, which they had shewed vnto the viceroy, that he might see it, for that he had praised it very much : and to bring also of their painted images. They did obey his commandement, and came vnto him when that he was at dinner with great maiestie. Then so soone as he had dined, he commanded that they should enter into the hal there where he was. The interpreter when he drew nigh vnto him did kneele down, and made signes vnto the Spaniards to follow him and do the like; but the captaine commanded them to arise and to couer their heads, and did very much behold the ara or (altar stone), making a showe of great admiration to beholde it: hee demanded of the fryers many things of great curiositie, and asked them if they would sell him that stone, and he would giue them for it what they would demande. The father Costodio answered, saying that they sold nothing, and much lesse that, for that it was consecrated and dedicated to the diuine colto (or sacrifice). The captaine replied and saide, that if they would not sell it, that they should giue it him, and hee would be gratefull vnto them in some other thing, that they should thinke well of.

The father Costodio answered, that by no manner of meanes he could not do it, for that vpon the same they did celebrate and say masse, at such time as they did sacrifice vnto the true God. At that instant the captaine did put his handes vppon it to feele it, and the father Costodio made signes vnto him to take away his handes, for that he sinned greatly therein. Then he seeing that they would not giue it him, he tooke his leaue, saying, that they should leaue it there with him, for that hee would looke vpon it more at leasure, promising to returne it them againe afterwardes. The father Costodio did consent thereunto, but first he requested him not to touch it with his handes.

So after that he had satisfied himselfe in the beholding of it, his affection was then much more to remaine therewith :

and for to accomplish the same, not fayling of his word and promise that he had made, hee deuised with himselfe a certaine slight and policie, and sent for the father Costodio, who came vnto him with great content, thinking verily that he would haue returned their ara. When he came vnto him, he did intertaine him verie ioyfully, and said that he was vpon his iorney to certaine warres by the commandement of the king, and that amongest those seruants that he carried with him for his seruice, there were two christened Chinos, which had beene captiues vnto the Portugales of the citie of Machao, from whence they ran away, of whom he had had vnderstanding in all thinges of the ceremonies of the Christians, and that their comming thether was to baptise such as would receiue the same: and hee being fully certified in many thinges touching the same, he liked well thereof and gaue great content, and hoped to be one of them that first should receiue the faith when the king should grant licence for the same.

All this (as it seemed) was that they should· let him haue the ara, vnto the which he was so affectioned, as aforesaid. But the father Costodio vsed the matter in such sort that hee got it out of his fingers, which was no small matter. Within a few dayes after, the captaine being readie to imbarke himselfe for to make his iourney, he sent vnto the Spaniardes that two of them should come vnto him, and that they should bring with them the blacke stone, for there were certaine friendes of his that would see it.

The father Costodio did straightwayes accomplish his commandement, and carried with him the ara (or altar stone), for that he durst not do otherwise, yet they did beleeue that in giuing him some pretie or curious thing, they should content him and quiet his mind: they carried also with them the image of Marie Magdalen, made of feathers, which was more woorthie than the ara (setting apart the consecration).

So when the religious fathers came wheras he was, he went foorth to meete them more then tenne paces, with signification of great ioy: and carrying them aside, he saide vnto them once againe, that the captiues had told him so many things of their vertuous maner of liuing, and of other things touching the heauen, that he had great affection vnto them, and desired that they might remaine in the countrie for to baptise the inhabitants therof, and that he wold be the first: but the cause wherfore he did delay the time is for to eschew the paines that is pronounced against all those that do receiue any law or strange ceremonie without particular licence of the king. And for that he went in hast to go and inhabite a certaine prouince, and that he was ready to depart; in the which, so soone as it was possible, he would do so much that al they should become Christians; and for as much as he tolde him that the blacke stone (vnto the which he was affectioned) was consecrated, that he would let him haue it to carry with him, that he might put it in the first church that the baptised should edifie, being made Christians: the which would be very shortly, for that he was determined before many daies to send to Machao for two friers such as were there, to be fully informed of them in thinges touching the Christian faith. Then the father Costodio sayde, if that which he had spoken came from his heart, that hee would foorthwith depart and goe with him and all his companie.

The captaine answered that as then hee could not doo it, till such time as the church was built, and licence had for the same of the king or vizroy, the which at that time he coulde not demande, for the great hast that he had to depart. The father Costodio replied and said, that his church being built, he would promise him of his worde to sende it him, and not to giue it to any other; and in pledge and token of the same, he should carry with him the image of Marie Magdalene made of feathers. The captaine receiued the same with great content: greatlic maruelling at the subtill and fine worke wherewith it was wrought: and after did so much, that almost perforce he remained also with the ara: and commanded to bee brought foorth two rich peeces of damaske, and to giue them vnto the father Costodio for to make an ornament in truck and ful satisfaction for the same; but the father Costodio woulde not receiue them, but was very much greeued to see howe that hee did remaine therewith, and with the image of feathers. The captaine did contende with him for to take the dameske, but hee would not.

Afterward they vnderstood that the interpreter was bribed by a seruant of the captaines, for to alter the friers words and to offer the captayne the ara, and any thing els that hee would desire. For to the contrary he durst not by any meanes to take it against the will of the fathers. To conclude he did imbarke himselfe vpon his voyage, and caried with him the ara and the image, with great ioy to himselfe: but vnto the fathers and their companions discomfort and sorrow, for they had lost the two thinges that they so much esteemed. The captayne at his departure did vse great thinges and curtesie, taking his leaue of them with signes, that signified he bare them great loue and good will, and that it greeued him to depart, and could not carie them with him as they requested.

The interpreter did comfort the Spaniardes, and sayd that they should not be sorrowful that the captaine had taken those two pieces; for that he was a mightie prince, and that he would fauour and helpe them with the vizroy, and that hee was certaine that he would accomplish that which he promised, that is, to become a Christian, for that he did beare great good will and affection vnto them: in the which the interpreter did not lie, for that it was told them by the seruants of the captaine, that were christened, as I told you before.

The frier Costodio remained so sad and sorowfull for the

carrying away of the ara and Madlin of feathers, as though he had lost a great treasure: and being desirous to recouer them againe, he did recommend the same vnto S. Antonio de Padua, who, for thinges that were lost, they knew by experience to bee the onely saint for aduocate, and did promise (the better to obtaine their desire) for to celebrate vnto him certaine masses, when they should come into place fit for the same.

Straightwayes it so fell out that the chiefe and principall interpreter did fall out with the other that did helpe him, about certaine profite that was comming to him, and did threaten him that he would tell the gouernor howe that they had giuen him much siluer for to conclude the matter about the ara, for that the fathers had giuen it them more by force then any good will. The interpreter fearing that hee shoulde bee for the same greeuously punished, and finding himselfe culpable in the things that the other threatned him for, he went vnto the captain, who was imbarked and readie to depart, tarrying onely for wether, and tolde him the falling out in all points as it passed, and of his threatnings: who likewise fearing what might succeede or happen, if it shoulde come to the vnderstanding of the aytao of the cittie of Canton, as could not be by any meanes excused: hee called vnto him one of his seruants and commanded him to take the ara and the image, and to carry them vnto the fathers, who accomplished his commande, and they receiued them with great comfort, and gaue great thankes vnto God for the same, and S. Antonio de Padua: by whose intercession they beleeued that they were restored.

CHAP. X.

The Timpintao dooth call the Spaniards before him, and dispatcheth them for to go to Canton; they tooke their leaue of him, and goeth from Aucheo: and at their comming to Canton, they are commaunded to make themselues readie to departe the kingdome.

The next day following, which was the thirde day of September, the timpintao did sende to call the Spaniards before him, who as we haue said was deputie vnto the vizroy, and he gaue them certaine dispatches, in saying, that there was in them all that they did aske, and gaue commandement to the gouernor of Canton that he should not neglect, but accomplish al things therin comprehended, so that they might depart when they pleased. When hee tooke his leaue of them, hee did intreate them verie curteously with words of great curtesie. The Spaniards departed his presence with incredible ioy: beleeuing that he had agreed and granted all that they did aske, and to remaine in the countrie to preach, so that the next day following they made all thinges in a redinesse to take their voyage, the which they finished in short time, by reason of their great contentment they had with themselues, as also for the good intertainement and good cheere they had by the way, which was made and giuen them by the commandement of the timpintao. So when they came vnto Canton, they went straightwayes to visite the gouernour, and to giue him the dispatches which they brought, who after that he had read the same, he bad them welcome, and saide that hee was very glad that the vizroy had shewed them so much fauour, and that the same was committed to his charge, for the execution of his commission, that they should perswade themselues that hee would performe it according vnto his commandement, without failing anie thing. And for to beginne the same, hee shewed vnto them a house of the kings which should be for their dwelling, which was in the suburbs halfe fallen downe, and there they were lodged, with a commandement that they should not go foorth, neither enter into the cittie without particular licence. Heere they remained many dayes being deceiued of their purpose, and maruelled very much that the gouernor would not giue them licence for to reedifie a monastery, neither for to enter into the cittie for to giue order in that which they beleeued was granted them by the vizroy, til such time as they vnderstood what was done by their interpreters, and relation giuen by the Chino boy which came with them from the Philippinas, who declared to them the truth in all things : how that the interpreters had neuer told the iudges how that they would remain in the countrie, neither made any mention thereof, but that they came thither as lost men, and that their request was to remaine in the country til it were faire wether, or the comming of the Portugall shippes. And this was that which the vizroy and his deputie had granted, and no other thing. But when the father Costodio and his companions (who verely beleeuing that their desire woulde take effect) vnderstoode the craft and wile of the interpreters, and the great falshood that they had vsed, they were very sadde, and beganne amongst themselues to remedie the same : so they determined to seeke a new interpreter, one that should faithfulle and truely declare their will vnto the gouernor. And although they did finde some that could doo it, for that they did reasonably vnderstande the Portugall tongue, yet there were none that woulde accept it, for any request or giftes that they did promise them.

The father Costodio seeing this, and that the time appointed did passe away without doing of any thing, one day hee and the rest of his companions did ioine togither, and entred in counsell to see what was best to be done, according vnto the necessitie in the which they were driuen. There was amongst them diuers opinions, for that of the father Costodio and of another religious man was, that they woulde go vnto Machao, which was not farre off, and there would administer the sacraments, and preach the holy gospel vnto the christened Chinos, and to learne the China language, and to tarrie there and abide the first occasion that should bee offered, or else they themselues to procure it, for, hauing the language, it were an easie thing to doo it: and they should not haue neede of any interpreter, neither feare to be deceiued as they had beene before. And besides this, they put the Portugals out of all doubt of the false opinion that the captaine generall had published abroade of them, and of other matters of like effect and purpose. The other two religious men and souldiers were of a contrarie opinion: which was, that they should returne vnto the Ilands Philippinas, and not vnto Machao, and saide, that they had departed without licence of the gouernor, and did aduenture themselues into the harme and damage that might happen vnto them by that enterprise, and all for to plant the faith of Christ in that kingdome. And now seeing that by the iust iudgement of God wee cannot put it in execution, wee are greatly bounde to returne againe vnto him, of whome we doubt not but with ease to get our pardon for the error passed, representing the zeale wee had to the honour of God, and the saluation of so manie soules, who did incite vs to giue that great enterprise: with the which we shall remaine blamelesse with them that had giuen wrong iudgement of vs, and accomplish our bounden duetie and obedience which wee doo owe vnto the gouernor. And in going vnto Machao wee shall runne in great danger to be holden and iudged for traitors to the king: and the intent wherewith wee went vnto China, euery one wil construe and interpret thereon at his pleasure.

The resolution of these contrary opinions, was by a common consent delated certaine dayes, in the which they prayed vnto God to put into their hearts that which was best for His deuine seruice. So in the end the father Costodio, and the religious man, who was of his opinion, did determine to go forwards with their pretence, and to go vnto Machao, as aforesaid, and the rest to returne vnto the ilands with the first oportunitie they might finde: but when it should come to effect, one of the religious friers that shoulde haue gone vnto Manilla was deade of an infirmitie that chanced him. They staid there longer then they did think they should, by reason that the iudges of the cittie were occupied with the examinations of students, the which is accustomed euery three yeares, and is in that manner and order as hath beene tolde you in the proper chapter for the same: the which examinations endured more then fiue and fortie dayes, with great feastes and banquets, without medling in any other particular businesse.

CHAP. XI.

The Father Costodio sendeth a messenger vnto Machao; he writeth vnto the bishop and vnto a priest for to bestow their almes on them for their departure. The captaine generall doth vnderstand therof, and commandeth them not to aid nor succour the Spaniards: and other matters appertaining unto them.

In the meane time of this their examination, the father Costodio did sende a messenger vnto the bishop of Machao, declaring vnto him his determination, and he also did write vnto the deuout priest, of whome we haue made mention before, and craued of them their almes wherewith they might make prouision for them that would depart for the Ilands Philippinas, and how that he and his companyon would go and see his lordship. This was not done so secretly, but it came vnto the vnderstanding and knowledge of the captaine generall of the Portugals, who with great choller went and demanded the lettèrs of the priest, those that were giuen him by the Chino : threatning him that if hee did not, hee woulde punish him with great rigor, and banish him out of the countrie as a suspected person. He answered him, that of truth he had receiued certaine letters, but that at the very instant hee sent them vnto the bishoppe vnto whom they were directed : about the which there was great holde and keepe, vntill it came to effect that the captaine did lay holde vppon the priest for to apprehende him : but when the bishop vnderstood thereof, hee with all speede possible went to remedy the danger that might insue, and to take him out of his power.

The captaine seeing that hee could not perseuer with his intent and purpose, he made many notifications vnto the bishop, requiring that he would not permit that any letters shoulde bee receiued from those religious Spaniards, for that he knew by very certaine relation that they were spies, and no friers ; and if so be that any damage should happen vnto them, by their order, that hee woulde lay the whole fault vppon him as a consenter and a helper. The bishoppe answered that he was fully perswaded and certified that they were true religious men, and seruants of God, and that he with a very good will would take vpon him the burthen of any damage that should happen to the country by their meanes, or vnto the king of Portugall. With this the captaine was somewhat quieted, but not so much but that continually hee did not let to imagine newe matters against the poore fathers, to haue occasion to apprehend them, and imagined in his minde for to write a letter vnto the interpreters, in the which hee did offer them great quantities of money, if that they would do so much as giue order that the iudges woulde sende the religious men and Spanish souldiers that were in Canton vnto the cittie of Machao, aduertising them howe and which way they shoulde vse the matter to put it in effect, and was, that he should tell the iudges, that the first time when as they went to speake with the gouernor, whercas they did aske and say that they would depart for the Ilands Philippinas, that they did interpret it contrary, for that their demand was for to go vnto Machao.

The interpreters straightwayes (with the desire of gaine) did take the charge vppon them, and did vse the matter in such sort that the iudges did sende them vnto Machao, whether it were with or against their willes. But God, who woulde not permit those his seruantes and Christians to bee deceiued, remedied the same at such time as it should haue beene put in execution, in the manner as you shall vnderstande in the chapter following.

CHAP. XII.

A Portugall of the cittie of Macheo doth discouer the euill intent of the captaine general: he giueth the Spaniards warning thereof by a letter without seale, by the which they remedie the danger that was so nigh at hand: they are called before the Aytao of the cittie, and he declareth vnto them such matters as haue passed with him, and the licence that was graunted for some of them to go vnto Machao, and the other vnto Luzon.

Being vnderstood by a Portugall, a good Christian of the towne of Machao, of such things as the captaine generall did imagine against the poore religious fathers that were in Canton, and their companions the souldiers, of whose holy zeale he was fully certified, and being greeued at the very soule that one Christian shoulde hurt and harme another: and more in the disturbing of the saluation of soules, hee determined with himselfe to giue them aduice therof with all speed that was possible, as in effect hee did by sending them a letter without anie name: wherein he gaue them to vnderstand that the captaine generall, by meanes of the interpreters, did pretende that they should be sent thither wheras he might apprehend them, and send them vnto the king of Portugall, or else to doo some hurt vnto their person, with some false information, and willed them to be wel aduised, and to keepe themselues from the deceit ordained.

The letter being seene, and wel aduised of all that was therein contained, they determined to giue notice thereof vnto a Chino, a verie friende of theirs, and perfite in the Portugall tongue: whome diuers times they proued by experience, and founde him a very honest man, and one that had doone them friendshippe: who promised them that before many houres, he would bring al things to light, and to know whether that were true or not.

So with this desire he went there whereas the iudge did sit in audience, and was there as one that knew nothing, vntill such time as he saw come thither one of the interpreters with a petition in his hand, and presented it vnto the supreme iudge, who was the Aytao, and which being read by a scriuener, hee prouided that all things should be granted and doone, that was therein contained. This petition the Chino aforesaid saw; and after that the interpreter was departed with contentment, and found that in the same petition he did request (in the name of the Spaniards) of the iudge to giue them leaue for to go vnto Machao, which was more for their purpose then to go vnto the Ilands Philippinas, which was granted by the iudge, and lacking nothing but to seale or signe the petition, but was delated vntil the euening, by reason of certaine businesse that chanced at that present: but sure it was the ordinance of God, for that if it had beene signed, they must needs of force haue accomplished the same, without any replication. So with this certaintie he went straightwayes vnto the Spaniards, to whom the interpreter had told that by petition he had asked licence for them to go to the Ilands Philippinas from whence they came; but the iudge woulde not graunt vnto that, but for to go vnto Machao, which was neerer hand, who commanded them to accomplish the same without any replication, vppon paine that they should be carried thither perforce.

The Spaniards asked councell of the Chino their friende, what meanes might be taken to auoide the danger that the interpreter had begun to bring them in, and was alredie gone to conclude the same. The Chino said that he was fully perswaded that the Aytao loued them well, and that he vnderstood hee did them great fauour and courtesie to graunt vnto the petition the which the interpreter did present in their name. But notwithstanding for so much as it was not signed, there was remedie to bee had, if that they woulde present another which hee would giue them, and go presently vnto the Aytao and present the same, and say when they giue it him, that they woulde go vnto Luzon and not vnto Machao, and that he himselfe would go with them for the good will he bare vnto them, if it were not for the great paine that is put vppon all them whosoeuer that shall speak for any stranger, without licence of the iustice, or is called and ordained for the same. So they being fully perswaded in this conclusion, with the petition made and all ready, there entred in at the gate wheras they were, a seruant to the Aytao, who in the behalfe of his master came to cal the Spaniards to come before him, for that he would see and talke with them before their departure. They straightwayes went forth in his company, and came vnto the gates of the cittie, after they had gon a good wayes in the suburbs: and there they were staied till such time as another came and brought their licence, written vpon a table (in such sort as in other places it hath beene told you). So when they had passed the gate, they passed thorough a long street, in the which they saw so great riches, and of so great curiosity, that the father Costodio with great admiration said, I haue beene in the principallest citties of all Flanders and Italie, and in all them I haue not seene so great curiositie and riches as in this streete alone: and according vnto the report of them all, hee had great reason to maruell thereat. So they comming vnto the end of this streete, and in sight of another gate, they sawe that the souldiers which kept and garded the same, did shut them in their presence with great hast, and let fall a percullis of yron before the gate, and demanded to see their licence at a window out of the saide percullis: and when they had it, although they saw with them the seruant of the Aytao and the interpreter, yet would they not open the gate vntill such time as it was acknowledged and newe firmed by another iudge; the which being done, they presently did open the gates and did conduct them vnto the house of one which is to be compared to a iudge of the court, and called in their language Tequisi, that he might go with them to the Aytao, for so it was commanded and ordained. Unto this Tequisi they gaue their petition that they had made, without giuing the interpreter to vnderstand therof, requesting him by signes and some words which they had learned of the language that he woulde giue it to the Aytao, and to procure that hee might accept and grant that which by the same they did demand. But when they gaue it him, it caused great alteration in the interpreter, for that they told the iudge that he was a theefe and a traitor, and how that he had sold them to the captaine general of Machao, and how that hee had presented a petition in their name: howe that they would go thither, and not to the iland of Luzon, where all their desire is to returne, and this hath he done by gifts that the saide captaine general hath promised to giue him, if that he do accomplish his desire. The Tequisi when he heard this, he forthwith departed with vs from his owne house, towards the house of the Aytao which was hard by, and as he went by the way he read their petition, and sawe that it was different to that which the interpreter had giuen before vnto the Aytao, he being present: whereat he made a stay and began to consider of the same, as also of that which the Spaniards had said vnto him at such time as they gaue him their petition, for by the signes and tokens they made, as by their semblant in speech, it seemed to him that they were marvellouslly indigned against the interpreter; but he did not wel vnderstand them, for that they could not plainly declare it in their language, till such time as hee found the contrarietie that was in the petitions, and the turbation of the interpreter, whom presently hee called vnto him, and asked him what the matter was? Hee trembling for feare, answered and saide, that hee vnderstood that the father Costodio (whome all the rest doo obey as their head, and with whom he alonely did communicate), that it was his pleasure, and gaue order to go vnto Machao, and that hee was certaine that all the rest were of that opinion, wherein he thought he had done well, and therefore he presented that petition in asking licence, whereby they might doo it liberallie, with this discharge. And againe the Spaniards seeing how he was terrified, and how that he requested them so humblie they would not proceed any farther with their complaint, wherewith the Tequisi was satisfied, who said vnto the Spaniards being in the gallerie of the Aytao his house, that they shoulde tarry there, and hee entred in with the petition in his hand. So within a while after they were commanded to enter into the hall there whereas the iudges were, and had seene the petition and had comoned about the same. And at their entring into the hall whereas the Aytao was, there were signes made vnto them that they should kneele downe, the which they did almost twenty paces before they came to the table that was before him: hee had in hande the petition that Tequisi had giuen vnto him, and although that he had read it before, yet did he returne and looked againe vppon it, and asked which were they that would go vnto Machao. The father Costodio signified himselfe and frier Iohn Baptista his companion; and said, that they, for that they were old and timorous of the sea, they would go thither for that it was nearer hande, and howe that the rest that were not of such yeares, neither so timorous, they woulde returne vnto the iland of Luzon from whence they came, and there dwell with other of their brethren and friends that were there. The interpreter, whose euill conscience did accuse him for the euils which he had done, was so timorous, that all men might see plainly his default, and without al doubt the iustices are so right in executing the same, that if their complaint had gone forwards, they would haue punished him and his companion, and that very cruelly: but the religious friers woulde not consent that the souldiers shoulde declare against them, although their will was good, but thought it a sufficient punishment to see in what affliction the poore men were in, and tooke pittie on them.

The Aytao was desirous to see their images and book, which was the chiefest occasion wherefore hee sent to call them; and when he saw them he receiued great content, and called the father Costodio to come nigh vnto him, and asked the signification of some of them, such as seemed vnto him most strangest, and being satisfied thereof, hee commanded the frier Costodio to reade on one of these bookes, hee harkening vnto it with great attention, and as one amased to see those letters, and the forme of them so farre different vnto theirs, which are all in manner of caractes, as hath beene told you. So after that they had passed away the time a while in this, hee saide, that those which woulde go vnto Machao shoulde put themselues on the one side, and they that woulde go vnto Luzon on the other: the which being doone hee tooke his leaue of them verie louinglie, and saide that hee would giue them the licence which they did aske at all times whensoeuer they woulde, and although hee coulde not grant it them without first to consult with the vizroy of Aucheo, yet he would doo it within tenne dayes, and then those which woulde go vnto Macheo might presently depart, and those which would go vnto Luzon, he would send them vnto Chincheo, that from thence the gouernour shoulde cause them to be sent in the first passage that goeth with merchandice.

This Aytao was very peaceable and humaine, who hauing compassion on the Spaniards, for that they seemed vnto him to be good men, he commanded to bee giuen to them, ouer and aboue the kings alowance, a hogge, and rice, and other kind of victuals. So herewith they went vnto their lodgings with content, and also the interpreter, who thought that hee was newe borne againe that day.

CHAP. XIII.

The Spaniards remaine certaine dayes in Canton, whither came certaine Portugals from Machao: at the first they feared them, but afterwards they were assured, by the contractation they had the one with the other, that they were friendes: the vizroy of Aucheo commeth to Canton, and dispatcheth the Spaniards, and giueth them good prouision and intertainment.

After that the ten daies were past appointed by the Aytao, and some more, and seeing that no more mention was made them, but as though they had neuer seene them, they were very sorowfull, and in ielousie that the captaine general of Machao aforesaide had knowledge howe that his craft and subtiltie was discouered, and thereupon to begin and frame some other: procuring for an instrument in the performing of the same, some iudge or some other person of power and authoritie. So they being with this care and discontent, there came vnto the cittie of Canton foure Portugals to buy and sell merchandice, with a safe conduct which they had for the same, which was the occasion that their sorow and trouble increased, suspecting what might happen conformable to the aduise which they had from thence: but for that they did comon and visit them many times, with intent to discouer their minds the one vnto the other, they presently did forget the euill suspection that they had of them, and not onely that, but they did giue them great almes and charitie, helping and aiding them in all things, as it was meete and reason amongst Christians. So being void of their first care, they put all their diligence and care in their departure: and seeing that there was no mention made thereof, by reason that the iudges were occupied in mustering the souldiers of that circuit in a great and mightie field, whereas they were trained vp in military exercises, some shooting in bowes, some with hargabushes, tossing the pike, running of horses, and many other exercises more: and after that they had many different proofes, as well of thinges past as at that present, they ordained captaines, such as were aduanced aboue all the rest, and most worthy: all which being finished, the Spaniards determined to put the Aytao in remembrance of his promise; and the better that they might doo it, and with most breuitie, they ordained a petition, and went with the same vnto the house of the Aytao, therewith to aske licence to put it in vre. The first iudge they met withall was the Tequisi aforesaid, who made signes that they should come vnto him, and asked of them what they would haue. The father Costodio answered, nothing but onely to present that petition vnto the Aytao, to put him in minde of their departure: the Tequisi did take the petition, promising them to giue it vnto him presently, the which he did accomplish in a short space. So being read by the Aytao, he made answere by the same petition, that he had a particular care of them, and tarried onely for order from the vizroy, which could not tarrie long: the receiuing whereof hee woulde aduertise them; the which hee did accomplish in fewe dayes, which came with great content vnto the Spaniards, for that he commanded that they should be sent away in verie good order, and to giue them all that was needfull for their iourney, and that in aboundance. The same day that this commission came, there came also newes that the vizroy would come vnto the cittie of Canton, and that within few dayes hee would bee there: the which did so much trouble the Aytao and the rest of the iudges, that day and night they neuer rested, but were occupied in the preparing al things necessary to receiue him, which were so many and with so great maiestie as though the king in person should come thither: with great and mighty triumphall arkes, rich hangings, with other things, the which 1 do not here make mention of, although they were very curious, because I would not be tedious, for that I haue a great desire to conclude this little historie: and if I should declare all that passed therin, it were requisite for the same alone to make a great volume.

Foure dayes after the comming of the vizroy, by his order there was giuen both to the one and to the other a prouision, in the which he commanded all iudges and gouernors to receiue the Spaniards into their iurisdictions whereas they should passe, and not to permit any to do them harme or iniury, but to giue them free passage with securitie till such time as they should come to the place appointed in the said prouision, which was vnto Machao and vnto Luzon: and iointly therewith he commanded two captaines to beare them company til such time as they had brought them out of all danger. And to giue vnto them that went vnto Machao (which was three daies iourney) sufficient prouision requisite for fiue dayes: and to them that went to Luzon their prouision for forty dayes, although the voyage is to be made in fifteene dayes, and in twentie dayes at the most. He also commanded them that had the charge to carry them, that they shoulde haue a special care vnto their healthes, in trauelling not too fast, but little and little. Likewise the Aytao gaue order vnto the interpreters for to sell the frigat, in the which the fathers came thither, and to giue vnto them the price that shoulde bee made thereof, to bestow it at their pleasure: the which they did, but kept still the halfe of that which they solde it for: and with many other things more, which by the commandement of the vizroy was giuen them for their iourney, and thought it well bestowed on them, for to see themselues free of their lyings and crafts. At the departure of the father Costodio, one of the souldiers mind was altred, who was called Pedro de Villa Roel, and was very desirous to go with him vnto Machao, the which hee did accomplish by apparelling himself in the habite of a Portugal, because he had no licence to go otherwise. So all things being in a redinesse for their iourney, they tooke their leaue the one of the other, in shedding many teares with the griefe of minde.

The father Costodio and his companions came safely and in health to Machao in foure dayes, as himselfe did afterwards write thereof, and were very well receiued of the bishop, and of all the rest: and within fewe dayes after they gaue them a place for to build a monasterie, wherein he and his companion might liue, and all such as should take the habite of that order. They came thither the fifteenth of Nouember.

And those which went vnto Luzon departed out of the cittie of Canton in a great barke, of the which there are many in all that kingdome, very well tilted and dressed, with many roomes and galeries and painted windowes, as hath beene told you: in the which they were very much made of by the patron of the said barke and of the passengers, which were many, and went vnto diuers partes with merchandice: some thinges that they saw by the way till they came vnto Chincheo, shal be told you in the chapter following.

CHAP. XIV.

They that were determined to go vnto Luzon, doo departe for the cittie of Chincheo: in which voyage they see many riuers and townes: and other particular things.

The Spaniards depart out of the riuer of Canton, and after they had sailed by sea the space of three leagues, they entred into another mighty riuer, in the which they trauelled four daies. And sure the great number of citties and townes that they saw alongst the riuers side is incredible, and so nigh the one vnto the other, that they seemed to be al one: so in the end of foure dayes they landed at one of the cities, where came so much people to see those strangers, that it seemed al the kingdome were there assembled together, and were so many in number, that before they could get to the inne wheras they should be lodged, there passed more then foure houres, and was in distance but a quarter of a league: but when they came thither, they were verie faint with the great thrust and throng of the people. They stayed in this cittie one day, and the next day, very early in the morning, was brought vnto them horse, for to trauel by land other two daies, the which was almost continually in villages and townes; and the third day they were imbarked in a smal barke, wherein they passed a riuer which had but litle water, the space of two houres; then after they were shipped in a bigger barke, and entred into another riuer, which seemed to be an arme of the sea, in the which they sailed fiue dayes, and sawe sailing vp and downe the said riuer so many barks and boats, that it made them to be greatly amased. These riuers were as wel replenished of cities and townes, as the other riuer whereof we haue spoken. Al which is a helpe to beleeue that which hath been said of the mightinesse and the great number of people that are in that mighty kingdom.

Concluding this riuer they entred into another, but not so broade as the last, but a swifter current, and beset with mightie trees both on the one side and the other, and were so thick that almost they could not see the sunne thorough them: and although the country was very asper there alongst the riuers side, yet was there many walled citties, and an infinite number of townes and vilages, in such sort that the suburbs did almost ioyne the one vnto the other. So when they were disembarked out of this riuer, they trauelled by land other foure dayes, and greatly maruelled to see the great fertilitie of the country, and many other things more, which they do passe ouer, for that in the relation of the Augustine friers it hath beene declared vnto you. In the ende of those foure daies they came to a cittie ten leagues from Chincheo, and were lodged in the suburbs of the same, whether resorted so much people to see them, that although they did shut the gates to defend themselues from the prease, yet could they not be disturbed of the entry, for that they broke the gates, and climed vp the wals and windowes to see them. The host of the house whereas they were lodged, when he saw that the people did spoile and destroy his house, he requested the Spaniards to go forth into a greene fielde which was there harde by, placed amongst a company of orchards, the which they did to satisfie them, and also to satisfie the multitude of people that were come thither only to see them. The noise of the people was so great, that the gouernor feared there had bin some other matter, and commanded a iudge to go and examine the cause and know the truth: but when that hee was certified thereof, hee commaunded the Spaniards to come vnto his house, for that hee was desirous and would see them. They presently did accomplish his commandement, and went their way, and as they passed thorough the streete, there were certaine representing a comedie, but so soone as the people that were there did see the Spaniardes, they left the players all alone and followed them. They entred into

the gouernors house, and found him with great maiestie of
seruants and souldiers of his gard : he entertayned them with
great loue, and asked them who they were, and from whence
they came. The interpreter presently showed the prouision
they brought from the viceroy, which was, in summe, their
licence giuen by him for them to go vnto Chincheo, and that
none should disturbe them in their iourney, but to ayde and
giue them all fauour possible, and that which was needefull
for their iourney. And when that he had read the same, he
saide that thereby he did vnderstand that which he desired
to know, and how that the viceroy did command all gouernors, and him as one of them, they should offer to do all that
lay in them : the which he did accomplish, and shewed them
great fauour and friendship.

The next day following, they departed out of this citie by
land, being giuen vnto them by the gouernor very good prouision for the way. The same day they came vnto a towne
that was very fresh, and fiue leagues from the place they departed, they were determined to tarrie all that night, fearing the passage through a citie which was but a league
before, suspecting that they should be as much troubled with
the people as they were in the other citie the day before. And
although this was but a small towne, yet was there so great
a concourse of people that came from the villages there
abouts, that it caused them to depart the next morning more
early than they thought, and all the night they could not
sleepe, because of the great noyse of the people.

So within a while after they departed from that towne,
they came vnto the citie aforesaide, the which for situation
and gallant buildings, was the fairest in all that province.
Through the midst thereof ranne a mightie riuer, ouer the
which were many bridges very great and most faire. Here
were they so oppressed with much people that came to see
them, that they were detayned in the presse a good while
before they could enter into the citie : and after they were

within they were compassed about in such sort, that they could not goe to seeke to eate, but were constrained to enter into a barke and go downe the riuer and shroud themselues amongst a company of trees, and although they did vse this policie, yet the number of people were so great that leapt into the same barke that they were readie to sinke, till such time as they who had entred the barke, to auoid that perill, returned and lept a shoore, leauing them all alone with the barkemen and marriners that did rowe, who went to seeke and bring them to eate, and they remained in the barke all that night.

So the next day in the morning, before the people could come to disturbe them, they rowed towards the great and huge citie of Chincheo, and entred into the same vppon a Sunday, in the morning, being the sixt day of December.

They remained still in the barke for their owne quietnesse and security, and sent their interpreter with their prouision vnto the Gouernour, that he might ordaine at his pleasure that which was therein commanded. The Gouernor when he had receiued commission he said vnto the interpreter that he should tell the Spaniards that he was very glad that they were come thither in safetie and in good health, and that hee should receiue great ioy to see them, and to shew them the courtesie that was commanded him by the viceroy, in their prouision or commission. But by reason that the great number of people that would come to see them, should not be troublesome vnto them, he would passe ouer his content in seeing them, and for their better comoditie they shall depart in the same barke wherein they came, vnto the port of Aytim, whereat were certain ships that were bound vnto Luzon, and that he would command they should be receiued into the said ships, and to be carried with as much speede as was possible: and for the accomplishing of the same hee kept the commission of the viceroy, and gave an other commission vnto the gouernor of the port, whether as hee sent them, in the which he commanded to be accomplished all that he had promised.

The Spaniards, although they would very gladly have seene the citie of Chincheo and the mightinesse thereof, yet did they accomplish that which the gouernor did command without anie reply, for that they considered that it should come then better to passe. So they came vnto the said port the next day folowing in the morning, whereas they did remaine in the barke, doing as they did at Chincheo, and sent their interpreter with the commission vnto the gouernor, who presently after he had read the same, sent and commanded that the Spaniards should come a shore and come and see him: who did accomplish the same, although with no lesse trouble than in other places, by reason of the people that came to see them. The gouernor intertained them with great loue and faire words, and before they departed from him, he sent to call a captaine of one of the ships that was there bound unto Luzon, and asked of him when he would depart from that place, who answered within ten daies: then the gouernor commanded that he should carrie them in his ship, and to giue them the best intertainement that was possible, who promised him to accomplish the same, and therwith he tooke his leaue of them, and sent them with the said captaine, who offered them all the fauour and friendship that was requisite. He presently carried them vnto his ship, who after he had shewed them the whole commoditie therof, he made them a colation or banket with great friendship.

They remained in this port more than fifteene daies, wheras they suffered very much colde, and seeing that the ship wherein they were appointed to go was not redie, neither any order for them to depart in many daies, considering the great desire they had to be amongst their own nation and to take their ease, and hauing knowledge of another ship that was ready and would depart, they altogither went vnto the gouernor (who was set in audience), and said vnto him with a loud voice (as is vsed in al that countrie), that the captaine whom he had commaunded to carrie them vnto Luzon, was not readie to depart, neither any signe that he would in many daies, and that he would giue them licence, and command a captaine of an other ship that was there readie to depart, and went vnto the same Iland of Luzon, that he might carrie them, because they were so ill at ease, and suffered so much colde that they felt great griefe.

When the gouernor heard this he was very angry, and with great choler he commaunded one of his officers that was there with him, to go presently and bring before him that captaine vnto whom he had committed the carriage of the Spaniards: the which was accomplished, and that in so short time that it caused great wonder: who when he came before the gouernor had so great feare, that he knew not whether he was in heaven or in earth. The gouernor straightwaies asked him what was the occasion that he did not depart within the tenne daies as he had sayde? The captaine answered, that they had had no wether, neither at that present, wherewith they might nauigate. He asked him againe and saide, seeing that the weather and time would not serue, how is it that there is an other ship readie to depart. The captaine at this demand did faulter in his speech, and answered friuolous wordes, wherefore the gouernor commanded that he should be whipped in his presence for the lie which he had tolde; and as they were pulling off his apparell for to execute the commandement, the Spaniards hauing pitie and compassion of him, for that he seemed to be an honest man, they fell all vpon their knees at the gouernors feete, and requested him to pardon his offence, who did presently consent therunto with a good will, and commanded to let him alone; but he spake vnto him very sharpe wordes, such as, so farre foorth as the Spaniardes could perceiue by the semblance both of the one and of the other, that was as much griefe vnto him as though he had beene whipped. Then presently he commanded to call the captaine of that ship that was readie to depart, and deliuered vnto him the commission that he had giuen vnto the other, with a great penaltie, and charged him to carrie the Spaniards vnto the Ilande of Luzon, and charged him to bring a testimoniall from thence, how that he had carried them in very good order and saftie, and left them at the place that they desired. This captaine vnderstanding what had passed with the other, and because he would not see himselfe in the like perplexitie, did accept the commandement, and thought the time long of his departure from thence, and did promise them more than they did demand, and made hast to depart out of the hauen because hee would not be called backe againe.

CHAP. XV.

The Spaniards depart from China and go to Luzon, they do passe some stormes at the sea: the mariners do call vpon the diuell, by lots: the religious men do reprehend them: in the end they come to their desired port, whereas they are received with much ioy.

The second day of Januarie, departed out of the porte of Aytim, with a prosperous wind, the shippe wherein was imbarked the Spaniardes, and two other which were their safe conduct: but by reason it was winter, the faire winde indured but a while, yet came they that day vnto the islande of Amoy, which was sixe leagues from the firme lande, and there they stayed one day. The next day following they went to sea, to prosecute their voyage, whereas they were taken with so terrible and foule weather, that the ship did driue they knew not whither, and many times in daunger to be drowned. This storme indured four dayes, although more stronger at one time than at an other: in the which storme was separated the three ships, the one from the other, in such sort, that euery one tooke his way, procuring to saue themselues, as commonly in such cases is vsed, without hauing any care the one of the other; and God was so pleased that the ship wherein the Spaniardes were, and one of the other two, entered into a sure port, although with great trouble and with so great a leake, that they could scarce keepe her aboue water; but in especiall that which came in their safe conduct. And afterwarde they understood that the other ship had taken port fiftie leagues from that place, with the like perill and danger. In this port they remained certaine dayes trimming their ships, and tarrying for a faire winde. So they departed from thence the three and twentie day of Ianuarie, and to their iudgementes with a settled and good winde, with the which they sayled fiue dayes, in the end whereof they discouered the iland of Luzon, with a singular ioy unto them all, for which the Spaniards gaue thanks vnto God, by whose fauour they had escaped the storme past.

But it so fell out, as they were going alongest the coast of the iland for to enter into the port of Manilla, and being within fiue leagues of the entrie thereof, vpon a soddaine there arose the north wind with so great furie, and caused so great a sea, that they found themselues in a great deale more daunger than in the other storme past, in such sort that they sponed[1] before the winde with their foresayle halfe mast hie, shaking it selfe to pieces, and in euerie minute of an houre readie to be drowned. The Chinos, for that they are superstitious and witches, beganne to inuocate and call vpon the diuell, for to bring them out of that trouble (which is a

[1] Incorrectly written for "spoomed." To spoom a ship is to put her right before the wind.

thing commonly vsed amongest them, at all times when they finde themselues in the like perplexitie); also they doo request of him to showe them what they should doo to bring themselues out of trouble.

But when the Spaniards vnderstoode their dealinges, they did disturbe them that they shoulde not perseuer in their lottes and inuocations, and beganne to coniure the diuells, which was the occasion that they would not answere vnto the inuocation of the Chinos, who did call them after diuerse manners (as hath been declared in the first part of this historie); yet they heard a diuell say, that they should not blame them because they did not answere vnto their demaunde, for they could not doo it for that they were disturbed by the coniuration of those Spanish fathers which they carried with them in their shippe.

So presently, when the night was come, God was so pleased that the storme ceased, and became, in fewe houres, very calme, although it indured but a while; for, as they beganne to set sayle to nauigate towardes the port, and almost at the point to enter into the same, a new storme seised on them, and with so great force, that they were constrayned to returne vnto the sea, for feare to be broken in pieces vpon the shore.

At this time they wanted both water and victualles, which was vnto them a newe torment; and they were brought into so great extremitie, that for ninetie and sixe persons that were in the shippe, there was not left victuals for two dayes.

The Chinos beganne a newe to inuocate the diuels by writing, which is a way that they neuer let but doo answere them, as they did at this instant, and were not disturbed by the coniurations of the fathers; yet, notwithstanding they lyed in their answere, for that they saide, that within three dayes they should be within the citie of Manilla, and after it was more then four dayes.

In conclusion, having by the fauour of Almightie God ouercome all their trauayles by the sea, and the necessitie of the lacke of water and victualles, they arriued at the desired port the second day of Februarie, anno 1580; whereas they were receiued by the gouernour, and of all the rest, with great ioy, in pardoning them the offence they had committed in going without licence, and shewed vnto them particular fauours, and were very sorrowfull that the father Costodio and his companions remained in Machao, for that hee was wellbeloved of all, and that with great desert, for his vnderstanding, learning, and holy life. Who, within fewe dayes after, did write a letter vnto the rest of the religious men in Manilla, aduertising them how that in a short time they came vnto Machao in good health; and how that the bishoppe and the captaine generall, with all the rest of the towne, were verie glad and ioyfull of their comming, and fully resolued to the contrarie of the false opinion that they had conceiued of them, and that he was in great hope to see his desire accomplished, for that he was daily in place whereas they did see and comon with the Chinos, whom, so soone as he can speake the language, he doth pretend to instruct them in matters touching the faith. Also he wrote, that he vnderstood by good originall or information (although it was comitted in secret), that the kingdom or province of Cochin China, which is four daies iourney from Machao, whereas the Portingals hath contraction, and port for all their ships that come from the Indias, hath sent vnto the bishop of Machao, and doth demand of him priests for to baptise them, with such determination and good will to be Christians, that in some portes they haue alreadie timber cut downe for to edifie churches. This you may belieue, for that the bishop himselfe hath tolde him, and in the latter end of his letter was written as followeth: They have inuited me to this enterprise, and (for to put my selfe therein) I would gladly haue with me many companions, which is the treasure that we go to seeke. It is a firme lande, there whereas God hath prepared a great haruest. They are politike people, and more easie to be conuerted then the Chinos, for that the diuell hath not put so manie disturbances against the gospel of Christ as in China, although it doth ioyne vpon it; and once entering the faith therein, with the fauour of God, their great and difficult doings which now they haue among them, will be broken with great ease; for they are not so many nor so great, whereby wee should be discomforted to see them ouercome, and principally they being men of so good wisedome and vnderstanding, as we haue seene by experience in the time that we haue beene amongest them; and so full of mercie and pitie, that although wee entred into the lande without licence, and for dooing of the same wee ranne in great daunger of our owne liues, they did intreat vs well, and gaue vs all that was needefull, and also did suffer vs to preach, if we could the language; the which, with the fauour of God, we will quickly learne, for that we are whereas continually we doo common and talke with the Chinos; wee doo verie earnestly commit it vnto our Lord to direct and guide the same, that his holy name may bee exalted, and the soules of these blinde Gentiles may knowe and beleeue, and beleeuing, may be saued.

This was the substance of the letter, with the which it seemeth vnto me great reason to conclude this second relation, and to begin the third, the which I do beleeue will be pleasant to the reader, and is intituled, *A Commentarie of the New World;* in the which is contayned many curious matters, as you shall perceive after the reading thereof, and is declared in substance and effect by the relation of the father, that did passe and see them all, who was named fryer Martin Ignacio, a religious man, of the order of S. Francis, who, after that he had compassed the whole worlde, came hither to Rome with Martin Simion, bishop of the Iland of

Pepper, in the orientall or East Indias, with whom I haue had communication diuers times, and is a Chalde borne, and of the citie of Ninivie in Babylon, and made bishop by the patriarke of Babylon.

THE END OF THIS BOOKE.

A

COMMENTARIE,

OR

SHORT DISCOURSE,

OF ALL SUCH NOTABLE THINGES AS BE BETWIXT SPAINE TILL YOU COME VNTO
THE KINGDOME OF CHINA, AND FROM CHINA VNTO SPAINE, RETURNING BY
THE ORIENTALL OR EAST INDIAS, AFTER THAT THEY HAD ALMOST
COMPASSED THE WHOLE WORLD.; WHEREIN IS CONTAYNED
ALL THE RITES, CEREMONIES, AND CUSTOMES OF
THE PEOPLE, THE RICHES, FERTILITIE, AND
STRENGTH OF MANY KINGDOMES: AND THE
DESCRIPTION OF THEM.

*Made and set fourth by the Author of this Book, as well by that which he hath
seene, as also by true relation that he had of the religious and barefoot
Fryers of the order of Saint Francis, who trauailed
the same the yeare* 1584.

CHAP. I.[1]

A Commentarie of the New World.

SAINT LUCAS DE BARRAMEDA, and the citie of Cadiz, from whence ordinarily goeth foorth all such fleetes and shippes that go vnto the occident, or West Indias, are distant the one from the other onely fiue leagues, and in thirtie seuen degrees of altitude; from whence vnto the ilandes called

[1] Nearly the whole of this chapter is entirely different from the original Spanish, and is translated by Parke from the French of Luc de la Porte. The following is translated from the original Spanish of Mendoza.

"The itinerary of Father Martin Ignatius, guardian of the order of the blessed S. Francis, who went to China with others of the same order, and of the province of S. Joseph, by command of our lord, King Philip,

the Canarias is two hundred and thirtie leagues, and alwayes doo rut to the southwest, and is ordinarily sailed in eight or

with his return by the East Indies and other realms, making the circuit of the world ; wherein are treated of the most remarkable things that he heard and saw in the journey, with the rites, ceremonies, and customs of the people, the riches, fertility, and strength of many kingdoms through which he passed, and the description drawn up according to the notice he took of them.

"CHAP. I.

" *Of the reason of his Majesty's commanding these friars to proceed to the kingdom of China; of their embarkation and arrival at the Canary Islands.*

" Our sovereign, King Philip, having been informed of the matters relating to the great kingdom of China by certain friars of the order of the blessed Doctor, S. Augustine, who came to his court ; and having seen the two accounts which they brought him from thence, of the entry of the Augustine and Franciscan fathers (as may be seen more largely in those accounts), and the letters of his governors of the Philippine Islands, and of the provincials of the Orders, in which they begged him, as has already been said in the first account, to send his embassy to the sovereign of that great kingdom, with friars and ministers for the conversion of the natives of the islands already discovered, and of the many others which were being discovered every day; and that, by the king of China giving opportunity for the preaching of the Gospel, they might be enabled easily to succour and assist the Augustine fathers, who were the first who entered those islands ; his Majesty having sent forty friars of the said order of Augustine, and many others of the order of the blessed S. Francis : and moreover, the embassy (which they had begged of him with so much earnestness), in order that there might be no want of ministers, in the year eighty, he determined to send forty barefooted friars of the province of S. Joseph, whose commissary was Miguel de Talavera, with instructions and orders to proceed to New Spain, thence to the Philippine Islands, and thence to the great kingdom of China, in case there should be an opportunity of introducing the Holy Gospel. According to the order of his Majesty, there were to have been fifty of these friars ; but from the prevalence of the plague of universal catarrh in Spain, not more than thirty-four could be assembled. These then were despatched and set forward by the order of the royal council of the Indies, and of Monsignor Sega, the Apostolic Nuncio. And arriving at Seville without the requisite licence to depart for the Indies, his Majesty's commercial officers, who were about to despatch the fleet, would not allow them to embark for want of the document ; they had been told at ten dayes. The seas are rough, which causeth great waues; for which cause it is called the gulfe of the Jeguas.

These ilands, which in ancient time were called Fortu- Fortunadas. nadas, are at this day called by the Spaniards the Canarias, which is derived of *canes*, or dogs; for that there was in them at such time as the Spaniardes did discouer them, great quantitie of dogges, very bigge, fierce, and braue. There are of them seuen ilands, which are called Gran The names of the Canarias. Canaria, Tenerife, Palma, Gomera, Yerro, Lancarote, and Forte Ventura; and are in altitude twentie-eight degrees,

> Madrid that it would be sent without fail. On account of this carelessness they found themselves in a most unpleasant position; for the fleet was departing, setting its sails, and leaving the bar of S. Lucar, and they could not go in it for want of the licence; nor could they return to their convents, because in Castile, whence they had come, they refused to admit any one from Seville, which was infested by the plague. The ships having got beyond the bar, there arose a sudden storm, in which one of the largest vessels of the fleet was lost, and another had its main-yard broken. The commander of the fleet, seeing that the damage could not be remedied in a short time, sailed in three days, leaving the ship which had its yard broken to refit, with orders to follow immediately. During this time, his Majesty's licence for the passage of the friars arrived at Seville, with an order to the officers that, at all events, they were to be furnished and despatched with the greatest possible celerity. This order arrived at 10 o'clock at night; and the friars were immediately informed that they were to embark in the said ship, which was ready to sail, having procured another yard. They appointed the day, immediately following which was Sunday, at three o'clock in the morning, and twenty-eight friars embarked, all preachers. God granted them such favourable weather that they overtook, at the Canary islands, the fleet which had sailed from S. Lucar some days before them. This course was always south-west; and, although the distance is two hundred and thirty leagues from S. Lucar to the islands, they reached them in seven days. These islands are in nearly twenty-eight degrees latitude, and are seven in number, all well provided with the necessaries of life: there is much corn and wine, and various kinds of pulse, with abundance of sugar, sheep, fowls, and camels, and all at much less prices than in Spain. They are all inhabited by Spaniards, who live comfortably. In one of them is a bishop, with prebendaries, a cathedral church, and convents of friars. In short, there is but little difference between these islands and Spain."

lacking very little, and haue in them many particular thinges, of which I will declare some of them in briefe.

In the Iland of Tenerife, at the farther part thereof, towards the north-west, there is a mountain called El Pico de Tereyra, which, unto the iudgement of them who haue seene it, is the highest in all the worlde, and is plainely seene before you come to it three score leagues: so that a ship going from Spaine vnto those ilandes, doth discouer that mountaine first. None can ascende or go vp that mountaine but in the moneths of July and August, for that all other moneths of the yeare there is very much snow on it, although in all those ilandes it doth neuer snowe, and to mount the height thereof is three daies worke; on the top of the same there is a round and plaine place, and being thereon at such time as it is faire weather, and the seas calme and in quiet, you may see all the seuen ilands, and euerie one of them will seeme but a small thing in respect; yet some of them are distant from that more than fiftie leagues, and it hath as much more in compasse as that. In the two monethes aforesaid, they do gather in the toppe thereof all the brimstone that is brought from that iland vnto Spaine, which is much in quantitie. This mountaine belongeth to the Duke of Maqueda, by particular gift of the king.

In one of these seuen ilands aforesaid, called the Hierco,[1] there is a continuall woonder, which in my iudgement is one of the greatest in all the worlde, and worthie to be knowen amongest all men, whereby they may exalt the mightie providence of God, and giue him thankes for the same. This iland being the greatest amongest the seuen, is a countrie very asper and vnfruitfull, and so drie that there is no water to be found in all the iland, but on the sea side, and that in fewe places, but very farre distant from the inhabitance of the ilande. But there naturall necessitie is

---

[1] Misspelt for Hierro, the Spanish form for Ferro.

remedied by the diuine prouidence of heaven (as aforesaide), and by a strange meanes, which is, there is a great and mightie tree (vnknowen, and the like hath not beene seene in any part of the whole world), whose leaues are narrowe and long, and are continually greene like iuie, vpon the which tree is seene continually a small cloud, which neuer augmenteth nor diminisheth, with the occasion that the leaues continually, without ceasing, doth distill drops of water, very cleere and fine, which doth fall into certaine sesternes, which the inhabitantes of the townes haue made for the conseruation thereof, to remedie their necessities, and to sustaine thereby not onely themselues, but also their cattell and beastes, and is sufficient for them all: yet doo they not knowe the originall and beginning of this continuall and strange miracle.[1]

[1] The following is a translation of what Leopold von Buch says of this tree in his "Description Physique des Isles Canaries, traduite de l'Allemand, par C. Boulanger." Par., 1836, 8vo., fo. 122.

"There was formerly in the Island of Ferro a gigantic til (*Laurus Fœtens*), whose pulpy leaves extended their thick foliage to a great distance. Every day, two or three hours after sunrise, the leaves of this tree began to condense the water, which falling from leaf to leaf, like drops of rain, collected together at the foot of the tree, in a very pure stream. The inhabitants of the island, being altogether destitute of spring water, used to go towards midday to draw this water, and return to their homes in the evening with their pitchers full. The tree being regarded as sacred passed for a wonder of the world: a keeper appointed by the inhabitants had it in charge to collect the water in cisterns, and presided at its distribution among all those who came to draw. This remarkable tree was still existing in 1689, and was situated to the east, above the little town of Valverde. Father Galindo, who saw it, has given its description in detail. It survived long after that period; but its leaves were diminished, and it lost its beneficent properties. Necessity compelled the inhabitants to find some other means of supplying themselves with water, and the tree was forgotten. Meanwhile, travellers going to the new continent of America, never forget (whatever may be the number or variety of objects that strike their imagination in those countries) to speak of the tree of the Isle of Ferro. It has therefore preserved a great reputation in Europe."

One hundreth leagues distant from these ilandes, towards the right hand, there is an other thing of little lesse admiration then the other that we haue spoken of, which is, that many times there is seen an iland, which they cal S. Borandon. Many being lost at the sea haue chaunced vpon the same iland, and do say that it is a very fresh and gallant iland, with great abundance of trees and sustinence, and inhabited with Christian people, yet can they not say of what nation or language. The Spaniards many times haue gone with intent to seeke it, but neuer could finde it, which is the occasion that there be diuers opinions touching the same. Some doo say that it is an inchanted iland, and is seene but certaine daies assigned or appointed: and others say that there is no other let or impediment for the finding therof, but because it is so little, and is continually couered with great cloudes, and that there runneth from it riuers which haue so great a current that it maketh it difficult to come vnto it. My opinion is (if it be any thing worth) that being true, that which so many haue spoken of this iland, according vnto the common opinion which they haue in all the seuen ilands of Canaria, it can not be without some great mysterie: for he which can cause it to be all in a cloud, and the swift current of the riuers to be an impediment to the finding therof, can find remedie for the inhabitants to come forth (if it be so for them that be without at the sea not to go into it), yet can it not be for them within the iland, but at some time there should haue some come foorth by chance, and haue bin seene of some there abouts, and declared vnto them the secret of that mysterie: from whence I do gather, that either this iland is imagined or inchaunted, or else there is in it other some great mysterie, for the which to giue credite vnto it, or to varie from the truth, it shal be wisdome not to proceed any further, but to conclude in that which toucheth the Ilandes of Canarias aforesaid.[1]

Opinions of this iland.

[1] For a very interesting chapter on this imaginary island, see No. 23

The clyme and temperature of them all is excellent good, and hath abundance of al necessary sustenance for mans life. There is gathered in them verie much wheate and other seedes, and wine: there is also made verie much sugar: there is nourished and brought vp great store of cattel, and that verie good. But in especiall camelles, whereof there is great store. Also all kinde of sustenance is better cheape there then in Spaine. Camelles.

All these ilandes are inhabited with Spaniardes, whereas they doo liue verie pleasantly, amongest whome, at this day, there be some that be naturall of the Guanchas aforesaid, who be verie much Spaniarde like. The principall of all these seuen ilandes is the Gran Canaria, in the which is a bishoppe and a cathedrall church, and counsell of the Inquisition and royall audience, from the which dependeth the gouernement of all the other sixe ilands.

CHAP. II.

They do depart from the Ilands of Canaria for the Ilande of Santo Domingo, otherwise called Hispaniola, and do declare of certaine things in the way thitherward.

After that the fleetes or shippes had taken refreshing in the Ilandes of Canarias aforesayde, they departed from thence, sayling by the same rutter, vntill they come vnto an ilande called the Desseada, which is fifteene degrees from the Equinoctiall, eyght hundreth and thirtie leagues from the Canarias: all which is sayled without seeing any other land: they are sayling of the same ordinarily eight and twentie and thirtie dayes. The Iland called Desseada.

of the Appendix to Washington Irving's "Life and Voyages of Columbus."

This Iland Desseado was called by that name by reason that the gulfe is great, and so many daies sayling, that when they do see it, is that after that they haue verie much desired the same, so that Desseado is as much to say, as "desired." This iland hath nigh and about it many other ilandes, one of the which is that which is called La Dominica, which is peopled and inhabited by certaine Indians who are called Caribes, by such as do nauigate that way, which are a kind of people that doo eate humaine flesh: they are very expert archers, and very cruell: they do anoint their arrowes with a deadly earth, and so ful of poison, that the wound the which is made therewith can not be healed by any humaine remedie. This ilande is in fifteene degrees. It is verie little and not of much people, yet notwithstanding it hath beene the death of many Spaniardes both men and women: such as haue come thither in shippes, not knowing the daunger thereof, haue gone a shore for fresh water, or else to wash their lynnen, and vppon a soddaine vnlooked for, haue beene be set by the Indios, who haue slaine them, and after eaten them: and they say that it is very sweete flesh and sauorie, so that it be not of a fryer, for of fryers by no meanes they will eate, nor would not after that happened vnto them as hereafter followeth.

There was a ship that was bound vnto the firme land, and did arriue at that ilande, in the which went two religious fryers of the order of Saint Francis, and hauing no care as aforesayde, but very desirous to be a lande, they went a shore without any feare or suspition of any harme that might happen vnto them; and being at a riuer side sporting themselues with great recreation, by reason of the freshnesse thereof, easing themselues of the long and painefull nauigation which they had comming from the Ilandes of the Canarias vnto that place, when the Caribes did see them, without uy feare, vpon a soddaine they descended from a mounyne, and did kill them all, without leauing any person

The Iland Dominica.

aliue. Many dayes they made great feastes and bankets, eating of those bodies which they had slaine, some sodde and some roasted, as their pleasure was. So on a day they would amongest them eate one of the fathers, who was very faire and white; but all that did eate of him in a little space did swell marueilously, and did die madde, with great gaspings that it was woonderfull to see: so that from that time, they remaine as warned neuer for to eate any more of the like flesh.

<small>They which did eate friers flesh did die madde.</small>

Of these euils they haue committed an infinite number, and haue at this day with them many Spaniardes both men and women, whose liues they pardoned for to serue their vses or euilles, because they were verie young, of the which they say that some haue fled away. They go naked like vnto the Indians, and doo speake their language, and are almost conuerted vnto their nature. This great inconuenience might be remedied, if that it did please his maiestie to command some generall that were bound vnto the firme land, or vnto the New Spaine, to make abode there a fewe dayes, and to roote out and make cleane that ilande of so euill and wicked people, which were a good deede, and they doo well deserue it, and to giue libertie vnto the poore Christians that are there captiue, a great companie of them. And it is saide of a truth that some of them be of good calling. There can none goe a lande on this ilande, but straightwayes they are discouered by such ordinarie spyes as they doo put to watch. And if they do see that those which doo come a land are many in number, and that they can not hurt them, they doo remaine in the highest part of the mountayne, or else amongest the thickest of woods and bushes, till such time as the shippes do depart, which is so soone as they haue taken fresh water or fire wood. They are great traytors, and when they see oportunitie they giue the assalt, in the manner as hath beene tolde you, and doo very much harme.

Nigh vnto this Ilande Dominica, towardes the northwest,

is the Ilande of S. John de Puerto Rico, the which is in eighteene degrees: it is fortie and sixe leagues long and fiue and twentie leagues brode, and in compasse about an hundred and fiftie leagues. There is in it great store of kyne, verie much sugar and ginger, and yeeldeth very much wheate. It is a lande of verie much golde, and is not laboured nor taken out of the earth for lacke of people; it hath verie good hauens and portes towardes the south, and towardes the north onely one, the which is sure and good, in respect whereof the Spaniardes did giue the name vnto the whole ilande, Puerto Rico, taking the name of the port or hauen. In it there is foure townes of Spaniardes, a bishoppe and a cathedrall church, and he that is prelat at this day is the reuerend father Don fryer Diego de Salamanca, of the order of S. Austin.

Much kine, sugar, and ginger: wheat and gold.

When the Spaniardes went first vnto this ilande, according vnto the report of the reuerende father de Las Casas, bishop of Chiapa, was in the year 1509. This iland was so full of trees and fruite that they gaue it the name of the Guertas;[1] and there were in it sixe hundredth thousande Indios, of the which at this day there remaineth not one.

Of sixe hundreth thousand Indians there remaineth none.

From this ilande vnto the ilande of Santo Domingo, is foure score leagues; I say, from one port vnto an other, and from poynt to point, but twelue leagues. They doo ordinarilie go from one port to an other in three dayes; but to returne they are more than a moneth, for because the winde is contrarie.

[1] Orchards.

CHAP. III.

Of the Iland of Santo Domingo, called Hispaniola, and of their properties.

The Iland Hispaniola, which by an other name is called Santo Domingo, by reason that it was discouered as that day, it is in eighteene degrees, and was the first that way discouered in the Indias, by the captaine Christopher Colon, worthie of immortall memorie; it was inhabited in the yeare of 1492. This iland is in compasse more than sixe hundredth leagues; it is diuided into fiue kingdomes, the one of them is now called the Vega, which, at the time that it was discouered was called Neagua; it hath foure score leagues in compasse, and stretcheth all of them from the north vnto the south; out of the which sea, as doth testifie the reuerende of Ciapa in his booke, doth enter onely into the kingdome, thirtie thousand riuers and running brookes, twelue of them as great as Ebro, Duero, and Guadalquiuer in Spaine. The foresaide bishop doth also speake of an other maruaile, which is, that the most part of these riuers, those which do distil and run from the mountaines, which is towardes the west, are very rich of gold, and some of it very fine, as is that which is taken out of the mynes of Cibao, which is very well knowen in that kingdome, and also in Spaine, by reason of the great perfection thereof: out of the which myne hath been taken out a piece of virgin golde, so bigge as a twopennie wheaten loafe, and did weigh three thousand and sixe hundred castillianos,[1] the which was sonke and lost in the sea, in carrying of it into Spaine, as doth testifie the aforesaid reuerend bishop. In this Ilande there is greater quantitie of cattell than in the other Ilande of Puerto Rico; and

---

[1] The castellano, which is still used in Spain and its dependencies as a weight for gold, is equivalent to 71 grains English.

218 A DISCOURSE OF THE

Canna-fistola.

Gold and pearles.

Bread of a roote called Casaue.

Of three millions of

there is made much sugar, and gathered much ginger and cannafistula, and also manie sortes of fruits, such as is in Spaine, as others different of the countrie, and that in abundance: there are also great store of hogs, whose fleshe is as holesome and as sauorie as is mutton in Spaine, and is verie good cheape: a heyfor is bought for eight ryalles of plate, and all other thinges of that countrie after the rate, although that the marchandice of Spaine is verie deere. It is a countrie of very much golde, if there were people for to take it out: and manie pearles. In all this ilande they gather no wheate, but in the bishopricke of Palensuela; although in many other places the ground would yeeld it very well if they would sowe it. But nature, which was woont to supplie necessities, dooth accomplish the lacke of wheate to giue them in steede thereof a roote, which dooth growe in that iland in great quantitie and abundance, and dooth serue them for bread, as it did vnto the naturall people of that countrie, when the Spaniards went thither. It is white, and is called casaue, the which being grinded and brought into meale, they doo make bread thereof for their sustinence, the which, although it is not so goode as that which is made of wheat meale, yet may they passe therewith and sustaine themselues.

This countrie is verie hoat, by reason whereof their victuals are of small substance. The principall citie of that iland is called Santo Domingo, (for the reason abouesaid), in the which is an arch-bishop and a royall audience, or chauncerie. This citie is built on the sea side, and hath to it a great riuer, the which dooth serue them for their port or hauen, and is verie secure. There is in it three monasteries of religious friers, and two of nunnes.

In this ilande (as saith the reuerende bishop of Chiapa in his booke) there were, when as the Spaniards came first thether, three millions of men naturall Indians, of the which this day there is not two hundred left, and yet the most part of them be sonnes vnto Spaniardes, and blacke mores borne of the Indians women. All their sugar milles and other places are inhabited with negros, of the which there may be in that ilande about twelue thousand. It is a holsome countrie vnto them that dwell therein. The sea is ful of whales, and that in abundance, which are seene by such as do come in their ships, and many times they are in feare of them. But aboue all other, there is an infinite number of great fishes called tiburones,[1] and are in great skuls:[2] they are marueilously affected vnto humaine flesh, and wil folow a shippe fiue hundred leagues, without leauing of it one day. Many times they haue taken of the fishes, and do finde in their bellies all such filth as hath beene throwne out of their shippe in many dayes sailing, and whole sheepes heads with hornes and all. If they chance to finde a man in the waters side he wil eat him all: if not, all that he doth fasten on he doth sheare it cleane away, be it a legge or an arme, or half his body, as many times it hath beene seene, and they doo it very quickly, for that they haue many rowes of teeth in their heads, which be as sharpe as rasers.

Tiburones.

CHAP. IV.

Of the way and the Ilandes that are betwixt this Iland of Santo Domingo and the kingdome of Mexico.

The first ilande, that is after you are departed from Santo Domingo, is that which ordinarily is called Nauala,[3] the which is one hundred and twelue leagues from the cittie of Santo Domingo, and is seuenteene degrees, and is but a small iland: and nigh vnto that is another, which is called

The Ilande of Nauala.

[1] Sharks.   [2] Schools.   [3] More properly Navaza.

The Iland of Iamayca. Vracans. Jamayca, of fiftie leagues in longitude, and fourteene in latitude: there was wont to be about them many vracanes,[1] which are spowts of water, with many blustering winds. This word *vracan*, in the Indian tongue of those ilands, is as much to say, as the ioyning of all the foure principall winds togither, the one forcing against the other: the which ordinarily dooth blow vppon this coste, in the monethes of August, September, and October, by reason whereof such fleetes as are bound vnto the Indies doo procure to passe that coast, before these three monethes or after, for that by experience they haue lost many ships in those times. From *The Iland of Cubá and the Port Hauana.* this iland they go vnto the ilande of Cuba, which is in twenty degrees, in the which is the port of Hauanha, which is called the Cape of San Anton: they doo put two hundreth and fiue and twentie leagues of longitude, and of latitude sixe and thirty; it is inhabited with Spaniards, who conuerted all the rest vnto the faith of Christ: there is in it a bishop, and monasteries of religious friers.

When that any ships do go vnto Noua Espania, they haue sight of them, and likewise when they doo returne: all those which do come from the Peru do enter into the foresaid port of the Hauana, which is a very good port and sure, and there is to be had all kind of prouision necessary and belonging vnto the fleetes and ships, some which the ilande dooth yeeld it selfe, and other some brought from other places: but in particular, there is great store of very good timber, as wel for the repairing of ships as for other thinges, with the which they do ordinarily balest their ships that come for Spaine. The kinges maiesty hath in this a gouernor and a captaine, with very good souldiers for the defence thereof, and of a fort which is in the same harbor, the best that is in all the ilands.

This iland of Cuba was discouered in the yeare 1511, and was in it (being of the bignesse aforesaid) a great number of

[1] Hurricanes.

naturall people, and now but a very fewe: it hath a riuer wherein is very much gold, according vnto the opinion of the natural people, and was tolde by the fathers vnto their children, the which was cast into that riuer by the natural people, in this order following.

There was a casique, called Hatuey, who, for feare that hee had of the Spaniards, came from the Iland Hispaniola, vnto this iland with many of his people, and brought al their riches, with much golde amongst them, who by the relation of other Indians of Santo Domingo (wheras he had been king), vnderstood that the Spanyardes were comming vnto that iland, whereupon he gathered togither all his people, and many of that iland, and made a parley vnto them, saying: It is said of a certeintie, that the Christians doo come into this iland, and you doo well vnderstand by experience, what they haue done by the people of the kingdome of Aytim (which was the Ilande Hispaniola), the like will they doo here by vs; but do you know wherfore they doo it? They answered and saide, because they were of their owne nature cruel. The casique saide No, that they did it not therefore; but because they had a God whom they did worship, and because they will haue him from vs, they doo kil vs: and in saying these words he tooke forth a basket with golde and iewels which he brought thither in secret, and shewed it vnto them saying, This is their God that I spake off; let vs make vnto them areytos, the which are sports and dances, and possible we shall please them, and then wil they command their people not to do vs any harme. For the accomplishing and furnishing of the same, euery one of them brought that which they had in their houses, and made therof a great mountaine of wheate, and danced rounde about the same till they were werie: when the casique saide, I haue thought with myselfe whilst we were dancing, that howsoeuer it be, these that do come wil kil vs: for whether we do keep our treasure or giue it vnto them, *The Spaniards god is gold.* *The Indians throwe all their gold and iewels into the riuer.*

with couetousnes to seek more from vs, we shall die; therefore let vs throw it into this riuer. The which they did with a common consent and good will.

The Port of Saint Iohn de Lua. From this point or cape of Sant Anton, they saile to the port of San Juan de Lua, which is on the firme land of Mexico, two hundreth and thirtie leagues from the said point: in all that bay there is great fishing, but in especial of one kind of fish which is called *mero*, the which are so easie to be taken, that in one day they may lade not shippes but whole fleetes; and many times it happeneth that they bring so many to their ships that they throw them again into the sea for lack of salt to salt them with. They *The Iland of Campeche.* passe in sight of an iland, called Campeche, the which is a gallant and fresh country, and nigh vnto the kingdom of *Honey and waxe.* Mexico: in it is great store of victuals, but specially hony and waxe, and is three hundreth leagues compasse; al the people of that iland are conuerted vnto the law of our Lord Jesus Christ. There is in it a bishop and a cathedrall church, a gouernor for his maiestie, and monasteries of friers. Within few dayes after they depart from this ilande, and come vnto the port of Saint John de Lua, in the which, by reason that it hath many flats, it is requisite to be carefull for to enter into it: his maiestie hath in it a fort which is good and *The citie of Vera Cruz.* strong. Fiue leagues from this port is the cittie of the Vera Cruz, whereas is the whole trade and traficke, and there is resident the king's officers: it is a hot country by reason that it is in the nineteene degrees, but well replenished of all kinde of victuals: it was wont to be vnwholesome, but now they say it is not so much; they know not what shoulde bee the occasion, whether it bee by the moouings of the heauens, or by the good gouernement and discretion of them that do dwel in it. This cittie is from the citie of Mexico, the which is metropolitan of al that kingdom, and by whom al the rest is gouerned, seuentie leagues, al the way inhabited and ful of townes, both of Indians, Spaniards, and so great store of prouision that it seemeth to be the land of promision. It is maruellous temperate, in such sort that almost throughout al the whole yeare it is neither whot nor cold, neither dooth night exceede the day, nor the day the night, but a very little, by reason that it is almost vnder the equinoctiall line. The mightinesse of this kingdome, and some particularities, you shall vnderstand of in the chapter following.

CHAP. V.

Of the bignesse of the kingdome of Mexico, and of some particular and notable things that are in it.

This kingdome of Mexico is the firme land: on the one side it hath the north sea, and on the other side the south sea: it is not possible to declare the bredth and length thereof, for that vnto this day it is not all discouered. Euery day they doo finde and discouer new countries, as in the yeare of fourescore and three, you may perceiue by the entry which was made by Antonio de Espeio, who, with his companions, did discouer a countrie, in the which they found fifteene prouinces, al ful of townes, which were full of houses of foure and fiue stories high, the which they did name Nuevo Mexico, for that it doth resemble the Old Mexico in many thinges. It is towards the north, and they do beleeue that that way, by inhabited place, they may come vnto that country which is called of the Labrador (of which shal be spoken more at large hereafter).

This kingdome towards the orient dooth ioyne vnto the country of Peru, and so running by the north sea, and reacheth vnto Nombre de Dios, which is a port of the saide kingdome, and from thence vnto Acapulco, which is a port in the kingdome of Mexico: and in the south sea it reacheth

Panama. vnto Panama, a port of the said Peru; and in the same sea
The Straites of Magellanes. it extendeth nigh vnto the Straights of Magellanes, and not farre from the river of Plata and Brasill.

To conclude, this kingdome is so great that vnto this day they cannot find the end thereof: but euery day doth discouer new countries, whereas all the Indians that they do finde are verie easie to bee reduced vnto the Catholike faith, for that they are people very docible, ingenious, and of a good vnderstanding. There is amongst them diuers languages, and verie different climes; although all generally doo vnderstande the Mexican tongue, which is most common. There are many prouinces inhabited by Indians and Spaniards, that euery one of them is as bigge as a reasonable kingdome; yet the greatest and most principall is that of Mexico, whereas are many Indians and Spaniards, which doo exceed all the rest in number: the names of them are Honduras, Guatimala, Campeche, Chiapa, Guaiaca, Mechuacan, Nueua Galicia, Nueua Viscaya, Guadiana, and others more, which I leaue out because I woulde not be tedious: in all the which, they haue either a royall audience and gouernors, or other justices, all Spaniards.

The naturall people whereof, neuer since they were conuerted haue beene found in any heresie, nor in any thing contrarie vnto the Romish faith. All these prouinces are subject and doo acknowledge that of Mexico as the principall: there whereas his maiestie hath his vizroy, an inquisition, an archbishop, and a royall audience or court of Chancerie.

This cittie of Mexico is one of the best that is in all the whole world, and is situated vpon water after the manner and fashion of Venice in Italie: in all this kingdome almost you cannot know when it is winter, or when it is summer, for that in al the whole yeare, there is smal difference betwixt the daies and the nights, by reason of the temperature of the countrie; the fieldes are greene almost all the whole yeare, and trees beare fruit also almost all the whole yeare: for when it is winter in Europa, then doo there fall dewes from heauen which dooth cause all things to budde and floure; and in the summer it doth ordinarily raine, but especially in the monethes of June, July, August, and September, in the which monethes it is a maruel when it raineth not euery day; and it is to bee wondred at, for that almost it neuer rayneth but from noone forwards, and neuer passeth midnight, so that it neuer troubleth them that doo trauell by the way, for that they may beginne their iourney at midnight, and trauell vntill the next day at noone. It raineth vnreasonably, and with so great furie and force, that the time that it dooth indure, it is requisite to flie from the showers; for that many times they are so hurtfull, that one sole shower taketh away the life of a man.

It rayneth almost euery day.

Almost all the whole yeare in this kingdome they do sowe and gather as wel wheate (wherof they haue great abundance) as maiz, which is the ordinary sustentation of al the Indians, blacke moores and horse, of the which they haue great abundance very gallant and good, both to the eye, and indeed, as in any kingdom in al the whole world that is knowne vnto this day. The brood of them was carried out of Spaine thither, when first they did discouer that country, and for that effect were chosen the best that could bee found: and for that they doo eate all the whole yeare greene grasse and maiz, which is wheat of the Indians, is the occasion that they do deserue to haue the praise aboue all other. In fine, this kingdome is one of the fertilest of victuals of al that euer we haue heard off, and of riches, for that there is in it an infinite number of siluer mines, out of the which is taken great abundance, as it is to be seene euery yeare when as the shippes doo come vnto Syuell. It is vnder the Torrida Zona, yet notwithstanding it is of the temperature as I haue said, contrarie vnto the opinion of ancient philosophers, who said that it was not inhabited. But now to excuse them, it shal

The best horses in all the world.

An infinite number of siluer mines.

not be from our purpose to declare the cause wherefore they were deceiued, and is, that in the foure monethes aforesaide, wherein the sunne hath his most force, it doth continually rayne, which is the occasion that the country is so temperate: and besides this, God doth prouide that it is visited with fresh windes, which come both out from the South and North Sea, and is so ordinarie a thing, that it is a maruell to see it calme, by reason whereof the whole kingdome is of that propertie; and although the sunne be very strong and causeth great heate, yet putting himselfe vnder any shadowe, although it bee but little, they straightwayes feele a fresh and comfortable winde, by reason of the temperature of the heauen in the manner aforesaid.

The inhabitants of this kingdome throughout al the whole yeare, neede not to augment nor diminish their apparell, neither their beddes. Also the aire and clime is so holesome, that you may lie and sleepe in the fieldes without any thing vppon you, as in any house, be it neuer so well hanged and close.

All that is discouered of this kingdome (except it be the lande of the Chichimecos, which is a kind of Indians that liueth as the Alarbes[1] do in Africa, without any house or towne)—all the rest, I say, are in peace and quietnes baptised and doctrined, and furnished with many monasteries of diuers orders of religious men, as of the order of S. Dominicke, of S. Francis, of S. Austen, and of Iesuits, besides a great number of priests that are reparted in al parts of that kingdome, so that the one and the other are continually occupied in doctrining of the naturall people and other Spaniards that are in that kingdome, of whome, although they be but a few in respect of the Indians, yet do they surmount in number more then fiftie thousand. In the principall citie of this kingdome, which is that of Mexico as

[1] Arabs? The word seems to have been misprinted in the original Spanish.

aforesaid, there is a vniuersitie, and in it be many schooles, *An uniuersitie in Mexico.* whereas is red any facultie, as is in Salamanca, and that by men of great sufficiencie, whose trauell is gratified with great rentes and honor. There bee also in it many great hospitals as well of Spaniards as of Indians, wheras the sicke men are cured with great charitie and comfort, for that euery one of them haue great rents and reuenues. I do not intreat of the churches and monasteries, both of friers and nunnes, which are in that cittie, nor of other particular thinges, for that thereof there is written a large historie, and my intent is to declare by way of a comentary that which the said father Costodio and frier Martin Ignacio did comon with me by word of mouth, and that I saw written and vnderstood of him at his returne from trauelling almost the whole world, and of other things that I my selfe haue experimented in certaine parts of it: so that this my discourse may more properly be called an epitome or itinerario then a historie. In this kingdome there are bred and brought vp more cattell then in any other parts knowne in all the world, as wel for the good climate and temperature of the heauen, as also for the fertility of the country. The kine and sheepe many times bring foorth twise a yeare, and the goates ordinarily thrise a yeare: so that because they haue many fields in that countrie, and much people that doo giue themselues vnto that kinde of gettings (as grasiers) is the occasion that there is so great abundance, and solde for a small price; and manie times it happeneth that the bringers vp of them doo kill tenne thousand head of them onely to profite themselues with the skinnes, in sending of them into Spaine, and leaue the flesh in the fieldes to feede the foules of the ayre, without making any more account thereof.

There is great aboundance of many sorts of fruites, some of them very different from those which are gathered in our Europa, and the most part of them: but amongst all notable things which are to be considered off in that king-

A strange kind of tree. dome (which are manie), one of them is a plant called maguay, and an ordinarie thing in all those prouinces and townes, of the which they make so many things for the seruice and vtilitie of them that do dwel therin, that it is hard to be beleeued of them that haue not seene it (although in al places you haue many witnesses to it). They take out of this plant wine, which is that which the Indians doo drinke ordinarily, and the negros: also excellent good vinegar, honie, a kinde of thride or yarne, wherewith they doo make mantels to apparel the naturals, and for to sow the same apparell: the leafe haue certaine pricks whereof they do make needels wherewith they sow their apparel, their shooes, and slippers. The leaues of that plaint, ouer and aboue that they are medicinal, they do serue to couer there in the place of tyles, and being dipped in the water, they make thereof a certaine thing like hempe which serueth for many thinges, and make thereof repaue; and the trunke of this plant is so bigge and strong, that it serueth for ioystes and beames whereon they doo build their houses, which commonly is couered with strawe, or else with brode leaues of trees, as is that of this plant.[1] All this, although it seemeth much, yet in respect it is nothing considering the great profite that is made of this plant: as shalbe declared vnto you when we come to intreat of the Ilands Philippinas, where as there is great aboundance of them, as I refer it vnto the iudgment of the reader.

CHAP. VI.

This chapter doth prosecute in the things of the kingdom of Mexico.

Properties of the Indians. The Indians of this kingdome are maruellous ingenious, and doo see nothing but they imitate the same, whereof

[1] This is evidently a palm, and probably the mocaya, macauba, or macaw-tree.

commeth that they are very good singers and plaiers vpon all sorts of instruments, yet their voices doo heale[1] them nothing. They are very much affectioned vnto matters touching ceremonies of the Church, and giuen vnto the diuine culto, and therein they doo very much exceede the Spaniardes. In euery towne there are singers appointed, which repaire euery day vnto the church to celebrate the offices vnto our Lady, the which they do with great consort and deuotion. Touching the dressing and adorning of a church with flowers and other curiosities, they are maruellous politike: they are reasonable good painters in some places: they make images of the feathers of small birdes, which they call in their language Cinsones,[2] which haue no feete, and feede of nothing else but of the dewe that falleth from heauen, and is a thing greatly to be seene, and was wont in Spaine to cause great admiration; but in especiall vnto such as were famous painters, to see with what curiositie and subtiltie they did make their pictures, in applying euery colour of the feathers in his place. They are people of great charitie, but in especiall vnto the ecclesiasticals, which is the occasion that one of them may trauell from sea to sea (which is more then fiue hundred leagues) without the spending of one riall of plate in victuals, or in any other thing, for that the naturals doo giue it them with great good will and affection: for the which in all their common places of resort, which is an inne for strangers, they haue men appointed for to prouide for all ecclesiasticall men that doo trauel, of all that they haue neede, and likewise vnto the common people, for their money. They doo not onely receiue great content with them, but they themselues doo go and request them to come vnto their townes, at the entrie whereof they make them great entertainement: they go all foorth of the towne both small and great in procession, and manie times more than halfe a league, with the sounde of

Pictures made of fethers.

---

[1] Misprinted for "help". [2] Probably humming-birds are meant.

trumpets, flutes, and hoybuckes. The principallest amongst them go forth with bowes and nosegayes in their hands, of the which they doo make a present vnto such religious as they doo receiue: and sometimes they cast them more flowers then they woulde willingly they shoulde. Generally, they doo reuerence all ecclesiasticals, but in particular those of such religious houses, which in that kingdome were the first that did conuert them and baptise them; and they do it in such sort, that if the religious man will for any offence punish or whippe any of them, they do it with such facilitie, as a master of a schoole doth beate his schollers that he doth learne.

<small>Hernando Cortes.</small> This great reuerence and subjection was planted amongst them by the worthy captaine Hernando Cortes, marques Del Valle, hee who in the name of the Emperor Charles the fift of famous memorie, did get and made conquest of that mightie kingdome. He who amongst other vertues that be spoken of him (and doo indure vnto this day in the memory of the naturall people of that countrie, and as I do beleeue his soule is mounted many degrees in glory for the same), hee had one that surmounted the other in excellency, which was, that he had great reuerence and respect vnto priestes, but in especial vnto religious men, and his will was that the same should bee vsed amongst the Indians: at all times when hee did talke with any religious person, he did it with so great humilitie and respect, as the seruant vnto his master. If he did at any time meete with any of them in the streete, he being on foote, a good space before hee came vnto them, hee woulde put off his cappe, and when hee came vnto them he would kisse their handes: and if hee were on horsebacke, he had the like prevention, and woulde alight and doo the like. By whose example, the naturall people of that countrie doo remaine with the same custome, and is obserued and kept in all that countrie vnto this day, and with so great devotion, that in what towne so euer that any ecclesiasticall or

religious man doth enter, the first that doth see them before they enter therein, doo runne vnto the church and ring the bell, which is a token knowne amongst them all that a religious man is comming, so that foorthwith all the women go foorth in the streete whereas they do passe, with their children in their armes, and bringe them before the religious men, that they should blesse them, although he be on horseback, and do passe a long thorow the towne.

In all this countrie there is great aboundance of victuals and fruit, that the mony being of so small estimation (by reason they haue so much), a ryall of plate is no more woorth there then a quartillo in Spain: you shall buy there a verie faire heafor for twelue rials of plate, and fiftie thousand if you will at the same price, and a calfe for sixe or eight rials of plate, a whole sheepe for foure rials, and two hennes, such as you haue in Spaine for one riall, and of Guiny hennes, otherwise called Turkey cockes,[1] and in Spanish Pavos, you shall haue an hundred thousande (if you please) for a riall and a halfe of plate a peece, and after this rate all other sortes of victuals whatsoeuer you will buy, although they be neuer so good: wine and oyl is very deare, for that it is brought out of Spaine, not for that the countrie will not yeeld thereof, and that in great aboundance (as hath beene seene by experience), but they wil not consent to it for diuers respectes. There be thorough out all the whole kingdome many hearbes that are medicinall, and the Indians very much experimented in them, and do always cure with them, in such sort that almost there is no infirmitie but they haue a remedy for the same, and do minister it, by reason whereof they do liue very healthfull, and do die verie seldome, but of leanenes, or when the radicall moistnessse is consumed. They vse little lettings of bloode, and lesse of compounded

Medicinall hearbes.

They vse no compounds.

---

[1] The word "Guiny" has been inserted here by the translator; the expression in Spanish is, "hens from the Indies, which in Spain are called Pavos," meaning Turkeys.

purgations, for that they haue amongst them other simples which they bring out of the fielde, wherewith they do euacuate their humors, applying them vnto the pacient. They bee for little trauell, and doo passe with little meate, and verie seldome sleepe but on a matte vpon the ground, but the most part in the fields in the open aire, which as wee haue saide hurteth not, neither themselues nor yet the Spaniards.

But now to speake in few words that which requireth a great discourse and many words, and yet notwithstanding not expresse well that which might be said of this mightie kingdome: I will conclude in comparing it vnto the most greatest and richest of all that is now knowne in all the world, except that of China, of the which in this historie hath beene mentioned so many thinges, and shall be more spoken off, when as we shall come to intreate of it; for that wee will intreate of the New Mexico, as I haue promised in the fifth chapter, and because it is a new thing, I do beleeue it wil be of great content.

CHAP. VII.[1]

Of the New Mexico, and the discouering thereof, and what they do know of it.

In the said chapter I said that in the yeare 1583 there was discouered fifteene prouinces, the which the discouerers therof doo call the New Mexico, vppon the firme lande of Nueua Espania, and I did promise to giue notice of the discouering thereof, the which I will do with as much breuitie as is possible, for that if I shoulde difusely declare

[1] This and the three following chapters are supplied by Parke from the French of De la Porte.

all that they did see and knowe, it were requisite to make of it a newe historie: the substance thereof is, that in the yeare of our Lord 1581, hauing notice there of a religious man, of the order of Saint Francis, who was called frier Austen Ruyz, who dwelt in the valley of Saint Bartholomew, by the relation of certaine Indians called Conchos, who did communicate with others their neighbors called Pasaguates, who said that towards the parts of the north (trauelling continually by lande) there were certaine ilandes very great, and neuer knowne nor discouered by the Spaniards, who being moved with great zeale of charitie for the saluation of those soules, did aske licence of the Counte of Corunnia, vizroy of the saide Nueua Espania, and of his owne superiors for to go togither, and to procure to learne their language: and knowing it necessarie to baptise and preach vnto them the holie evangelist, hauing obtained the licence of the aforesaide persons, taking with him other two companions of the same order, with eight other souldiers, who of their owne good wil would beare them company, he departed to put in execution his Christian zeale and intent: who after a few dayes that they had trauelled, they came into a prouince which was called the Tiguas, distant from the mines of Saint Bartholomew (from whence they began their iourney) two hundred and fiftie leagues towardes the north, in the which by a certaine occasion the naturall people thereof did kill one of the friers companions: who, as also the souldiers that went with him, seeing and perceiuing the successe,[1] and likewise fearing that thereof might happen some other greater danger, they determined with a common consent to returne vnto the mines from whence they departed, with consideration that the company which went with him were very fewe to make resistance against such successes as might happen, being so farre distant from the dwellings of the Spaniards,

The prouince of Tiguas.

[1] This word is evidently coined from the Spanish word "suceso", an event or occurrence. It is used in the same sense a few lines further on.

and from their necessarie succour. The two religious men which remained did not onely refuse their determination, but rather seeing good occasion to put their good desire in execution, and so much ripe mies[1] or dainties for the Lordes table, and seeing they could not perswade the souldiers to proceed forwards in the discouering thereof: they alone remained in the saide prouince with their Indian boyes, and a Mestizo that they carried with them, thinking that although they did remaine alone, yet were they there in securitie, by reason of the great affabilitie and loue wherewith the naturall people did intreat them.

So when the eight souldiers came vnto the place that they desired, they straightwayes sent the newes of al that happened vnto the cittie of Mexico, vnto the vizroy, which is distant from the mines of Saint Barbora one hundred and three score leagues. But the friers of S. Francis were very much agreeued for the remaining there of their brethren, and fearing least they should be slaine, for that they were there alone, they began to moue the hearts and minds of other souldiers, that were in the company of another religious frier of that order, called Frier Bernardino Beltran, for to returne to the said prouince, to deliuer the aforesaide two religious men out of danger, and from thence to prosecute and go forwards with their enterprise begun.

At this time there were at the said mines by a certaine occasion, an inhabitant of the cittie of Mexico, called Antonio de Espeio, a very rich man, of great courage and industrie, and verie zealous in the seruice of the maiestie of King Philip: hee was naturally borne of Cordoua, who, when that he vnderstood the great desire of the saide friers, and howe much it did import, did offer himselfe to go on that iourney, and to spend thereon part of his substance, besides the venturing of his life. So licence being granted

[1] We do not find this word. The literal translation is, "so great a harvest ripe and ready to offer at the table of God."

vnto him to prosecute the same, by some that did represent the king's person, and was procured by the saide friers, there was appointed and giuen him for captaine, John de Ontiueros (who was chiefe bayley for his maiestie, in the townes which are called the foure Cienegas, which are in the gouernement of the new Biscay, seuenty leagues from the aforesaid mines of S. Barbora), and he to go with him, and gather togither men and souldiers, such as he could, for to accompany him, and helpe to follow their Christian intent.

The saide Antonio de Espeio was so earnest in this matter, that in a few dayes he had ioyned togither souldiers, and made prouision necessarie for the iourney; and spent therein a great part of his substance, and departed altogether from the valley of Saint Bartholomew the tenth of Nouember, 1582, and carry with him (for whatsoeuer should happen) one hundred and fifteene horses and mules, great stoare of weapons and munition, with victuals, and certaine people of seruice in this iourney necessarie. He directed his iourney towards the north; and at two dayes iourney they came whereas were a great companie of Indians, of those which he called Conchos: they were in raches[1] and in houses made of straw, who, when they vnderstoode of their comming, by relation of long time before, they went forth and entertained them with shewes of great ioy. The feeding of these people, and of al the rest of that prouince, the which is great, is of conyes flesh, hares, and venison, of the which they haue great aboundance. They have great store of maiz, which is wheat of the Indians, pompines and mellons, very good and in aboundance. They haue many riuers full of fish, very good and of diuers sorts: they go almost al naked; and the weapons that they doo vse are bowes and arrowes; and liue vnder the gouernement and lordship of caciques as they of Mexico: they found no idols amongst them, neither could

The prouince of Conchos.

Great store of conies, hares, and venison.

---

[1] Rushes for thatching. See Halliwell's *Dictionary of Archaic and Provincial Words*.

they vnderstande that they did worship any thing; for the which they did easilie consent that the Spaniards should set vp crosses, and were very well content therewith, after that they were informed by the Spaniards the signification thereof; the which was done by interpreters that they carried with them, and by whose meanes they vnderstood of other inhabitances, whether as the said Conchos did conduct them, and did beare them company more then foure and twenty leagues; all which way was inhabited with people of their owne nation: and in al places whereas they came, they were receiued with peace, by aduice that was giuen by the caciques from one towne to another. So hauing passed the foure and twenty leagues aforesaide, they came vnto another nation of Indians called Passaguates, who liue after the manner and fashion of the other aforesaid Conchos, their borderers, who did vnto them as the others did, conducting them forwarde other foure dayes iourney, with aduice of the caciques as afore. The Spaniards found in this iourney many mines of siluer (according to the iudgement of them that vnderstand that faculty), and of very rich mettall. One iourney from this they came to another nation called the Tobosos, who, when they discouered the Spaniards, they fled vnto the mountaines, and left their townes and houses void: but more after they vnderstood that, certain yeares past, there came vnto that place certaine souldiers for to seeke mines, and carried with them captiue certaine of the natural people of that country, for which occasion they remaine as scared and feareful. The captain forthwith gaue order, that they should be called backe again, with assurance that there should be no hurt done to them; and did so much that many of them returned, of whom they made much on, and gaue them giftes, declaring vnto them by the interpreter, that they came not thither to do hurt to any; with the which they all returned and were in quiet, and consented that they should set vp crosses, and declare the mysterie of

Passaguates.

Mines of siluer.

Tobosos.

them, and they made shew that they were content therewith; and did accompany them, as the other their borderers did, vntil they had brought them into the inhabitance of another different nation, which was distant from them twelue leagues. They vse bowes and arrowes, and do go naked.

CHAP. VIII.

Here he doth prosecute the discouering of the New Mexico.

The nation that the saide Tobosos did conduct them to is called Jumanos, who, by another name are called by the Spaniards, Patara Bueyes; their prouince is very [large] and full of townes, with much people: their houses made of lime and stone, and their townes traced in very good order: al the men and women haue their faces raced,[1] and their legs and armes: they are corpulent people, and more decent then any that they had seene vntil that time: they haue great store of prouision, and hunt both of beasts and foules; great store of fish, by reason of mightie riuers that commeth from the north, and some of them as big as Guadalquiuir, the which doth enter into the North sea: they haue many lakes of salt water which, in certaine times of the yeare, do congeale, and they do make thereof good salt. They are warlike people, and made shew thereof presently; for the first night that the Spaniards had placed themselues, with their arrowes they slew fiue horse, and hurt as many more, and would haue left not one aliue if they had not been defended by the guarde. When they had done this mischiefe, they left the town, and went to a mountain which was hard by; whether as presently in the morning went their captaine with other fiue souldiers, well armed, with an

[1] Streaked. See Minsheu's *Ductor in Linguas*.

interpreter called Peter, a naturall Indian borne, and with faire words and perswasions he quieted them and made peace, and caused them to descend into their towne and houses; and perswaded them to giue aduice vnto their neighbours, that they were men that would hurt no bodie, neither came they thither to take away their goods; the which he obtained easely by wisedome, and in giuing vnto the caciques certaine glasse beades and hartes[1] which they carryed for that purpose, and other trifles: so with this, and with the good intretement done vnto them, there went many of them in the company of the Spaniardes many dayes, alwayes trauelling alongst the riuer side aforesayde, whereas were many townes of Indians of this nation, the which indured twelue dayes iourney: in all the which, the caciques gaue aduice from one towne to another, out of the which they came forth and entertained the Spaniards without their bowes and arrowes, and brought with them victuals and other prouision and giftes; but in especiall hides and shamway skins, very well dressed, so that those of Flanders do nothing exceed them. These people are all clothed; and they found that they had some light of the holy faith, for that they made signe vnto God, looking vp vnto heauen, and they do cal him in their language *Apalito*, and doo acknowledge him for Lord, by whose mightie hand and mercie they confesse to haue receiued life, and to be a natural man, and al temporall goods. There came many of them with their wiues and children to the religious frier (that came with the captaine and souldiers, of whom we haue spoken off), for to crosse and blesse them; of whom being demanded, from whence and of whom they had the knowledge of God: they answered, that of three Christians and one negro that passed that way, and remained there certain daies amongst them, who, according to the signes and tokens they gaue them,

---

[1] Misspelt for "hats", De la Porte mentioning "chapeaux" among the presents.

should be Aluar Nunnez Cabesa de Vaca and Dorantes, and Castillo Maldonado, and one negro, the which escaped out of the fleete wherewith Panfilo de Naruaz entred into Florida; and after that they had bin many dayes captiue and slaues, they escaped and came vnto these townes, whereas God by them did shew many myracles in healing (by the onely touching with their handes) many diseases and sicke persons, by reason thereof they left great fame in all that countrie. All this prouince remained in peace and quietnesse; by which demonstration they did accompanie and served the Spaniardes certaine dayes, trauelling alongest the riuer side aforesaide.

Within few dayes after they came vnto a great inhabitation of Indians, where they came foorth to receiue them, by newes that they had of their neighbours, and brought with them many curious thinges made of feathers of different colours, and many mantles made of cotton, barred with blewe and white, like vnto them that are brought from China to truck for other thinges. All of them, as well the men as women and children, were clothed with shamway skins, very good and well dressed; yet could the Spaniardes neuer vnderstande what nation they were, for lacke of an interpreter that vnderstood their language. They dealt with them by signes; and they shewed vnto them certaine stones of rich metall, and being demaunded if they had of the same in their countrie: they answered by the same signes, That fiue dayes iourney from thence, towardes the north-west, there was great quantitie thereof; and howe that they would conduct them thither and showe it vnto them, as afterwardes they did performe. and did beare them companie two and twentie leagues, the which was all inhabited with people of the same countrie.

So following the saide riuer they came vnto an other inhabitance of much more people than the other past, of whom they were well receiued, and welcomed with many presents, especially of fish; for that they haue great store by reason of certaine great lakes not farre from thence, wherin is bred great abundance. They were amongest these people three dayes; in the which, both day and night, they made before them many dances, according vnto their fashion, with a particular signification of great ioy. They knew not how this nation was called, for lacke of an interpreter: but yet they vnderstoode that it extended very farre and was very great. Amongest this nation they found an Indian, a Concho by nation, who tolde and made signes that fifteen iourneys from thence, towardes the north-west, there was a lake which was verie broad, and nigh vnto it very great townes, and in them, houses of three and four stories high; the people well apparelled, and the countrie full of victuals and prouision, who did offer himselfe to bring them thether; whereat the Spaniards reioyced, but left to giue the enterprise, only for that they would accomplish their intent and begon voiage, which was to go to the north to giue ayde vnto the two religious men aforesaide. The chief and principall thing that they noted in this prouince was, that it was of a good temperature, and a rich countrie, great store of hunt, both of foot and wing, many rich metals, and other particular thinges of profite.

From this prouince they folowed their iourney for the space of fifteene daies without meeting any people: they trauelled amongst high and mightie pine trees, like those of Spaine; at the end wherof, after they had traueiled to their iudgments four score leagues, they came vnto a small village of very few people, very poore, and their houses made of strawe: they had great quantity of deere-skins, as well dressed as those that are brought out of Flanders; great store of excellent white and good salt. They gaue them good intertainment for the space of two daies that they remained there; after the which they did beare them companie twelue leagues, vnto certaine great habitations, always trauelling alongst the riuer side towarde the north, as aforesaide, till such time as they came vnto the countrie which is called the New Mexico. All alongst this riuer side was planted full of white salow trees;[1] and in some place it was foure leagues brode. Likewise there was many walnut-trees and peare-trees, like vnto those in Spaine.

In the ende of two dayes trauaile amongest these trees, they came vnto tenne townes, the which were situated alongst this riuer side on both partes, besides others that appeared, but farther distant. It seemed vnto them to haue much people, and as appeared to be more than tenne thousande soules.

In this prouince they did receiue them courteously, and carried them vnto their townes, whereas they gaue them great store of prouision and hennes of the countrie, with many other things, and that with a great good will. In these townes were houses of foure stories high, verie well wrought and gallant chambers, and most of them had steuues or hote houses for the winter. They are all apparelled with cotton and of deares skinnes; the manner and apparell both of the men and of the women, is much like vnto the Indians of the kingdome of Mexico. But that which did cause them most for to woonder was, to see both men and women to weare both bootes and shooes of very good lether, with three sooles of neates leather: a thing which they haue not seene but onely there. The women go without any thing vpon their heades; but their haire trimly kembed and dressed. Euerie one of these townes had caciques, by whom they were gouerned, as amongest the Indians in Mexico, with sergeantes and officers to execute their commandement, who goe through the streetes of the towne, and declare with a loude voice the will of the caciques, the which is straightwayes put in vre.

Houses of 4 stories high.

In this prouince the Spaniardes founde many idolles that

[1] Willows.

VOL. II.   I I

they worshipped; and in euery house they had a temple wherein they do worship the diuell, whereas, ordinarily, they do carrie him to eat. Likewise, as amongst Christians, in the high wayes they doo put crosses; so have they chappelles, whereas they say, the diuell doth recreate and rest himselfe, when as he trauelleth from one towne to another; the which chappelles are maruellously well trimmed and painted.

<small>They worship the diuell.</small>

In all their tyllages and ploughed groundes, of the which they haue many and very great, they haue on the one side of them, a portall or shedde built vppon foure pillers, whereas the labourers do eate and passe away the heate of the day, and are people verie much giuen to labour, and doo continually occupie themselues therein: it is a countrie full of mountaynes and woods of pine trees. Their weapons are strong bowes and arrowes, with their heads or pointes made of flint stone, wherewith they will pierce and passe a shirt of mayle or plate coate. They vse also macans, the which is a staffe of half a yeard long, made of flint, and verie smoth, wherewith they may cut a man a sunder in the midst; they vse also bucklers and targets made of rawe hides.

CHAP. IX.

Still doth hee prosecute the New Mexico, and declareth of such things as were there seene.

So after they had beene four dayes in this prouince, they departed; and, not farre distant from the same, they came vnto another, which was called the prouince of the Tiguas, in the which they found sixteene townes; in the one of the same, called Poala, they vnderstood that the Indians had slaine the two friars, Francisco Lopez and Frier Augustine, whome they went to seeke : and with them, three boyes and a Mestizo. But when they of this towne and their neighbours vnderstoode, being pricked in conscience, and fearing that the Spaniards came to plague them, and to be reuenged for the death of the saide fathers, they durst not abide, but left their houses voide and fled vnto the mountaines that were nighest hande, from whence they could neuer cause them to descende, neither by giftes nor policie. They founde in their houses great store of victualles, and an infinite number of hennes of the countrie, diuers sortes of metals, and some of them seemed to be very good: they could not perfectly vnderstande the number of people that were in that countrie, for that they were fled vnto the mountaines, as aforesaid.

Being fully certified of the death of them that they went to seeke for, they entred into counsell to determine whether they should returne vnto New Biscaya, from whence they came, or to proceede forwarde; in the which there were diuers opinions. But by reason that they vnderstoode there, that towardes the port of the orient from that place, and not farre distant from that prouince, there were very great townes and rich, and finding themselues so nigh them, the captaine Antonio de Espero,[1] with the consent of the religious fryer aforesaide, called Bernardino Beltran, and the most part of his souldiers and companions, determined to proceede forwardes in the discouerie thereof, till such time as they did see to what end it would come, that they might the better giue perfect and iust notice thereof vnto his maiestie, as witnesses that had seene it.

So being in conformitie they determined, they remayning there sentenela, or royall companie, the captaine, with other two companions with him, should go forwardes in the demand of their desire, which foorthwith they put in execution. So, at the end of two dayes of their trauaile, they came vnto a

[1] Misspelt for Espejo.

prouince where they discouered aleuen townes [sic], and much people in them, which, in their iudgement, did passe fortie thousand soules. It was a countrie very well replenished and fertile, whose confines are ioyned vnto the lands of the Cibola, whereas as is great store of kyne, of whose skins they do apparell themselues and with cotton; hauing the vse of gouernement amongest them as their neighbours haue. There are signes and tokens of many rich mynes, and found in their houses certaine metalles; these Indians do worship idols: they received the Spaniardes with peace, and gaue them to eate. Seeing this, and the disposition of the countrie, they returned vnto their sentenela from whence they departed, to giue notice vnto their companions of all that hath beene saide.

So when they were come vnto their companions aforesaide, they had notice and vnderstanding of an other prouince, called the Quires, which was vp the riuer on the north, sixe leagues distant. So they departed thitherwardes; and when they came within a league of the place, there came foorth in peace a great companie of Indians, and requested that they would goe with them vnto their townes; the which they did, and were verie well entertayned, and had great cheare. In this prouince they sawe but onely fiue townes, in the which there was a great number of people, which, vnto their iudgement, did passe fifteene thousand soules; and doo worship idolles as their neighbours doo. They found in one of these townes a pye in a cage, as is the vse in Spaine; and tirasoles, as those which are brought from China, and painted on them the sunne and the moone, with many starres: and taking the altitude thereof, they founde it to be in seuen and thirtie degrees and a halfe vnder the north poole.

They departed from this prouince, and trauelling by the same course or rutter, fourteene leagues from thence, they came to another prouince called the Cunames, whereas they discouered other fiue townes: and that which was the principal and biggest of them is called Cia, which was of such huge bignesse that it had in it eight places: their houses be plastered with lyme, and painted with diuerse colours, much better than they had seene in any prouince past. It seemed that the people that were there did passe in number twentie thousande soules. They gaue presentes vnto the Spaniardes with many curious mantelles, and of victualles to eate maruellously well dressed, and iudged the people to be more curious, and of more estimation of themselues, than any that thitherto they had seene, and of greater gouernement. They shewed vnto them rich metalles, and the mountaines that were hard by whereas they did take it out. Here they had notice of an other prouince which was towards the northwest, and determined to go thither. Rich metals.

So after they departed from thence, and had trauailed sixe leagues, they came to the said prouince, which was called Ameias, in the which was seuen great townes, and in them, according to their iudgment, thirtie thousand soules: they said that one of these seuen townes was very great and faire; the which they would not go to see, for that it was situated behinde a mountaine, as also they feared some euil successe, if that they should be deuided the one from the other. They are people after the fashion of the other prouince their neighbours, with as much prouision, and as well gouerned. Fifteene leagues from this prouince, trauelling continually towards the north-west, they came to a great town, called Acoma; it had in it more than sixe thousande soules. It was situated and placed upon a high rock, the which was more than fiftie fadam in height, and had no other entry but by a payre of staires, the which was made and cut out of the same rocke, a thing the which did cause great admiration vnto the Spaniardes: all the water that they had in this towne was in cesternes. The principallest hereof came with peace for to see the Spaniards, and brought them many mantles, and shamwayes very well dressed, and great quantitie of prouision: they haue their corne-fields two leagues from that place, and for to water them they take water out of a small riuer there harde by. Upon the saide riuer side they sawe many fields with roses, like vnto those that are in Spain. There are many mountaines which shewe to haue mettals, although they went not vp to see it, for that the Indians be many, and very warlike people.

The Spaniards remained in this place three daies, in one of the which the naturall people thereof did make vnto them a solemne dance, and came foorth in the same with gallant apparell and with maruellous ingenious pastimes, with the which they reioyced exceedingly. So four and twentie leagues from this place, they came vnto a prouince called in their naturall language Zuny, and the Spaniards do call it Cibola, there is in it a great number of Indians. In the which was Francisco Vazquez Coronado, and left there erected many crosses and many other signes and tokens of Christendome, which continually did remaine standing. They found there three christened Indians, which were left there at that time, whose names were, Andres de Cuyoacon, Gasper de Mexico, and Antonio de Guadalaiara, who had almost forgotten their own language, and could speake very well that of this countrie: yet with a little vse after they had talked with them they did easily vnderstand them. Of these they vnderstood, that three score iourneyes from thence was there a lake, very great, about the which was situated many excellent good townes, and that the natural people thereof had very much gold, and it seemed to be true for that they did all weare braslets and eareringes of the same. The fore-saide Francisco Vazquez Coronado hauing certaine intelli-gence of the same, he departed from this prouince of Cibola, and went that way: and hauing trauelled twelue iourneyes, his water did faile him, so that he determined to returne backe againe as he did, with pretence to returne an other time, when better oportunity should be had: the which afterwards he did not put in execution, for that by death all his determinations and pretences were cut off.

CHAP. X.

Still doth he prosecute the discouery of the New Mexico.

Vpon the newes of this great riches aforesaide, the sayde captaine Antonio de Espeio determined to go thether, where were of his opinion the most part of his companions: but the religious fryer was of the contrarie opinion, and sayd that it was high time to returne vnto New Bizcaya from whence they came, for to giue notice of all that they had seene, the which they did put in execution within few daies after, the most part of them, and left the captain with alonely nine companions that would follow him. Who, after that hee had fully certified himselfe of the riches aboue said, and of the great quantitie of good metals that were there, he departed out of this prouince with his companions, and trauelled towardes the northwest.

So after that they had trauelled eight and twentie leagues, they came into an other prouince, the which was very great, in the which to their iudgment were more than fifty thousand soules: whose inhabitants, when they vnderstood of their comming, they sent them a messenger, which said, that if they would not be slaine of them, that they should not approch any nearer vnto their townes. Unto the which the said captaine answered, that they came not thether to do them any harme, as they should well perceiue, and also did request them that they would not disturbe them in the prosecuting of their pretence, and gaue vnto the messenger certaine things such as they carryed with them, who did praise so much the Spaniardes, that he did appease the troubled minds of the Indians, in such sort, that they did of their owne good wil grant them licence for to enter into their townes. The which they did with one hundreth and fiftie Indians their friends, of the prouince of Cibola aforesaide, and with the three Indians of Mexico of whom we made mention.

Before they came vnto the first towne by a league, there went foorth to meete and receiue the Spaniards more than two thousande Indians laden with victualles and prouision, vnto whome our captaine did giue thinges of small price: yet it seemed vnto them to be of great estimation, more than golde. So when they came nigher vnto the towne called Zaguato, there came foorth to receiue them a great number of Indians, and amongest them their Caciques, and made a great showe of mirth and ioy, and threw vppon the ground much flower of maiz that their horse might tread vpon it. With these feastes, ioy, and pleasure, they entred into the towne, whereas they were very well receiued, lodged, and made much of: the which the captaine did partly recompence, in giuing vnto all the principallest amongest them, hattes, and glasse beades, and many other thinges more, which they carried with them to serue the like oportunitie.

The Caciques did forthwith dispatch and send aduise vnto all those of that prouince, giuing them to vnderstande of the comming of their new guestes, and how that they were verie curteous men, and did no harme. Which was occasion sufficient to cause them all to come laden with presentes vnto the Spaniardes, and did request them for to goe vnto their townes to sport and recreate themselues: the which they did, but alwaies with great care and respect of what soeuer might happen. For the which the captaine did vse a policie with them, which was, that he tolde vnto the Caciques, that for so much as his horse were verie fierce and furious, and that they had told them that they would kill them, therefore for to shunne the damage and harme that might happen vnto the Indians, it were requisite to make a fort with lyme and stone, to put them in. The Caciques did giue such credite vnto his words, that in a few houres they had ioyned together so much people, that they made a fort according as the Spaniardes did request, and that with an incredible breuitie. Besides this, when the captaine sayd that he would depart, they brought vnto him a present of fortie thousand mantles of cotton, some white, and some painted, and a great quantitie of hand towels with tassels at the corners, and many other thinges, and amongst them rich metals, which shewed to haue much siluer. Amongst these Indians they had great notice and knowledge of the lake aforesaide, and they were conformable vnto the other, in that touching the great riches and abundance of gold.

The captaine hauing great confidence in this people and of their good dispositions, he determined after certaine daies that he had bin there, to leaue fiue of his companions and the rest of the Indians his friends, that they might returne vnto the prouince of Zuny with all their bagage: and hee himselfe, with the other four that remained, would go more at quiet to discouer certaine very rich mynes, of the which he had true notice. So according vnto his determination he departed with the guides he had, and hauing trauelled toward the northwest fiue and forty leagues, he came vnto the sayde mynes, and tooke out of the same with his owne hands rich metals, and very much siluer: the mynes had a great and brode veine, it was vpon a rocke whereas they might go vp to it with great ease, for that there was a way open to that effect: nigh thereunto were certain townes of Indians amongst the mountaines, who shewed friendship vnto them, and came foorth to receiue them with crosses in their hands, and other signes and tokens of peace: nigh vnto the same they saw two reasonable riuers, vppon whose bankes there were many vines full of excellent good grapes, great walnut trees, and very much flaxe, like vnto that of Spaine, and it

Rich metals.

was tolde them by signes, that on the other side of the saide mountaines there was a riuer of 8 leagues brode. But they could not vnderstand how nigh it was, yet did they make demonstration that it did run his course towards the North Sea, and vpon both sides thereof was situated many townes, and of so huge bignes, that in comparison those wherein they were, were but suburbes in respect.

So after the captaine had taken all this relation hee departed towardes the prouince of Zuny, whither he had commanded his other companions to goe, and at their comming thether in health, which was by an other excellent way, he found therwith his other fiue companions: the father fryer Bernardino with the souldiers that were determined to returne backe againe (as aforesayde), for as yet they were not departed from thence for certayne occasions. Unto whom the naturals of the countrie had giuen good intertaynement and all thinges necessarie, and that in abundance: and afterwardes did the like vnto the sayde captaine and vnto them that came with him, and went foorth to receiue him with demonstration of great ioy, and gaue them great store of prouision for their iourney pretended, requesting him to returne againe with breuitie, and to bring with him many Castillas (for so they doo call the Spaniardes), and they would giue them all to eate: for the which (the better to accomplish the same) they had sowed that yeare more wheate and other graine, then they had done in any other yeare past.

At this present the sayde religious fryer and the rest of the souldiers did ratifie their first determination aforesaide, and concluded to returne vnto the prouince from whence they came, with the pretence before spoken of, and there ioyned with him in that iourney, Gregorio Hernandez, who was standert bearer in that attempt.

So when they were departed, the captain, who remained but with eight souldiers, did fully resolue himselfe to prosecute his begun pretence, and to take his course vp alongst the north riuer : which being put in execution, and hauing trauelled about sixty leagues towards the prouince of Quires aforesaid, twelue leagues from thence towards the orient they came vnto a prouince called Gubates, whereas the Indians receiued them with peace, and gaue them great store of prouision, and also notice that not far from thence there were certayne rich mynes, the which they founde, and tooke out of them glystering metals and very good, with the which they returned to the towne from whence they departed.

They iudged this prouince to haue nigh vpon fiue and twentie thousande soules, all well apparelled with painted mantles of cotton, and shamwayes skins very well dressed. There are many mountaynes and woodes of pine cedar trees, and their houses of foure and fiue stories hie. Heere had they notice of an other prouince that was but one daies iourney from thence, which was called of the Tamos, in the which was more than fortie thousand soules, but when they came thether the inhabitants would not giue them any victuals, neyther permit them to enter into their townes; for the which, to auoyde the danger wherin they were, being but a few souldiers (as aforesaid) and some of them sicke, they determined to depart thence towardes the countrie of Christians, the which they put in execution the beginning of Iuly in the yere 1583, and were conducted by an Indian that went with them, who carried them by a contrarie way and different from that they came, downe alongest the riuer side, which they called of the Vacas, by reason that there was great store of kine all alongest the same. By the which they trauelled one hundred and twentie leagues. From thence they came vnto the riuer of the Conchas there whereas they first entred, and from thence vnto the vale of S. Bartolmew, from whence they departed to begin this discouerie. And when they came thether they vnderstood that many dayes before were arriued there in health, frier Bernardino Beltran and his companions, and were gone from thence vnto the village of Guadiana. In this towne the captaine Antonio de Espeio made a certaine and true information of all this aforesaide, the which presently he sent vnto the Earle of Corunnia, viceroy of that kingdome: and he sent it vnto his maiestie, and vnto the lords of the royall counsell of the Indians, that therin they might ordaine that which seemed them best, the which they haue done with great care. I beseech the Lord God, if it be his pleasure that it may go forwardes in such order, that so many soules redeemed by his precious bloud be not condemned: whose wits and vnderstanding do farre exceed those of Mexico and Peru, as by the information of those that haue delt with them appeareth, wherby we may presume that with great facilitie they will imbrace the law of the gospell, and leaue the idolatrie that the most part of them do vse, which God for his mercies sake permit, so it may be for his glorie and exalting of the Catholike faith.

I haue bin tedious in this relation, more than a commentarie doth require, but I haue doone it by reason it is a newe thing and little abrode as yet, and it seemeth to mee not to giue discontent vnto the reader. And now me thinketh it shall bee well that I doo returne vnto my matter first begunne, and to proceede and go forwardes in the voyage and description of the new worlde, returning vnto the citie of Mexico, there where as I did digresse for to declare the discouerie of the Newe Mexico.

CHAP. XI.

Departing from the citie of Mexico, they go vnto the port of Acapulco in the South Sea, whereas they doo imbarke themselues from the Ilandes Philippinas; they passe by the Ilandes of Theeues, and do declare the rites and condition of that people.

From the citie of Mexico they go to imbarke themselues or take shipping at the port of Acapulco, which is in the South Sea, and is eleuated from the poole nineteen degrees, and ninetie leagues from the citie of Mexico: in al which way there be many townes inhabited with Indians and Spaniards.

Being departed from this port, they sayle towards the south-west, till they come into twelue degrees and a halfe, to seeke prosperous wind to serue their turne, which the mariners do cal Brizas, and are northerly windes, which are there of such continuance and so fauourable that, being in the moneths of Nouember, December, and Januarie, they haue no neede to touch their sayles, which is the occasion that they do make their voyages with so great ease. So that for that, and for the few stormes that happened in that passage, they do cal it the Mar de Damas (which is the sea of Ladies). They sayle alwayes towards the west, following the sunne when as she departeth from our hemispherie. In this South Sea they sayle fortie daies without seeing anie lande: at the end whereof they came to the ilandes of Velas, which by another name are called De los Ladrones; there are seuen or eight of them; they doo lye north and south, and are inhabited with much people, in the order as you shall vnderstand.

These ilands are in 12 degrees, but there are different opinions of the leagues that are betwixt the port of Acapulco and those ilands; for vnto this day there is none that hath

The sea of Ladies.

vnderstood the certaintie thereof, for that their nauigation lieth from the east vnto the west, whose degrees there haue bin none that euer could measure. Some say, this iourney hath a thousande and seuen hundred leagues, others a thousand and eight hundred; but the opinions of the first we vnderstand to be most certaine.

<small>White people as bigge as gyants.</small>

All these ilands are inhabited with white people, of comely faces, like vnto those of Europa, but not of their bodies, for that they are as bigge as gyants, and of so great force and strength: for one of them hath taken two Spaniardes, of a good stature, the one by one foot, and the other by the other, with his handes, and hath lifted them both from the grounde with so great ease, as though they had bin two children. They go naked from top to toe, as well women as men; yet some of them were woont to weare an aporne made of a deares skinne before them of halfe a yeard long, for honesties sake, but they are but a fewe in number, in respect of those that weare nothing before them. The weapons which they do vse be slinges, and darts hardened in the fire, and are with both the one and the other very expert throwers.

They do maintaine themselues with fish which they do take on the coast; and of wild beasts which they do kill in the mountaines, in ouertaking of them by swiftnesse of foot.

In these ilands there is one the strangest costume that euer hath bin heard of or seene in all the whole world, which is, that vnto the young men there is a time limited for them to marrie in (according vnto their custome), in all which time they may freely enter into the houses of such as are married, and be there with their wiues, without being punished for the same, although their proper husbands should see them: they doo carrie in their handes a staffe or rodde, and when they do enter into the married mans house they do leaue it standing at the doore, in such sort, that if any do come after they may plainly see it: which is a token that, although it be her proper husband, he cannot enter in till it be taken away. The which custome is obserued and kept with so great rigour and force, that whosoeuer is against this lawe, all the rest do kill him.

In all these ilands there is not as yet knowen neyther king nor lord, whom the rest should obey; which is the occasion that euery one do liue as he list and at his pleasure. These ilandes were woont to haue warre the one with the other, when occasion did force them. As it happened at such time as the Spaniardes were there in the port of the said iland, there came abord their ships to the number of two hundred small barkes or botes, in the which came many of the inhabitants thereof to sell, vnto them of the ships, hens, and nuts called cocos, patatas, and other thinges of that iland; and to buy other such things as our people did carrie with them, but in especiall yron (vnto the which they are very much affectionated), and vnto things of chrystall, and such like of small estimation. But there grew a great contention amongest them, which people of what ilande should first come vnto the shippes, and was in such order that they fell vnto blowes, and wounded the one the other maruellously, more liker beastes than men; of the which there were many slaine in the presence of the Spaniards, and would neuer leave off their contention a good while, till in the end, by way of peace, they consented a conclusion amongest themselues, but with a great noyse, which was, that those of one iland should go to the larbord of the ship, and those of the other iland should go to the starbord; with the which they were pacified, and did buy and sel at their pleasure. But at their departure from our people, in recompence of their good intertainment, they threw into the ship of their dartes hardened with fire, with the which they did hurt many of them that were aboue hatches: yet went they not away scotfree, for that our people with their hargabushes did paye them in readie monie their bold attempt.

Marginal note: Without king or gouernor.

256   A DISCOURSE OF THE

Iron more esteemed than siluer or gold.

These people do more esteeme yron than siluer or golde, and gaue for it fruites, nnames,[1] patatas, fish, rise, ginger, hennes, and many gallant mattes very well wrought, and all almost for nothing.

These ilandes are verie fertile and healthfull, and very easie to bee conquered vnto the fayth of Christ, if that at such time as the ships doo passe that way vnto Manilla, they would leaue there some religious men, with souldiers to garde them till the next yeare, and might be doone with small cost. It is not as yet known what ceremonies and rites they do obserue; for that there is none that doo vnderstande their language, neither hath any beene on those ilandes, but onely as they haue passed by, which is the occasion that they cannot be vnderstood. The language which they doo vse, to any mans iudgement, is easie to be learned, for that their pronunciation is verie plaine; they call ginger *asno*, and for to say Take away your hargabush, they say, *arrepeque*. The pronunciation of their wordes is neither in the nose nor in the throte. It is vnderstood that they be all Gentiles, by certaine signes and tokens that our people haue seene them do, and that they doo worship idols, and the diuell, vnto whom they do sacrifice such as they do take in the warres of their borderers. It is thought that they doo descend of the Tartares, by some particularities that is found amongst them, the which do draw very nigh vnto some that they do vse.

These ilandes are south and north with the land of Labrador, which is nigh vnto the new found lande, and not farre distant from the ilande of Japon. It is knowen for a trueth that they do deale with the Tartares, and that they do buy yron for to sell it vnto them. The Spaniards did giue name vnto these ilandes as they passed by, the ilandes of Ladrones (which is of theeues), for that they are very bolde and subtile in their stealinges, in the which facultie the Egyptians, that are in our Europa, may go to schoole with them

[1] The Spanish word is "ñames", in all probability meant for "yams".

for the verie facultie thereof. I will declare vnto you one thing that happened in the presence of many Spaniardes, the which did cause them greatly to maruaile, which is,—there was a marriner commanded by the captaine of the ship to keepe the sterneborde side, and not to suffer any of them to enter therein; and being as one amased to see so many canoas that came thether (the which be small barkes or botes made all of one peece) one of them diued downe vnder the water, till he came there whereas the marriner was (vnmindfull of any such matter should happen) and vpon a soddaine, without seeing the other, he snatched his sword out of his hand, and went vnder the water againe therwith; the marriner made a noise, and declared the knauerie that the ilander had done vnto him, whervpon there were certaine souldiers that made their hargubushes ready to shoot at him when he appeared from vnder the water. This ilander perceiuing it, came foorth and swimmed aboue the water, shewing his handes, and made signes that he had nothing in them, which was the occasion that they did not shoot at him.

So after a while that he had beene there resting of himselfe, he returned and diued vnder the water againe, and swam so farre as he thought that the bullet of the hargubush could not reach to hurt him, and finding himselfe in securitie, he tooke the sword from betwixt his legges whereas he did carrie it in secret, and beganne to florish with the same, mocking our people whom he had so easily deceiued.

This kind of stealing, and many others which they had done, and that with great subtiltie, is the occasion that they beare the names of theeues, and all the ilandes whereas they doo dwell doo beare the name thereof, the which they will easily pardon, if they might ordinarily finde where as they might execute their inclination.

CHAP. XII.

They departe from the Ilandes of the Ladrones, and come vnto them of Luzon, or Philippinas by an other name, and doo declare the particular thoughts of those ilandes.

From this Iland of Ladrones nauigating towards the west, almost two hundred leagues, till they came to a mouth called of the Holy Ghost, they straightwaies doo enter into the Archipelago (which is an infinite number of ilands), almost all inhabited with their own naturall people; but many conquered by the Spaniardes, eyther by force of warre or friendship. Four score leagues from this is the citie of Manilla, which is vpon the Iland of Luzon, there whereas ordinarily dwelleth the gouernor of all those ilandes, and the officers of his maiestie: therein is a bishop and a cathedrall church. This citie standeth in fourteen degrees and a quarter, and round about the same there are so many ilandes, that vnto this day there is none that euer could number them: they do extend all of them northwest and southwest, and north and south, in so much that the one part stretcheth vnto the Straight of Sincapura, which is fiue and twentie leagues from Malaca, and the other part vnto the Malucos, and other ilandes, whereas they gather a great number of cloues, pepper, and ginger, of the which there are great mountaines full. The first that discouered these ilands were Spaniards, which came to them in the company of the famous Magellanes, and made no conquest of them, for that they knew better to nauigate then to conquer; by reason whereof, after they had discouered and passed the straight (which vnto this day beareth the title of his name) and came vnto the Ilande of Zubu, whereas they did baptise certaine of the inhabitance, and afterwards in a banket, the same ilanders did kill him and other forty of his companions, which was the occasion that Sebastian de Guetaria, a naturall Biskin borne,[1] for to escape with his life, did put himselfe in a shippe that remained of the voyage (which afterwards was named the Victorie), and in her and with a few people that helped him, with the fauour of God he came vnto Siuell, hauing compassed the whole world, from the Orient vnto the Ponient, a thing which caused vnto all men great admiration, but in particular vnto the Emperor Charles the Fift of famous memorie, who after he had giuen many gifts and fauours vnto the said Sebastian de Guetaria, hee gaue order that a new armie should be made ready, and to returne againe in demande of the said ilands, and to discouer that new world.

So when all things were in a readinesse for to depart on their voyage (the which was done with great breuitie) they ordained for generall of all that fleete one Villa Lobos, commanding him to go by the Nueua Espania. This Villa Lobos arriued at the Ilands of Malucas, and at those of Terrenate, and at other ilands ioyning vnto them, the which ilands were laid to gage by the aforesaid emperor vnto the crowne of Portugal.

In these ilands they had great wars by meanes of the Portugals, and seeing themselues with little helpe and small resistance for to go forwards with their conquests, they left it off, and went to the most part of them with the aforesaide Portugals vnto the India of Portugall, from whence afterwards they sent them as prisoners vnto the said king of Portugall, as offenders that had entred his ilands without his licence: who did not onely leaue to do them any harme, but did intreate them very well and sent them vnto their owne country of Spaine, and gaue them al thinges necessary for their iourney, and that in aboundance.

Then certaine yeares after, Don Philip king of Spaine being very willing that the discouering shoulde go forwards, which the emperor his father had so earnestly procured, sent

[1] A native of Biscay.

and commanded Don Luys de Velasco, who was his vizroy of the Nuoua Espania, that he would ordaine an army and people for to returne and discouer the said ilands, and to sende in the said fleete, for gouernor of all that should bee discouered, Miguel Lopez de Legaspi, who did accomplish all that his maiestie had commanded, and made the discouerie thereof in such order, as in the first relation of the entrie of the fathers of the order of Saint Austen into the China dooth more at large appeare.

Of ancient time these ilands were subiect vnto the king of China, vntill such time as hee did deliuer them vp of his owne free will, for such reasons as were spoken off in the first part of this historie: and that was the occasion that when the Spaniards came vnto them, they were without lorde or heade, or anie other to whome they shoulde showe duetie, but hee which had most power and people did most command: so that this (and that there were so many of equal power) was the occasion that ciuill warres continued, without any respect of nature, kinred, or any other duety, but like vnto brute beastes, killing, spoiling, and captiving one another, the which was a great helpe vnto the Spaniards for to subiect that countrie with so great ease vnto the king, and called them the Ilands Philippinas in respect of his name. They did vse amongst them to make captiues and slaues such as they did take in vnlawfull wars, and for trifling matters, the which God did remedie by the going thither of the Spaniards : for you should haue a man with fortie or fiftie other friends in his company, or seruants, that vpon a sodaine would go and set vpon a small village of poore people and vnprouided, and take and binde them all, and carrie them away for slaues without any occasion or reason, and make them to serue them all the dayes of their life, or else sell them to other ilands. And if it so chanced that one did lende vnto another a basket or two of rice (the which might bee woorth a ryall of plate), with condition to returne it againe within ten dayes; if the debter did not pay it the same day, the next day following he should pay it dooble, and afterward to double it euery day so long as he did keepe it, which in conclusion the debt would grow to be so great, that, to pay the same, he is forced to yeeld himselfe for captiue and slaue.

But vnto all such as were captiued in this order, or in such like, the king of Spaine hath commanded to giue libertie; yet this iust commandement is not in euery point fulfilled and accomplished, because such as should execute the same haue interest therein. All these ilandes were gentiles and idolaters, but now there is amongest them many thousands baptised, vnto whom the king hath shewed great mercie, in sending vnto them the remedie for their soules in so good time: for if the Spaniards had stayed any more yeares, they had beene all Moores at this day, for that there were come vnto the Ilande of Burneo some of that sect that did teach them, and lacked little, for to worship that false prophet Mahomet, whose false, peruerse, and corrupt memory, was with the gospell of Christ easily rooted out.

In al these ilands they did worshippe the sunne and moone, and other second causes, figures of men and women, which are called in their language Maganitos, at whose feastes (which they do make very sumptuous, with great ceremonies and superstition) they doo call Magaduras. But amongst them all, they have in most veneration an idoll whome they called Batala, the which reuerence they had for a tradition; yet can they not say what should be the occasion that he should deserue more then any of the rest to bee had in so great estimation. In certaine ilandes not farre off, called the Illocos, they did worship the diuell, and made vnto him many sacrifices, in recompence of a great quantitie of gold hee had giuen vnto them; but nowe by the goodnesse of God, and the great diligence put and done by the fathers of the order of Saint Austen (who were the first that passed into

The diuell was worshiped.

these parts, and liued worthely) and also by the friers of Saint Francis, which went thither tenne yeares after, all these ilands or the most part of them are baptised, and vnder the ensigne of Jesu Christ: and the rest which doo remaine and are not, is more for lacke of ministers and preachers, then for any obstinacie of their parts. There is nowe gone thither certaine fathers of the order called Iesuits, who will be a helpe vnto them with their accustomed zeale and labour. And nowe goeth thither many other religious men, very well learned and apostolike, of the order of Saint Dominicke, who will doo their indeuour to conuert them vnto Christ, as it behooueth Christians to do.

CHAP. XIII.

Here is declared of some notable things that are, and haue beene seene in these Ilands Philippinas.

Witches.
They of these ilandes were accustomed to celebrate their feastes aforesaid, and to make sacrifices vnto their idols, by the order of certaine women which were witches, whome they do call in their language Holgoi, that were had in as great estimation amongst them, as be the priests amongst Christians. These did talke ordinarily with the diuell, and many times in publike, and do diuellish witchcrafts both in words and deeds: into whom it is to be beleeued that the diuell did enter, for that straightwayes they did answere vnto all things that were demanded of them, although for the most part they woulde tell a lie, or els such wordes that might be giuen diuers interpretations of, and of diuers vnderstandings. They did also vse to cast lottes, in such sorte as hath bene declared in the first part of this history: they were great Agorismers[1] or observers of times: in so much that if

[1] The Spanish word is "agoreros", soothsayers or superstitious persons, from *aguero*, an omen.

they begin any iourney, and at the beginning they meete with a cayman, or lyzarde, or any other sauage worme, they knowe it to be a signe of euill fortune, whereupon they would straightwayes leaue off their iourney, although it did import them very much, and returne vnto their houses, saying, that the heauen will not that they shoulde go forwards on that iourney: but all these lies and falsenes which beene taught them, and they perswaded to, by the diuell, is ouerthrowne and taken away by the law of the gospel (as aforesaide), and haue now amongst them many monasteries full of religious men, of the order of Saint Austen, Saint Francis, and of Iesuits. According vnto the common opinion, at this day there is conuerted and baptised more then foure hundred thousand soules, which is a great number: yet in respect of the quantitie that are not as yet conuerted, there are but a few. It is left vndone (as aforesaid) for want of ministers, for that, although his maiesty doth ordinarily send thither without any respect of the great charge in doing the same, yet by reason that there are so many ilands, and euerie day they doo discouer more and more, and being so far off, they cannot come vnto them all, as necessitie requireth. Such as are baptised, doo receiue the fayth with great firmenesse, and are good Christians, and would be better, if that they were holpen with good ensamples: as those which haue beene there so long time are bounde to doe: that the lacke thereof doth cause some of the inhabitantes so much to abhorre them, that they would not see them once paynted vpon a wall. For proofe whereof (and for to moue such as haue power and authoritie to put remedie in the same, I will declare vnto you here a strange case, the which royally did passe of a trueth in one of these ilandes, and is verie well knowne amongst them: that is, there chanced to die an ilander, a principall man amongst them, a few dayes after that he was baptised, being very contrite for his sinnes the which hee had done against God before he was baptised; and 'after hee died. So after by the diuine permission of God he appeared vnto many of that ilande, whom he did perswade forthwith to receiue the baptisme, with reasons of great efficacie, and declared vnto them (as one that had experiencd the same) the rewarde of that good deede which without all doubt shoulde bee giuen vnto them, if they would receiue the same, and liue after conformable and according vnto the commandements of Christ; for the which he told them and said, that forthwith so soone as he was dead, he was carried by the angels into glorie, there whereas all things were of delite, pleasure, and content, and did communicate onely in the sight of God, and that there was none that entred therein, neither coulde enter, except hee were baptised, according vnto the preaching of the Spaniards, of whome and of others that were like vnto them, there was infinite number. Therefore if so be that they would go and inioy of those benefites and delights, it is necessarie that first they should be baptised, and afterwards to obserue and keepe the commandements that be preached vnto them by the fathers, that are amongst the Castillas, and therewith he vanished away, and they remained treating amongst themselues concerning that which they had hearde, and was the occasion that some of them forthwith receiued the baptisme, and that others did delay it, saying, that because there were Spaniard souldiers in glory, they would not go thither, because they would not be in their company.

The Indians would not go into heauen because there were Spanish souldiers.

All this hurt is done by one peruerse or impious man, and with one euill ensample, the which amongst many good, as you haue in those parts; but in especiall amongst them in particular, it ought to bee reprehended and punished seuerely with rigour.

These ilands, at the first discouery of them, had the fame to bee *mal sanos*, or vnholesome, but since experience hath shewed and prooued it to the contrarie. It is a countrie maruellous fertill, and yeeldeth very much rice, wheate, goates, hennes, deere, buffes, kine, and great stoare of hogges, whose flesh is so sauorie as the mutton they haue in Spaine: there be also manie cattes that yeelde siuet, great stoare of fruites, which be very good and sauorie: great aboundance of honie, and fish, and all solde at so small price, that almost it is solde for nothing. Also there is great stoare of synamom, but no oile of oliues, but that which is carried thither out of the Nuoua Espania: they haue much oyle of algongoli[1] and of flaxe seede, the which they doo spende ordinarily in that countrie, so that the oyle of oliues is not missed with them.

Siuet.
Honie.
Sinamum.
Linseed oile.

There is great stoare of cloues, saffron, pepper, nutmegges, and many other drugges: great stoare of cotton and silke of all colours, the which is brought vnto them by merchants of China, euerie yeare a great quantitie, from whence commeth more then twenty shippes laden with peeces of silkes of all colours, and with earthen vessell, powder, saltpeter, iron, steele, and much quickesiluer, brasse, copper, wheate, flower, walnuts, bisket, dates, linnen cloth, counting chestes[2] very gallantly wrought, calles of networke, buratos, espumillas,[3] basens and ewres made of tinne, parchment lace, silke fringe, and also of golde, the which is spunne and twisted after a fashion neuer seene in all Christendome, and manie other of great curiositie, and all this aforesaide is solde verie good cheape. Likewise such things as the ilands do yeelde are sold very good cheape, for you shall haue foure roues[4] of wine which commeth of the palme tree for foure rials of plate (the which for lacke of that made of grapes is very good), twelue haneges of rice for eight rials of plate, three hennes

Cloues, saffron, pepper, nutmegs, cotton, and silke.
Powder, saltpeter, iron, steele, quicksiluer, brasse, copper.

---

[1] More properly spelt "ajonjoli", the Spanish name for "sesamum orientale", or oily-grain.

[2] Escritoires.

[3] These words are both used for a fine gauze or muslin, of which ladies' veils are made in Spain.

[4] The original word is *arroba*, containing from three to four gallons.

for one rial, a whole hogge for eighteene rials, a whole buffe for foure rials, a deere for two rials, and yet it must be both great and good, foure roues of sugar for sixe rials, a botiia[1] of oile made of algongoli for three rials, two baskets of saffron for two rials, sixe pounds of pepper or cloues for one riall, two hundred nutmegs for one rial, a roue of synamum for sixe rials, a kintal[2] of iron or steele for tenne rials, thirtie dishes of very fine earth foure rials, and all other things after this rate.

But amongst all other notable thinges that these Spaniards haue seene in those ilands, and in the kingdome of China, and other places whereas they passed, there is one thing which hath caused them most to maruel at, and to haue it most in memory; which is a tree, ordinarily called palma de cocos, but doth differ from that which beareth the dates, and with great reason, for that it is a plant so full of mysterie and profite, that there hath come a ship vnto these ilands, and the said ship, and all that was in her to be sold, with ropes, cords, masts, sailes and nailes, were made of this tree, and the merchandice that she brought was mantels made of the rind of the saide tree, with great subtiltie and fine works. Likewise all the victuals that was in the said ship for the sustentation of thirtie men that came in her, yea their water was of the same tree.

The merchants that came in this ship did certifie of a truth, in all the Iland of Maldiuia from whence they came, they haue no other sustainment, but onely that which this tree yeeldeth: they do make houses hereof, and tyles for to couer the same, the fruit doth yeeld a meollio or curnell, which is very sauory and healthfull, the sauor thereof is much like to greene hasell nuts, and if you do cut the branch there whereas the coco commeth forth is the principall fruite, and euery one of them hath ordinarily a pinte of water, the which is very sweet and delicate: al the said substance doth returne

[1] A jar.   [2] Quintal, a hundredweight.

into the trunke of the tree, whereas they doo bore a hole, and thereat they do draw out all that water, which is much: and mingling it with other thinges they make thereof good wine, the which is drunk in al those ilands and in the kingdome of China. Of the same water they make vineger, and of the meollio kernell aforesaide, oile verie medicinall, milke like vnto almon milke: hony and suger very sauorie. These and many other vertues hath this palme, whereof I haue declared part, for that they are notable, and do cause admiration vnto all men that passe into those partes: I doo leaue to declare the rest because I would not be tedious. Nigh to the cittie of Manilla, on the other side of the riuer, there is a towne of Chinos that be baptized, such as haue remained there to dwell to inioy the libertie of the gospel. There are, amongst them many handicrafts men, as shoomakers, taylors, goldsmiths, blacksmiths, and other officers, and some merchants.

CHAP. XIV.

The barefoote friers depart from the Iland of Luzon vnto China, and is declared such as was there seene.

For that the principall intent of these religious men, when they went out of Spaine, was for to go vnto the mightie kingdome of China for to preach the holy gospell, and did perseuer continually with that desire, they woulde neuer intreat of any other thing, but onely to put it in execution: and for the accomplishing of the same, they sought many meanes and waies, sometimes in requesting the gouernor of his aide and helpe to procure the same, for that it was an easie thing to be performed, hauing continually ships of the merchants of China in the port of Manilla.

The gouernor did driue them off with many reasons, but

principally he laid before them that rigorous lawe, which they knew was established against such as did enter into that kingdome without particular licence; yet notwithstanding, all this was not sufficient to abate the louing desire of those friers, which was only setled in their mindes for to go and preach the holy gospel in that kingdome by one meanes or other, although it were to put their liues in hazard : and for the prosecuting hereof, the comissary of those ilands, who was frier Geronimo de Burgos, did elect sixe religious men for the same purpose : amongst them was the father Ignatio, of whome I (as I haue said) vnderstood by writing and relation many thinges, the which is declared in these [sic] itinerario or comentarie : so that there was with him seuen religious men, all seruants of God, and very desirous of the saluation of soules, which was the occasion that they put themselues in so long and tedious a iourney, leauing their owne countrie and quietnesse. These seuen, with the good will of the gouernor Don Gonsalo Ronquillo and of the bishop, whom they did ouercome and winne with requests and perseuerance, and carried in their company a Spaniard their friende, called Iohn de Feria, of Andolozia, and other two souldiers that went with pretence to become friers, one Portugall, and sixe Indian ilanders : all the which, the eight day after Corpus Christi, which was the one and twentie day of Iune, in anno 1582, they departed from the port of Cabite, whereas they did imbarke themselues in a barke of the saide Iohn de Feria, and making saile at fiue of the clocke in the afternoone, in the morning betimes they founde themselues twentie leagues ouerthwart the port that is called Dol Fraile, whereas they determined to go to sea, leauing the coast of the Ilande of Manilla, which lieth north and south with China : from the which cittie, which is (as I haue saide) in fourteene degrees and a halfe, vnto the Cape of Boxeador, which is in nineteene, it is one hundreth leagues sailing, and from this cape to the firme land of China, they count it scarce fourescore leagues. And God was so pleased, although they had two dayes calme, the seuenth day, which was the day before the apostle Saint Peter and Saint Paule, at eight of the clocke in the morning, they discouered the firme lande of China: then straightwaies vpon the sight thereof, the comissarie commaunded to bring foorth the habites which hee carried readie made for to put vpon the friers, for that when the Chinos shoulde see that they were all friers, they should be voide of all suspition, to thinke them to be spies, as they thought when the first friers went thither (as hath beene tolde you); and not contented herewith, hee threw all the souldiers apparell into the sea, and one hargabus of Iohn de Feria, with the flaske wherein he carried his powder, and all other thinges such as he thought woulde be a hurt and hindrance vnto them, if it should so fall out that they shoulde erre out of the port whereas the Portugals doo vse, and fall vppon the coast, as afterwards it so fell out: they left nothing but a match, which they forgot, which lacked very little to haue cost them full deere. But when they had sight of the lande, they did not well knowe it, for that they had neuer seene it before, and were also ignorant of the ports; although they were very neere to the bay of Canton, they tooke their course vnto the northwest, wheras they should haue gone to the southwest, which was the occasion that they came vnto the prouince of Chincheo. This day, at fiue a clocke in the afternoone, they discouered a port that was not farre from them, whither they sailed and entred in, and came to an anker on the outmost side, yet with great feare and dread, for that they knew not the securitie thereof, neither the trouble that might happen.

They were not so soone at an anker, but they saw come forth of the said port many barkes, both small and great, and in them many souldiers with hargabusses, lances, swordes, and targets, and in their foreshippe some small peeces of ordinance. And when they came nigh vnto the barke wherein the Spaniards were, within musket shot, they stayed and discharged great stoare of hargabus shot. But they, who carried no armor to offende others, neither to defende themselues, the answere that they gaue vnto the shot, was making of many signes of peace, calling them with their handes to come nearer vnto them, that they might see and vnderstand that they came not thither with any pretence to do harme: yet all was not sufficient to cause them to leaue off their shooting, neither to come any nearer vnto their barke. At this present there was amongst the souldiers one Chino, that had beene at Luzon, and did knowe the Spaniards, being of God inspired: hee made signes vnto the rest to leaue off their shooting, which presently they did: and hee came with his brigantine vnto their barke, and after him all the rest: who, when they sawe that they had neyther armour nor weapon, neither will to flie from them, they entered into the barke, and with their naked swordes in their handes flourishing with them ouer the heads of the Spaniards, with a great noise and tumult, they carried them into the port, which was called Capsonson, whereas was a generall of a great armie of shippes that were at an anker in the saide port, who straightwaies commanded that there should be carried on borde his admirall foure of the Spaniards, the which they vnderstoode was doone to take their liues from them: for the which, by reason they did not name any person, foure religious men did offer themselues to goe, and after they had confessed themselues, they tooke their leaue of their companions, and carried euery one of them a crosse in his hande, and his breuiarie, without any other thing else.

So when they came before the captaine, they founde him more meeker and milder than they thought to haue done (surely a worke done by God, in recompence of the great perill that those his seruants did put themselues in to doo his seruice and commandement). He asked of them, from whence they came, and wherefore? with many other questions in effect; but when that hee was certified of the truth, hee commanded them to returne againe vnto their barke, without doing vnto them anie other harme; yet with a straite precept that they should not go forth without his expresse licence.

So with this commandement they remained in their barke three dayes, guarded with many barkes and souldiers: and the last of them, the captaine sent for two of the religious men; and when they came before him, he commanded them to be carried before a iustice, a friend of his there hard by. These iustices did talke with them with so great grauitie, and signes of cruelty, that euery time they came before them they thought verely that forthwith they would command them to be carried to be executed: and without all doubt, either they had wil to do it, or else to put them in great feare of death, for that it was plainely seene in diuers things they commanded: but especially in one day there came vnto them a iudge, with many armed men, and compassed their barke round about with a great number of brigandines, with plaine signes to giue them assalt, or else to sinke them: but within a little while they were all in quiet, and the iudge entred into a shippe that was thereby at anker, and being set in a rich chaire, guarded with many souldiers about him, hee commanded the rest that were in the brigandines forthwith to go to visite and search their barke, and sent with them an interpreter, one of Chincheo, who did a little vnderstande the Portugall tongue. These souldiers carried in their handes blacke banners, and other heauie and sorowfull signes (which is vsed in that kingdome, when at any time they doo execute anie person). So after they had made their visitation, although they founde in their barke not anie prohibited thing, but onely the match which I haue spoken off, they commanded that they shoulde forthwith bee imbarked two and two into the brigandines, whereas the armed souldiers were, who did direct their foreshippes towardes a towre, which was a prison, wherein was put all such theeues as were taken vpon the coast, out of the which there commeth none forth but vnto execution. But when the Indians of the ilands saw it, they wept bitterly, which moued the Spaniards vnto great compassion; although they were themselues in the same trance and perill, and as nigh their death, and made no other reckoning; insomuch that two of the religious men seeing them so nigh the towre (although when as they were farre off, they made shewe as though they cared not for it), yet at that time they were so farre from all reason and vnderstanding, that al the night one of them knewe not what he did, without any knowledge of the people wherein he was, but lay as a deade man: and the other with pure imagination and melancholike humour fel into a great infirmitie, whereof within a few dayes after he died in the cittie of Canton. But in conclusion, the stowtest of them all had feare enough, and would haue giuen his life for a small matter, for that he was without all hope, and thought verely that they carried them vnto execution: which was the occasion that a Spaniard, one of them that went with pretence to be a frier, and the habite on, hauing in his power a thousand and sixe hundred rials of plate, he threw them into the sea, saying, Seeing that I am going to dye, I wil that it be in the habite of S. Francis, with the pouerty in which the glorious saint liued and died, for to follow him in his steps aright. With this feare aforesaid they were carried towards the tower: but when they came nigh to it, there followed after the souldiers that carried them, a skiffe with many oares, in great hast, and called a loud vnto them, saying, that the captaine general commanded that they should bring backe againe those prisoners to his shippe, the which forthwith they accomplished: and after he had demanded of them certain questions, he commanded to carry them to the said tower; the which was done, as they could perceiue, for to put them in more feare. So after they had feared and scared them with this rigorous temtation, the saide captaine himselfe went into one of the brigandines, and went with them on land; whereas presently when he came on shoare, hee carryed the Spaniards into a temple of their idols, vnto whome hee did his accustomed reuerence; yet the religious men, although they were with great feare of death as aforesaide, they woulde not imitate him, but turned their faces from their idols and did spit at them, giuing the captaine to vnderstande by signes, that he should not worshippe them, for that they had no more goodnesse in them then was giuen by man; so that, by good reason to the contrary, those idols should giue reuerence vnto men, because they made them; and to whome they ought to giue their true worship is vnto the true God, the Creator of heaven and earth.

By this act it is plainely to bee seene the gift of strength, the which the Holy Ghost doth giue vnto his baptized Christians, as in these religious men that were at deathes doore, yet had they strength and spirit for to resist and reprehende them that could take away their liues. The captaine, although he made a shew that he was offended with that which hee had seene them do, yet he did them no harme, but presently brought them out of the temple, and commanded the souldiers to remaine there and guard them all that night: the which they passed lying vpon the grounde, and yet thought themselues happie, and gaue thankes to God for that he had deliuered them from the death that was so nigh vnto them.

CHAP. XV.

Here hee doth prosecute in things which the saide Fathers did see, and vnderstand, the second time they entred into the kingdome of China, and of the troubles they passed.

The next day in the morning, the priest of the idols did open the temple, whereas presently they put in the Spanish religious men, who sawe him and his ministers lighting of little candels, and making perfumes vnto their idols, with manie superstitious ceremonies; the which being done, they cast cértaine lottes (a thing much vsed amongst them), as they vnderstoode it was done for to consult with the diuell (who was within those idols) to know what they should do with them, yet this they could not perfectly vnderstand; but straightwaies they were carried out of the temple, and brought by the souldiers before a iudge, who was the chiefe and principall of all the sea of that prouince, and was sixe leagues from the place in a cittie called Quixue: the way thither was very plaine and brode, and paued, and vpon both sides there were fields both of corne and flowers. So with the helpe of God the Spaniards came before the presence of this general in eight days, although it was with great trauell, by reason they had neither force nor strength for to trauell, for that they had lost it with the heauie and sorowful newes as aforesaid.

Yet notwithstanding, at their comming to the citty Quixue, the souldiers had them in continuall guard and keeping till the next day following; then they were carried before the generall, where he was in a very great and faire house, the which had two courts, one of them was next vnto the doore of the streete, and the other was towards the farther partes of the house; both of them were railed round about in manner of grates: they were planted full of diuers sortes of great trees, wherein did feed a great number of deere and other wilde beasts, but yet as tame as sheepe. Right ouer against the inwarde court there was a gallerie, whereon was many souldiers which did guarde and keepe the person of the generall, who was in a mightie great and gallant hall, set in an iuorie chaire with great maiestie. Before they entred into the seconde court, there was discharged within, both artilerie and hagabus shot, and played vpon a drum, which was as bigge as those which they vse in Spaine: that being doone, there was a great sounde of hoybuckes and trumpets, and of many other instrumentes: the which being doone, they straightwayes opened the gates of the innermost court, whereas the gallerie was aforesaide, from whence they might see the throne whereas the generall was set. There was before him a table whereon was paper and other necessaries for to write (a thing commonly vsed in all that countrie): the souldiers that were his guarde were all in one liuerie of silke, and were in so gallant consort, and had so great sylence, which made the Spaniards greatly to maruell: the first order was of the hargabushes, and the seconde were pikes, and betwixt the one and the other was placed a sworde and a target; there might be about foure hundred souldiers. Behinde them were placed the officers of iustice, or executioners, with their instruments for to whippe and punish offenders: and in the midst of them were the scriueners and proctors.

About thirtie paces, more or lesse, from the chaire where the generall was set, was placed certaine gentlemen, and to the number of a dozen pages, bare headed, verie gallantlie apparelled in silke and golde. In the middest amongst these souldiers were the Spaniards carried, and before them such tokens and shewes as they doo vse when as they doo present before the iudges such as bee condemned vnto death. A good way before they came nigh vnto the place whereas the general was, they caused them to kneele downe: at which instant there was brought foorth certaine Chinos, that were prisoners, to be iudged; and so soone as their inditement was read, and iudgement giuen, the executioners did execute the rigour of the sentence in the presence of the Spaniards, first pulling off their apparell, and then making fast their hands and feete verie fast with cordes, in such sort, that they shriked that the noise reached vnto heauens: they kept them so bounde vntil they sawe farther what the iudge woulde commaunde, who, when hee had heard his inditement, if hee woulde that hee should be whipped, hee striketh a blow with his hand vppon the table that is before him: then the executioners doo strike fiue blowes vppon the calues of the legges of the offender with a broad cane, in the order as hath beene saide, and is so cruell that none can suffer fiftie of them but he dieth. The blowe being giuen vppon the table by the generall, straightwayes one of the proctors maketh a crie or noise, whereat presently commeth the executioner for to excute his office. And if the offender dooth deserue more, then the iudge dooth strike another blowe vppon the table: then is there giuen him other fiue blowes, and in this sort dooth the iudge so manie times as his offence dooth deserue. At the lamentations and shrikes that these miserable offenders doo giue, the iudges shewe no more signe of pittie then if they were stroken vppon a stone. So the audience being concluded and doone with the naturals of the countrie, the generall commaunded that the Spanyardes shoulde come a little nearer, and looked and searched their garments and all the rest, as also their breuiarios and books: that being done, they were informed by those that brought them, how and in what order they were apprehended, and of all other thinges touching their comming into that kingdome: vnderstanding thereof, he commaunded them to be carried vnto prison, where they were put in sure holde, and with great watch and guard for certain dayes, in the which time they passed incredible trouble, as well of hunger as of thirst and heat, which was the occasion that the most part of them fell sick of agues, and of the laske.[1]

So after these dayes that they were in prison, they were carried once againe to the audience, and many other more were brought forth to be uisited, all people beleeuing that the Spaniards should no more returne, but bee executed, for the which they receiued great content, to be cleared by one death, of so many as dayly they had before their eyes. In the conclusion of this audience the generall did decree, that they should be carried by sea vnto the cittie of Canton, whereas was the vizroy of that prouince, and he to commande them to be executed or punished according as hee thought best, according vnto the penalty put vppon whatsoeuer straunger that should enter into that kingdome without licence (as they did enter). But when they saw that they were carried out of the prison vnto the sea, they verelie beleeued that it was to drowne them therein; for the which (hauing a newe confessed themselues, and commended themselues vnto God) they did animate one another with the representation of the reward which was prepared for them: but when they came vnto the barre whereas they should imbarke themselues, vppon a suddaine the sea beganne to waxe verie loftie and troublesome, that it seemed almost a myracle, and it increased in such sort that the souldiers and mariners said, that neuer before they had seene the like torment, the which endured the space of tenne dayes: the which was the occasion that they did not imbarke themselues, and that the generall did change his pretence, and determined that they shoulde be carried by lande vnto the great cittie of Sancheo-Fu, the which was presently put in vre: they were manie dayes on this iourney, with fiftie souldiers that did guarde them: in the which they sawe so manie curious thinges, and of so great riches, that they iudged it to bee the best countrie in all the world.

[1] From "laxitas", an immoderate looseness of the bowels.

So when they came vnto the citty, with no small trouble and werinesse, by reason of their long iourney and euill intreatings by the souldiers, they were presently carried (as might be sayde) from Herode to Pylate, and escaped not one day, but they were carried to the publike audience, or else before some particular iudge. This citie was very fresh both within and without, and full of many orchards, whereas were an infinite number of fruite, with gardens, stanges of water, and other thinges of great recreation. This citie is three times so bigge as Siuell, and compassed about with a mightie strong wall, their houses are verie great and well wrought, their streets are exceeding faire, brode and long, and so straight, that from the one end vnto the other they may see a man. In equall distance the one from the other, there are built triumphall arkes (which is an ordinarie and common thing vsed in the cities of that kingdome): vpon their gates there are little towers, whereon is planted all the artilerie that they haue for the defence of the citie (as hath been said), all the which is inuironed and compassed about with a riuer which is great and faire, on the which is ordinarily sayling an infinite number of barkes and brigandines, and is of so great depth, they may come and lye harde vnto the wall, yea, ships of great burden. On the one side of the citie there is a little iland of great recreation, vnto the which they do passe by a very faire bridge, the one halfe made of stone and the other of timber, and is of a great length; that on the part that is made of stone, the father Ignacio did tell thirtie innes, or victualling houses, whereas was to be bought, not only flesh and fish, but also great store of marchandice, of great estimation and valure, as amber, muske, peeces of silke, and cloth of golde.

CHAP. XVI.

The Spaniardes are sent vnto the citie of Hucheofu, and doo declare what happened there vnto them.

From the citie of Sancheofu they were sent vnto Hucheofu, the which is more principall and greater than the first, alwayes hauing with them in companie and garde the number of souldiers aforesaid: sometimes they trauailed by lande and sometimes by water, whereas they saw so many rich thinges, which in respect to them, all that they had seene vnto that time was nothing. Of the which, although I haue had particular relation of many of them, I leaue off here the declaring thereof, for that of an itinerario or commentarie I will not make a historie. But principally for that many of them doo seeme to be incredible, and will be more vnto those that haue not had any notice of the mightinesse of this kingdome.

In the discourse of this their iourney, the cities and townes they sawe were many and verie bigge, and all compassed with strong walles: and at one of them there was a mightie riuer, on the which was edified more than five hundreth engynes or wheeles, and they were made with so much art, that alonely with the violence of the streame of the riuer that dooth force them, they water all the groundes there abouts for the space of two leagues and more, without any other helpe or humaine force.

In this citie they were certaine daies in visiting and complementes, after the which they were commaunded to goe vnto Canton, of the which in the two relations before, is made particular mention. So when they came vnto the citie they were carried vnto the prison of the Thequixi, which is whereas are put such as are condemned to die, the which they plainely perceiued. There they remayned verie manie dayes, and the most part of them were carried vnto the tribunall seate of the iudges, in companie with others that were condemned to die.

At this time there was in the citie the Tutan, who was the viceroye of the prouince, and the Chacu, who is the generall visitor, and that was at such time as was doone great iustice for to cleare the prisons, whereas were thousandes of men, and some that had beene there more than tenne yeares. There was some day at that time that in the presence of our people were brought foorth to be iudged, two thousand prisoners, some to the death, and others to be whipped, and other to be banished, with other kinde of penalties, according vnto the disposition and rigor of their lawes. That day wherein they make capitall audience, they vse particular ceremonies, as shooting of certaine peeces of artilerie, and to shut the gates of the citie, not permitting anie to enter in, neither go foorth, till such time as that act and iustice be finished, and many other thinges, as hath beene declared in the first part of this historie.

The Spaniards being in the citie at this time of so great calamitie, it so fell out that the same time there was a gentleman of Portingall called Arias Gonsalo de Miranda, chiefe captaine of the citie of Machao (very deuout vnto religious men, and a friende vnto Spaniardes), who vnderstanding the great trouble and danger wherein they were, hee tooke order by all meanes possible to set them at libertie, and had so great care therein, that hee went through with his intent, in such sort that they were deliuered out of pryson, and from the great feare in which they were, and all by the intercession of this gentleman, who did vse so good persuasions for the loue he did beare vnto them, that he made voyde the euill opinion they had against them, and with compulsion to reuoke the rigorous sentence of death pronounced against them. I do not here in particular treate of such thinges as happened vnto these religious men the servants of God, as well in the prison as on their iourney, for that they were many, and to declare them is requisite a long time, and to make a new historie.

And although in the bookes before, haue been declared the riches of that kingdome, and all thinges in particular, yet for the better certification, I thought it good (and not without purpose) to declare in the chapter following some of those which the father fryer Martin Ignatio did communicate with me, vsing in the treating thereof so much breuitie, that it shall seeme rather an epilogo then a new relation. And for a more verification of the truth, whereby better credite may be giuen therevnto, seeing that the persons who did see it doo agree in that which shall be here declared; and again, for that the saide father and his companions did see more thinges than the others, whose relations be alreadie set downe. The occasion wherefore they put confidence in them, and to let them see and vnderstand many secretes, was for that they were sentenced and condemned to die: for without all doubt if they had vnderstood that they should haue returned out of the kingdom, they should neuer haue seene them, for they haue great care that any other nations should know their secrets, their manner of gouernement, and liuing.

CHAP. XVII.

Here it doth intreat of the mightinesse, goodnesse, riches, and fortitude of the kingdome of China.

This kingdome is vnder the tropike of Capriçorne, and stretcheth foorth on the sea coast, south west and north east, more than fiue hundreth leagues: it hath on the partes south west the kingdome of Cochinchina, and on the north east, it dooth confine on Tartaria, a kingdome which dooth compasse the most part of the lande; on the other part of the northwest there is an other mightie kingdome of white people, which is beyonde the kingdome of Persia, it is called Catay: there be in it Christians, and the king thereof is called Manuell. It is sayd of a truth, that from the furthest part of this kingdome vnto Ierusalem, is sixe moneths trauaile by lande, the which they vnderstoode by certaine Indians which came from that kingdome by Persia, whose testimonials were made in Ierusalem sixe moneths before, wherein was declared how that they had trauelled by Arabia Felix, and passed the Red Sea. The other fourth part of this kingdome is compassed with a verie asper and high mountaine, which is fiue hundreth leagues vpon a right line: but nature had left certaine places open towards the northwest, which might be fourscore leagues, little more or lesse, towards the Sea of Iapon, which is towards the Septentrion. The great riches of this countrie, and the great number of people that be therein, did supplie the same (as in the first part of this historie is more at large declared). And for that the king of this countrie seeing himselfe oppressed and troubled by the mightie Tartaro, and seemed that easily he might defende himselfe from him, in shutting vp of those gates which nature had left open betwixt the mountaines, he did shut it vp with the death of many thousande of people, for that hee vsed therein great tyrannie, which afterwardes was the occasion of his owne death.

This mountaine, with the supply by man, is the famous wall of the kingdom of China, that is of fiue hundred leagues long; yet you must vnderstande it in the manner aforesaide, the better to giue credite thereunto, for alonely foure score leagues were made by mans handes with great industrie, and there is vpon it an infinite number of bulwarkes, which maketh it the more fayrer and stronger, but yet not so strong as is the other four hundreth and twentie leagues which were made by nature.

Nigh vnto the same there is a great desert full of ditches *Great ditches and lakes.*
and lakes of water, which is the occasion that this kingdome
hath been conserued for more than two thousand yeares, as
doth appeare by their owne histories, which they holde to
bee verie true.

All is imparted into fifteene prouinces, with that of Aynao,[1]
and euerie one of them hath a principall citie, of the which
it beareth the name. In the middest of this kingdome there
is a great lake, out of the which proceedeth many great and *A mightie lake.*
mightie riuers, which runne through all the kingdome, and
are so big that there sayleth vp and downe in them barkes,
fregats, brigandines, and many other vessels of an other
kinde of making. This great abundance of water is the
occasion that it is so fertile, and so well prouided of all
thinges; and againe, the most part of their cities and townes
are situated on the riuers side, so that by them the one prouince doth communicate with an other, carrying the one
vnto the other great store of marchandice and other thinges
of great curiositie, and is done with little cost, for that all
things are done very good cheape.

This sea cost of this kingdome is the biggest and the best
that is knowen in all the world; there is vpon it fiue prouinces, which be these: of Canton, Chincheo, Liampon,
Nanquin, and that of Paquian, which is the furthest towardes
the northwest, in the which is resident the king and his
counsell with all his court ordinarily, and the most part of
the men of warre that it hath, for that this prouince doth
confine vpon the Tartaros their enemies. Some will say,
that the kings ordinarie dwelling there, is for that it is the
best and most fertilest of all the kingdome. But I beleeue
(according to the saying of some of the Chinos) that he doth
it not but because it is so nigh vnto Tartaria, and to finde
himselfe there whereas hee may supply all necessities which
might happen vpon a soddaine by his enimies. In these

[1] The island of Hainan.

riuers there are certaine ilandes, the which are very profitable vnto all the kingdome, for that there is nourished and brought vp in them great store of deare, hogges, and other beasts, which is the occasion that the cities are so well prouided and serued.

But one of the things which causeth most admiration to them that go to this kingdome, is to see so infinite a number of ships and barkes that be in euerie port thereof, and are so many, that there hath beene a man in the citie of Machao that hath layde a wager, that alonely in the riuer of Canton there be more ships and vessels than in all the cost of Spaine.

More ships in one port than in all Spaine.

One thing I may affirme, that I haue heard declared by persons of great credite, that haue beene in that kingdome (but in especiall of the father Ignacio, whom I do follow in this Itinerario) that it is an easie thing in any one of these fiue prouinces that be vpon the sea cost, to ioyne together a thousande ships of warre, and all of them (as they say in Spaine) dedicated for that purpose. The occasion why there be so many, is alreadie declared in his proper chapter. There are diuers opinions touching the greatnesse of this kingdome, but the most are conformable with the father fryer Martin de Herrada, who, like a good geometrician and mathematician, went nighest the pricke. This opinion is declared in the first part of this historie whereunto I referre me, and in that which toucheth in particular things of that kingdom, for that it is there declared at large as it was taken out of their bookes. But one thing I cannot let passe but declare, for that it seemeth woorthie to make thereof a particular memorie: and I vnderstood it by the mouth of the said father Ignacio, which is that he doth affirme it to bee certaine true and approued, that euery day in the yeare one with an other (besides wars and the plague, the which in this countrie they remember not to haue any, neither do they finde written in their histories for 2,000 yeares, neither by

They neuer had the plague.

famin nor any other accidentall occasions to consume the people) yet doth there die many thousands of people both smal and great, in al the fifteen prouinces of this kingdome : which is no small griefe vnto them, who with a Christian zeale doth consider this heauie tribute of so many soules that the diuell doth recouer euerie day, and carrie them vnto his mansion or dwelling.

All this kingdome is so fertile, as well for the ordinarie watring as also for the temperature of the heauen, that almost all the whole yeare they do gather fruits, but in especiall of wheat and rice : so that both the one and the other are very good cheape, that our people in the discourse of their trauaile or pilgrymage did buy one pyco of rice or of wheate meale, which is fiue roues of Spaine, for one ryall and a halfe; and according vnto this rate al other thinges beare their prices, as hath beene before declared. They say that in this countrie there be many elephants, lyons, tygres, ownses, and other brute beastes, of the which these fryers sawe verie few aliue, but manie skins of them, which is a signe that it is of truth. There are many beasts whereof come the muske, the which are of the tygres, and like vnto a litle dogge, the which they do kill and put them vnder the ground certaine dayes, and after that it is putrified and rotten, the flesh and bloud is conuerted into that sweete powder. There be also many cyuet cats and little worth, a great number of horse, and although those which the said friers did see were litle, yet is it a common voice and fame that in some of the fifteene prouinces there are very good : but they were not there, so that they cannot say they had seene them. But the hens, geese, duckes, and other poultrie that are in all partes of this kingdome are without number, which is the occasion that they are of small estimation: the abundance of fish is no lesse, as well of the sea as of the riuers, in the which they are conformable. All they that do declare of the thinges of this countrie, and the small price that it is solde for, is such, that the saide frier doth affirme, and others that haue bin in that kingdome, that for the value of sixe marauadies (which is a pennie) may four companions eat very wel of flesh, fish, rice, and fruits, and drinke good wine of that countrie.

Mynes of golde and siluer.

In all this kingdome there are many mynes both of gold and siluer, and all verie rich : but the king will not let them be labored but with great lymitation (saying) that which is in those mynes be in his house, and that they should procure to bring it from other kingdomes : yet notwithstanding the abundance is so great both of the one and the other, and so common, that there is no man, although he be of an occupation, but hee hath in his house things both of gold and siluer, and other very rich iewels. They do esteeme for his value more the siluer than the golde: and they say the cause is, for that the prices of golde are variable, as in Italie : but the siluer is alwaies at one staye and price.

Siluer for his value more esteemed than gold.

There are great store of pearles, but in especiall in the Iland of Aynao; and great abundance of quicksiluer, copper, yron, steele, laton,[1] tyn, lead, salt peter, brimstone, and other things which were woont to beautifie a kingdome, but aboue all, there is very much muske and amber gryce.

Amber gryce.

The king of this kingdome, besides the great rent the which he hath, it is saide that he hath great treasories in all the principall cities, those which are the head cities of the prouinces; for the confirmance thereof, it was affirmed vnto the saide fryer for a verie certaintie, that in the citie of Canton, all the money that hath entred into the same for the space of fiue hundred yeres (as well by way of the Portingals, as by those of the kingdom of Cyan,[2] and others their borderers, and all the tributes of that prouince) is altogether in the king's treasure house of that citie, which amounteth vnto, by good account, many more millions than may be well numbred for to giue credite thereunto. It is as common for the people of this countrie to weare silke, as in Europe to weare

Wonderfull treasure.

---

[1] Latten, iron covered with tin. [2] Siam.

lynnen; yea, they doo make their shooes thereof, some of satten, and many times of cloth of golde, of verie gallant colours: the cause is by reason of the great abundance that they haue thereof, and is of so great quantitie, that it is carried from the citie of Canton vnto the Portingall Indians more than three thousand kintals euery yeare, besides a great quantitie which is carried vnto Japon, and ordinarily more than fifteene ships laden for the Ilandes of Luzon. The Sianes, and other nations, doo also carrie away a great quantitie: and although there are carried away ordinarily as afore saide, yet there remaineth so great quantity in that kingdome, that many fleetes may be laden therewith.

Fleetes may be laden with silke.

There is also great store of flax, cotton, and other kinde of webstrie,[1] and al so good cheape that the aforesaide fryer dooth affirme that he hath seene solde a canger,[2] which is fifteene fadom, for foure ryals of plate. The fine earthen dishes that are in this countrie, cannot be declared without many wordes. But that which is brought from thence into Spaine is verie course; although, vnto them that hath not seene the finer sort, it seemeth excellent good: but they haue such with them, that a cubbard thereof amongest vs would be esteemed as though it were of golde. The finest cannot be brought foorth of the kingdome vpon paine of death; neyther can any haue the vse thereof, but onely the loytias, which be there gentlemen (as hath been tolde you). There is great quantitie of sugar, honie, and waxe, and verie good cheape as aforesaide. And in conclusion I say, that they liue with so great abundance, that all things do flow so that they lacke nothing necessarie for their bodies: but for their soules, which is the principallest, they do lack (as you haue vnderstoode in the discourse of this historie): God remedie the same at his pleasure.

Sugar, hony, and waxe.

[1] Articles for weaving.
[2] The original word is "canga", probably a local word for the measure referred to.

The rent which the king of this kingdome hath, is declared vnto you in a proper chapter of it selfe; so that in this I will declare that which the sayde fryer tolde me, and is onely of one riuer, which is called the riuer of the salt, and is in the prouince of Canton, and is worth vnto him, euerie yeare, a million and a halfe. And although the ordinarie rent, the which he hath euerie yeare, dooth exceede the greatest king that is nowe knowen in all the world in quantitie; yet, in his treasories which he gathered together and kept (if it be true that the Chinos do say), in euery principall citie of these fifteene prouinces, is more than a great number of kings togither haue or can procure, no, nor come nigh vnto it by a great deale.

A riuer that yeeldeth a million and a halfe euery yeare in salt.

All the cities and townes of this kingdome are walled about with stone walles, and at euerie fifteene paces a bulwarke; and without the wall commonly all of them haue a riuer, or else a great deepe moote, wherein they may bring water at all times, with the which they are very strong: they doo vse no fortes, neyther haue they any, but onely ouer the gates of the cities, towers (as hath been declared), and in them is put all the artilerie, the which is for the defence of that citie or towne.

All cities are walled.

They vse many sortes of weapons, but in especiall hargabushes, bowes, lances of three or foure manners, swords like vnto faunchers, and with them targets. All the souldiers when they go to fight, they weare long garments down to their knees, very wel stuffed with cotton wooll, the which doth resist the thrust of a lance, or a stabbe: all such souldiers as haue the king's ryall pay weare, in token thereof, red and yellowe hats, of the which there is so great a number, as well horsemen as foot men, that almost it is impossible to number them. And it is a common opinion of all them that haue bin in this kingdome, and haue seene them, that all Spaine, France, and the Great Turke, hath not so many as this kingdome hath. They haue amongst them captaines of

They vse hargabushes, bowes, and lances.

Englande, France, Spaine, and the Turke hath not so many souldiers as this kingdome.

ten souldiers, some of a hundreth souldiers, some of a thou- *Captaines of few aud many souldiers.*
sand, of ten thousand, of twentie thousand, and in this sort
to a hundred thousand. The number of souldiors that these
captains do leade, are knowen by certain ensignes that they
beare. They muster and make show of their people euery
new moone; and the same day they do pay them royally,
and their pay must be in siluer, and in no other money. It
is saide by such as have seene this pay, but especially the
aforesaid father, Fryer Ignacio, that they giue them a peece
of siluer, which may weigh so much as a ryall and halfe of
Spaine, and is as much worth there as foure crownes amongest
vs, in respect of the value of all things. But both in the
one and in the other kingdom, that day that they do receiue
their pay, euery one must make a show of some act in armes,
the which is done in the presence of viewers or muster-
masters: and such as are found that doo not his exercise
with dexteritie, they are reprehended and cruelly punished:
they doo skirmish with great consort, and in that which
toucheth obedience to their captaines, and vnto the ensignes,
the which they do vse in their wars, they may compare with
all nations of the world.

CHAP. XVIII.

This Chapter doth treat of certaine rites and ceremonies, and other signes and tokens which be found, and do show that they haue had notice of the holy law of the Gospell.

Such ceremonies as vnto this day haue bin seene amongst
the people of this kingdom, are gentilicas,[1] without any mix-
ture with the Moores, nor with any other sect: yet there is
found amongst them, that is a sufficient indition,[2] that they
haue had in some time past, some particular notice of the

[1] The original Spanish word, meaning "pagan", left untranslated.
[2] From the Spanish *indicio*, "proof".

euangelical law, as is plainly seene by certaine pictures which haue beene found and seene amongest them, whereof we haue made particular mention, the which they beleeue was knowen by the preaching of the Apostle S. Thomas, who passed through this kingdome when as he went vnto the Indians, and from thence to the city of Salamina,[1] which, in their language, is called Malipur, whereas he was martyred for the name and faith of Jesus Christ: of whom, at this day, they do remember in that kingdome, by the tradition of their antecessors, who said, that many yeares past there was in that kingdome a man that did preach vnto them a new law, whereby they might goe vnto heauen: who, after that hee had preached certaine daies, and saw little fruit thereof (for that they were all occupied in ciuill wars) he departed from thence vnto the Indians. But first he left certaine disciples behind him that were baptised and well instructed in matters of faith, that they might preach vnto them whenas occasion did serue for the same. In many places they do worship the diuell, only for that he should do them no harme; and so the said fryer did tell me, for that hee was diuers times in presence whereas they did obsequies of certaine Chinos that lay a dying: and he saw that they had painted before the dead man a furious diuell, having in his left hand the sunne, and in his right hand a dagger, with the which he made a show as though he would strike him. This picture was put before him at the point that hee should yeelde vp the ghost, strengthening him that he should put great trust thereon.

And as the fryer did demand of them what reason they had to do the same; some of them answered and saide, be-

[1] More properly Calamina. Tillemont upon this subject says: "Les Portugais pretendent qu'il y a une ancienne inscription à Maliapur dans les Indes, où l'on apprend entre autres choses que Saint Thomas fut percé d'une lance au pié d'une croix près de cette ville. C'est peutêtre ce qui fait dire aux auteurs nouveaux que Calamine est la même ville que Maliapur."

cause the diuell should do no harme vnto the dead man in the other world they put his picture before him, that he might knowe him, and take him for his friend.

That which is vnderstood of these Chinos is, that although they haue amongst them many errors of the Gentiles; yet with great ease they would be reduced vnto our faith, if they might haue libertie for to preach, and they to receiue it.

When as the sunne and the moone is in eclypse, they beleeue verily that the prince of the heauen will destroye them, and for verye feare they put them selues in that colour: the people generally doo worshippe vnto them, and beleeue verily that the sunne is a man, and the moone a woman. And therefore, when as they beginne to bee eclypsed, they make great sacrifices and inuocations unto the prince afore said, desiring him not to kill nor destroy them, for the great necessitie they haue of them. All generally beleeue the immortalitie of the soule; and that in the other world they shall be rewarded or punished according as they liued in this worlde, in company of the bodie. Aud therefore they do vse to make in the fields sepulchres, wherein they command themselues to be buried after they bee dead. When they should be buried, they command to kill all their seruants or their wiues, those that best he loued in his life, saying, that they do it that they should go with them to serue them in the other world, whereas they beleeue they shall liue eternally and die no more. They put with them into their sepulchres things to be eaten and great riches, beleeuing that they do carry the same into the other world, and there to serue their necessities. In this error were the Indians of the Peru of old antiquity, as the Spaniards haue seene by experience. There is in this kingdom many vniuersities and colleges, wherein is taught philosophie, both naturall and morall, and the lawes of the countrie, for to learne to gouerne by them; vnto the which the king doth send ordinarily visitors to see and vnderstand the order that is amongst them, and to reward or punish the students according vnto the desert of eyther of them. They are greatly ashamed when they see any euil thing committed, although they bee not punished for the same, and are people that do permit with ease correction, as the father Ignacio and his companions did see by experience; who going alwayes as condemned men to die, yet at all times when they did see them do reuerence vnto their idols or vnto the diuell, or any other euill thing, they did reprehend them with great liberty, who did not onely seeke to hurt them for the same, but did greatly reioyce to heare their reasons wherewith they did prohibite or forbid them. The said frier did tell me that, one day, passing by an hermitage, whereas dwelled an hermite who had, vpon the altar in the same, an idoll for his saint: before whom was there a Chino, a principall man, worshipping the same; the saide father, without any feare, went vnto him, and began to reprehende him, and to spit at the idoll, and caused him therewith to leaue off his worshipping, whereof he was greatly amazed, both he and all the rest of his companie, to see with what boldnes it was done, and no harme done vnto him for the same, eyther they supposed that the Chino did thinke him to be a mad man, or else (which is most to be beleeued) that God did worke with his seruant whereby he would giue him his reward for that which he had done, in returning for his honour, in mittigating the furie of that man, and to giue him vnderstanding that he was reprehended with reason. There are many Chinos conuerted to the faith as well in the Ilands Philippinas, as in the citie of Machao, and they baptise of them daily, who giue tokens and outwarde showes to bee good Christians, and say that the greatest difficultie for to conuert all the whole kingdome, will be in them that doo gouerne in the same, for they had neede of a particular ayde and helpe of the mercie of God to bring them vnto the faith; for that they are had in reuerence and obeyed as Gods vpon the earth. Besides this, they do giue themselues to all delightes that any humaine creature can imagine, for that they put all their felicitie therein, and doo it with so great extremitie, that it is supposed there is no people in all the worlde that may be compared vnto them.

For besides that they are alwayes carried in little chayres, and vpon mens shoulders, which are covered with silke and golde; yet are they giuen much vnto bankets, wherein they haue so many different sortes of meates as their appetites doo require. And it is greatly to be maruailed at, that the women of this kingdome are marveilous chast and secret as any whatsoeuer; and to the contrarie the men are as vicious, but in especiall the lords and gouernors: and for that our faith do reprehend with rigor and terror the excesse of these thinges, it is to be beleeued that it will be a great impediment to the entrie of the Gospell amongst them: yet God may so touch them, and in such sort, that there will be no difficultie. Amongest the common people there will be no such impediment; but rather they will embrace with great content our holy law, for that it will be an occasion to cleare and set them at libertie from the tyrannie of the diuell, and from their iudges and lords, who do intreate them as slaues. This is the opinion of all them that haue entred into this kingdome, and haue intreated of this matter with the Chinos. They haue amongest them some good thinges, and woorthie to be imitated and folowed, of the which I will here set downe two, which are thinges of great purpose to my iudgement. The one is, that vnto none they do giue the office to gouerne, by no manner of wayes nor meanes, although they be suborned by friendship, but onely by his owne merites and sufficient abilitie. The seconde, that none can be viceroy, gouernours, nor iudge of a prouince or citie, in the which hee is naturall borne, the which they say is done to take away the occasion of dooing any iniustice, beeing carried away or led by parentes or friendshippe. All other thinges of this kingdome I do remit vnto that which hath bin before declared, for to passe vnto the rest, the which in this Itinerario is promised to be mentioned and declared.

CHAP. XIX.

This Chapter doth treate of the Ilands of Japon, and of other thinges in that kingdome.

The Ilands of Japon are many, and altogether make a mightie kingdome, that is divided amongest many lords: it is distant from the firme land of China, three hundred leagues, and in the middest betwixt both kingdoms is the prouince of Lanquin, which is one of the fifteene afore named; although going from Machao, a city of the Portingals, and ioyning vnto Canton, which is of the Proper China, they do make it but two hundred and fiftie leagues, trauelling towards the north, and commonly they do account the same leagues from the Ilands of Luzon or Philippinas, vnto the said Ilands of Japon: whereunto they may go by Noua Hispania, for that it is better and surer nauigation, and shorter voyage, for according vnto the reckoning of the pylots that do nauigate those seas, they make it no more then 1750 leagues, which is not halfe of that which the Portingalls make in their nauigation.

[marginal note: Japon is 300 leagues from China.]

These ilands are many (as aforesaid), yet are they populared with much people, who in their bodies and faces differ very little from the Chinos, although not so politike: [by the which it seemed to be true, that which is found written in the histories of the kingdom of China, saying, that these Japones in old time were Chinas, and that they came from that mightie kingdome vnto these ilands, whereas they do now dwell, for this occasion following. A kinsman of a king of China, a man of great countenance and valour, hauing conceiued within his brest for to kill the king, and thereby to make himselfe lorde of the countrie, the better to put this in execution, he gaue to vnderstand of his euill intent vnto others of his friends, requesting their fauour to execute the same, promising that he would do his best. This being done, and hauing them alwaies for his especiall friends, unto whom it seemed no difficult thing, and againe moued with ambition, they did promise him: and for the better confirmation thereof, they began to prepare souldiers, and to haue them readie against the day appointed. And for that this their pretence could not be brought to effect with such secrecie as the matter required, their treason came to be discouered vnto the king, at such good oportunitie that he might very well seeke remedie for his owne safegard at his pleasure, vnlooked for of his kinsman and the rest of his followers, who were all taken with great ease.

Then was it determined by those of the royall councell, that all the traitors should haue their throts cut according vnto the lawes of the countrie: but when their sentence was carried vnto the king to be confirmed (he vnderstanding that they much repented, and were sorie for their sin and treason that they had pretended against him), he determined to remedie the same with less damage, fearing what might happen by their deaths, so that he comanded they should not die, but be banished for euer out of the kingdome, with precise band, that they, their wiues and children, and al that should come of them, should for euer liue on those ilands that are now called Iapon, which were at that time desert and without people. This sentence was executed, and the offenders did accept the same for mercie. So they were caried to the said ilands, wheras when they saw themselues out of their naturall countrie, and without any possibility euer to returne againe, they ordained their comon wealth as a thing to last for euer: directing all their lawes which were for their conseruation and gouernment, contrarie vnto the Chinos from

The first inhabiting of the Iapon.

whence they came. But in particular they made one, wherin they did prohibite for euer their descendants to haue any frindship with the Chinos, and did admonish them to do them all the euill that was possible, which is obserued and kept vnto this day inuiolable, shewing themselues their contraries in all they may, euen in their apparell, speech, and customes: for the which there is no nation so abhorred of the Chinos as is the Iapones, so that they are payd their hatred with the like. And although at that time the said Iapones were subiectes and tributaries vnto the king of China, and so continued long time after, now at this day they are not, but do all harme that may be vnto those of that kingdome.][1]

They haue much siluer, but not so fine as that is of our Indians, likewise great abundance of rice and flesh, and in some parts wheate: and although they haue all this, with many fruits, and hearbs, and other things which be their ordinary victuals, yet are they not so well prouided as are their confines or neighbors, and no default in the lande, for that it is verie good and fruitefull. But that the naturall people do giue themselues verie little vnto the tilling and sowing thereof, for that they are more affectioned vnto the warres then vnto that: and this is the reason that many times they do lack prouision and victuals, which is the verie same reason that the naturall people and others do report of them.

In the Iapones are 66 kingdomes. There be in these ilandes three score and sixe kingdoms or prouinces, and many kings, although it may be better said, rulers or principals, such as the Spaniardes found in the Ilands of Luzo: for which cause, although they be called kings, yet are they not, neither in their contractation nor rent, for they haue verie little in respect of the multitude of people. The king Nobunanga, who died in the yeare 1583, was the most principall and greatest lord amongst them all, as well of people as of riches: who was slaine by a captaine of his, and punished by God by this meanes for his luciferine

[1] The whole of the passage included in brackets is inserted from the French of De la Porte.

pride, for that it did farre exceede that of Nebuchadonozor, and was come vnto that point that he would haue beene worshipped for a god: for the which he commanded to make a sumptuous temple, and to put in it thinges that did well declare and showe his follie: of the which that you may see how farre it did extend, I will declare here onely that which he did promise vnto them that did visite his temple.

First, the rich men that came vnto the saide temple, and did worshippe his picture, should be more richer: and those that were poore, should obtaine great riches: and both the one and the other, that had no successors to inherite their goods, should also obtaine them, and also long life for to enioy the same, with great peace and quietnesse.

A luciferine pride.

The second, that their life should be prolonged to eighty yeares.

The third, that they should bee hole of all their infirmities and diseases, and shall obtaine full accomplishment of all their desires with health and tranquillitie. And the last he commanded that euery month they should celebrate a feast for his birth day, and therein to visite his temple, with certification that all those that did beleeue in him, and in that which hee promised, should without all doubt see it accomplished, and those which in this life were faultie and did not doo in effect his commaundement, in the other they should goe the way to perdition. And the better to accomplish this his will, he commaunded to be put in this temple, al the idols in his kingdomes that were most worshipped, such as to whom frequented most pilgrimes: the which being done, he presently forbad that not one of them all should be worshipped, but he onely that was the true Fotoque and vniuersall god, the author and creator of nature.

[This foolishnesse did this proud king a little before his miserable death, and many other more, that I do leaue out, for feare that I should be too tedious in this itinerario. There did succeed this proude king in the kingdome his sonne, called Vozequixama, who for that he is very yong, at this day it is gouerned by a worthy captaine called Faxiuandono.][1]

All men that are borne in this land are naturally inclined to warres and robberies, and it is vsed ordinarily amongst themselues, alwayes he that hath most power and strength doth carry away the best part; and yet he doth enioy it with little securitie, for that as the prouerbe saith "he findeth a last for his shoo, or the length of his foote is found," and another commeth (when he thinketh least off) and carrieth away their spoile with victorie, reuenging iniuries the one for the other, without being requested thereunto: which is the occasion that they are neuer without ciuill warres, and that seemeth to bee the influence of the clime of that land. This, and the continual exercise in armes and in robberies, hath giuen them the name of warriers, and do terrifie all their borderers and neighbors.

They vse many weapons, but especially hargabusses, swords, and lances, and are very expert in them. On the firme land of China they haue done many suddaine robberies and thefts, and haue gone thorough therewith at their pleasure: and would haue done the like at the Ilands of Luzon, and vsed for the same all meanes possible, but yet it fell out contrary vnto their meanings, and returned their backes full euill against their wils, with their hands vpon their owne heads.

On a time they came vnto the Illocos, who with the fauour of the Spaniards (whose vassals they are) did defende themselues worthily: that the Iapones thought it best to returne vnto their houses and to leaue their begun pretence, with determination neuer to put themselues in the like perill, for that they had lost many of their companie. Not many yeares since there happened vnto them the like disgrace in China: there went tenne thousande of them to robbe and

[1] The whole of this paragraph included in brackets, is inserted by the translator from the French of De la Porte.

steale, and at their going on lande, they did sacke a cittie with little hurt and smal resistance, who with the content of that pray, forgot themselues and did not preuent the harme that might chance vnto them: the Chinos being offended did compasse them about in such sort, that when the Iapones remembred themselues, they were in that case that they were constrained to yielde vnto their enimies, who at their willes did repay themselues very well of the iniurie receiued, and a very good warning vnto all those that shall heare thereof, to flie from putting themselues into the like trance : so the Chinos were very wel reuenged of the iniury by them receiued.

The faith of Christ is very well planted in some of these ilands, by the good diligence and trauell of the fathers and Iesuites, but in particular by that which was doone by Master Francisco Xabier, one of the tenne companions of the father Ignacio de Loyola, a founder of the saide religion: hee trauelled with great zeale in the conuerting of the saide Ilands, and that which was a great helpe vnto the same was his holy doctrine and apostolike life, as vnto this day the Iapones doo confesse, attributing vnto him (next vnto God) the goodnesse that hath come vnto them by receiuing the baptisme, whome the fathers of that companie haue followed in all pointes, such as remained after his death, as also such as haue gone thither since that time.

So that vnto them may be attributed the thankes for the mollifying of such adamantine hearts, as are those of the natural people of these ilandes, whose wittes (although they be good and subtil) are naturally knowne to be inclined vnto warres, robberies, and doing of euill : and at this day, being Christians, they do followe their euill inclinations, yet notwithstanding, by the good doctrine and ensample of the saide fathers, they are much better Christians then those of the Orientall or East Indians.

I do not set downe here the number of those that are

baptised in these ilands, for that there are therein diuers opinions, as also for that the fathers of the name of Iesus or Iesuits doo distinctly declare in their letters. The Portugals say that in respect of the number of people that are to bee conuerted, the number that are baptised are very fewe, and that there are many that are not, for lacke of ministers and preachers; the which may easily be remedied, in commaunding to go thither more religious men of other orders, for to aide and helpe the saide Iesuites, the which shoulde be vnto them a particular content and comfort as I doo beleeue, as hath beene seene by experience in all partes of the Indians, whereas haue come religious men vnto places of their doctrine, for that the quantitie of people is so great that are in these ilandes, that although there shoulde go thither many laborers of the gospell, and all the orders of religious men, the one should not be a let or hindrance vnto the other, and they shoulde all of them finde enough to occupie themselues, especially if that the successor of Nobunanga were conuerted with his subjectes. All the men of these ilands are well set and well proportioned, and go well apparelled, although not in so good order as those of China: they liue verie healthfully and long, by reason that they doo vse verie few diuersities of meates: they doo not suffer amongst them any phisitians, and doo not cure themselues but with simples.

They haue amongst them many priests of their idols, whom they do call Bonsos, of the which there be great couents. Likewise they haue amongst them great witches, who do ordinarily talke with the diuell, and are not a small impediment for them to receiue the lawe of God in that kingdome. The women or wiues of these Iapones do keepe themselues very close, and very seldome go forth of their houses, in the which they do resemble those of China much (as hath beene said), yet haue they many wiues, for that by their lawes it is lawfull for them to haue as they please and can sustaine; yet are they so prudent, that they do restraine themselues,

<small>Many witches.</small>

and liue in great peace. Both men-seruants and women-seruants do serue their masters, as though they were slaues, and they may kill them at their pleasure without incurring any penalty of their lawes, a thing far different from any good policie. Many other things more could I declare of this kingdome, the which I do let passe, for the reason aforesaid: and again, for that the fathers of the company of Iesus haue intreated thereof at large and vere truely.

Not farre from these Ilands of Iapon, they haue discouered of late certaine ilandes which are called of the Amazones, for that they are all inhabited by women, whose ordinary weapons are bowes and arrowes, and are very expert in the same: they haue their right brest drie, the better to exercise their bow. Unto these ilands, in certaine monethes euery yeare, goeth certaine shippes from Iapones with merchandice, and they bring from thence such as they haue there: in the which time the men do deale with the Amazones as with their own proper wiues, and for to auoide dangers that might happen amongst themselues they deale in this order following. *Ilands of Amazones.*

After that their shippes are aryued, there goeth on shore two messengers for to giue aduice vnto the queene of their arriuall, and of the number of men that are in their shippes, who dooth appoint a day when they shall all come on shoare: the which day shee doth carrie to the waters side the like number of women, as they bee of men, but the saide women doo first come thither before the men doo disembarke themselues, and euery one of them dooth carry in their hande a paire of shooes, or a paire of slippers, and on them their own seuerall marke, and do leaue them on the sands at the waters side, without any consort or order, and presently departe from thence. Then the men come on shoare, and euery one take the first paire of shooes that he commeth vnto, and put them on: then presently the women come forth, and euery one of them carryeth with her him who hath fallen vnto her by lot, to put on *A strange custome.*

her shoes, and maketh him her guest, without any other particularitie, although it chanceth vnto the most vilest of them all to meete with the queenes shooes, or otherwise to the contrarie.

So when the monethes are expired set downe by the queene, in the which are permitted the men aforesaid, they doo depart, euerie one leauing with his hostis his name, and the towne where hee dwelleth, for that if it so fall out that they bee with child, and be deliuered of a sonne, that hee may bee carried the yeare following vnto his father, but the daughters do remaine with them.

This is very doubtfull to bee beleeued, although I haue bin certified by religious men, that haue talked with persons that within these two yeares haue beene at the saide ilands, and haue seene the said women; and that which causeth me more to stand in doubt, is for that the fathers of the companie that dwell at the Iapones, haue not in their letters made any particular mention of them: therefore let euery one giue credite to this as liketh him best.

CHAP. XX.

They haue notice of certaine kingdomes borderers vnto these Ilands of Iapon, and it treateth of some thinges of them, according vnto the truest intelligence that hath come from those parts, and of certaine miracles that happened in the kingdome of Cochinchina, that were notable.

From the cittie of Machao, which is inhabited by Portugals, and situated on the skirt of the firme lande of China, in two and twentie degrees, the aforesaide father Ignacio did trauell for Malaca, passing by the gulfe of Aynao, which is an ilande and prouince of China, and fiue leagues from the firme lande, and from the Philippinas one hundreth and foure score. It is a very rich prouince and of great prouision, and in the straight that is betwixt them and the firme lande, there is great fishing of pearles and aliafar,[1] and those which are there founde do in many killats[2] exceede them that are brought from Baren, which is on the coast of Arabia, or those that are brought from Manar, which is another kingdome from whence is brought many vnto that of China.

Great fishing of pearles.

This prouince of Aynao is very good and strong, and the people thereof very docible and well inclined. From this ilande to the kingdome of Cochinchina, is fiue and twentie leagues, and from Machao, one hundreth and twentie fiue: it is a mightie kingdome, and is in sixteene degrees of altitude, and the one part therof is ioyned with the firme land of China. The whole is deuided into three prouinces. The first dooth enter forty leagues into the lande, and hath in it a mightie king. The second is more farther within the land, and he that is lord thereof is a king of greater power than the first; and ioyning vnto the sun, more towards the Septentrion, is the thirde, the which is more greater and of more riches, whose king in respect of the other two is an emperor, and is called in their language Tunquin, which doth signifie the same. Unto him be subiect the other two kings: yet notwithstanding his mightinesse, and called emperour, hee is subiect vnto the king of China, and dooth pay him tribute and parias.[3] It is a countrie well prouided of victuals, and as good cheape as in China. There is great stoare of a wood called palo de Aguila, and of another woode called Calambay, and both of them are verie odoriferous.[4]

Parias is a duetie for the kinges owne person.

[1] More correctly *aljofar*, a corruption from the Arabic "seed pearls".
[2] From the Spanish *quilate*, a carat.
[3] Spanish. An acknowledgment or tribute from one prince to another.
[4] The following is from a notice by the late T. H. Colebrooke, Esq., appended to a paper by Dr. Roxburgh, which will appear in the forthcoming part of the "Linnæan Transactions." "It may be remarked by the way, that the Portuguese *pao de aguila*, as noticed by Rumphius, is an undoubted corruption, either of the Arabic *aghaluji*, or of the Latin

304

<small>Aboundance of silke and gold.</small>

Great aboundance of silke and gold, and of other things very curious: all these kingdomes are at a very point to be reduced vnto our faith, for that the principall (he whom they giue title of emperor) hath sent diuers times to Machao, and vnto other parts whereas are Christians, and haue requested to send them persons both learned and religious, for to instruct them in the law of God, for that they are all determined to receiue it and be baptised: and doo desire it with so great feruentnesse, that in manie citties they haue the timber ready to build and edifie churches, and in a redinesse all other kind of necessaries for the same.

There was in Machao a religious man of the order of barefoote friars of S. Francis, who, vnderstanding the great and good desire of this king, did sende him by certaine Portugal merchants that did trade into his countrie, a cloth whereon was painted the day of iudgement and hell, and that by an excellent workeman; and also a letter, wherein hee did signifie vnto him the great desire he had with some other of his companions to go into his kingdome to preach the gospel. The which being receiued by the said king, and informed the signification of the picture, and of the religious man that sent it him, he reioyced very much with the present; and did send in returne of the same an other that was very good, vnto the same religious man, and a letter of great curtesie, and did accept the offer that hee sent in his letter, and did promise that all that went thither shoulde haue good entertainement, and that he would presently make them a house next vnto his.

This religious man, although he had a desire to put in execution the kings will, yet at that time hee coulde not, by

<small>*agallochum*, and it is from a ludicrous mistake, that from this corruption has grown the name of lignum aquilæ, whence the genus of this plant now receives a botanic appellation, and which many authors have vainly attempted to distinguish from the lignum aloes and Calambac. The latter is a Malay name of the aloe wood, derived, according to the conjecture of Rumphius, from the Chinese Kilam."</small>

reason that he had but few companions: the which the king did vnderstande, and caused him to sende vnto the bishoppe of Machao three or foure letters, requesting him to send him the saide religious men, with certification that hauing them there, both hee and all the rest of his kingdome woulde receiue the faith of Christ and the holy baptisme: vnto the which letters they did alwaies make answere with promises that he would send them vnto him: but after, because they did not accomplish the same, the king did complaine of him vnto certaine Portugall merchants with great griefe, saying, this your bishop of Machao doth greatly lye; for that I haue requested him by foure letters to send me religious men for to preach the law of the gospell, and he consenting vnto my wil, did neuer accomplish nor performe his word. Unto this day they haue not accomplished this desire, for the great lacke they haue of such ministers as they doo demande, and are requisite in those parts, and cannot supply their want and necessitie, except they should leaue them vnprouided that bee already baptised. They doo driue them off with faire words and promises, that with as great breuitie as is possible, their desire shal be satisfied. And this was the answere that was giuen in Machao vnto certaine messengers or ambassadors that were sent by the aforesaid king, for the same demand, the which was required with great instance. The which messengers for their comfort, and for his who sent them, did carry with them al such images as they might haue, but specially that of the crosse, in which form and likenes (as hath bin informed) they haue made in the kingdome an infinite number, and set them in all their streets, highwayes, and houses, whereas they are worshiped and reuerenced with great humilitie, as well for that it is in an ensigne of Christ, whose faith they do desire to receiue, as also for a notable miracle which happened in that kingdome worthy to make thereof a particular mention, the which I will set downe here, in such sort as the ambassadors aforesaide did declare in publike before the inhabitants of Machao, when as they came to demande religious men for to instruct them in the gospel.

<small>A myracle.</small> There was a man naturally borne in this kingdome, who, for certaine occasions went forth of the same, and came and dwelt amongst the Portugals, who, seeing the Christian ceremonies, and being touched with the hand of God, was baptised, and remained certain yeares in the same towne, giuing outwarde shewes to bee a good Christian, and one that feared God; at the end thereof he changed his minde, and determined to returne vnto his owne countrie, and there to liue according vnto that which he had learned of the Christians, the which he beleeued to doo with ease, without any gainesaying or contradiction. Whereas when hee came thither, hee did obserue all such things as a Christian was bounde to doo: but amongst other signes and tokens of the same, he made a crosse and set it by the door of his house, whereunto he did reuerence at all times, when he passed by the same, with great devotion. His neighbours when as they saw that signe, a thing of them neuer seene before, and howe that that Christian did make particular reuerence, they beganne to mocke and scorne him and the crosse, and pulled it downe from the place whereas it was set, and did other things in dispite thereof, and of him that had set it there in that place, whose hatred and discourtesie was so much that they determined in their minds to burne it, and to put the same in execution, who, at the same instance, did all miraculously die; I say those that would haue burnt the same, the which was seene of many other, who haue giuen sufficient testimony thereof. And within fewe dayes after, all the whole linage of those dead persons did follow the same way, and not one escaped. This miracle being spread throughout all the kingdome, the naturals thereof did set vp many crosses in all parts.

This they say was the principall motion that God put into

their hearts for to moue them to demande for such as shoulde baptise them, and preach the holy gospell. Likewise, a great helpe vnto the same was the declaration of the painted cloth, which the aforesaid religious man did send to the king. Since that time, there hath gone vnto the cittie of Machao certaine naturals of that kingdome, who, being affectioned vnto our faith, were baptised there : with the which, and with the hope aforesaid, they are all sustained, till such time as it is the pleasure of God to send them the remedie for their soules, the which hee hath caused them to desire, which cannot be long, according vnto that which hath beene seene, and the miracles that God doth worke, the more for to kindle their desire, as the myracle of the crosse before spoken off, and others the which certaine Cochinchinos did declare in the cittie of Machao, in anno 1583, and happened the same yeare, and was very fresh in the memorie of all those of the saide kingdome. The one of them was, that one of the Christians aforesaid went to visite a principall man that had *Another myracle.* the palsie, and kept his bed many yeares before : and conferring with his long sicknesse, he told of certaine myracles, such as he had vnderstanding that was done by Christ our Redeemer, when that he was man amongst men whome hee redeemed : but in particular those which he did in the healing of the like infirmities, such as he lay sicke of: alonely with his deuine vertue, in touching of them with any part of his garments or shadow. The iudge hearing this, hee had a particular faith and devotion to him that had doone these myracles that the Christian had told him, and asked what his name was, and what signes and tokens he had : he told him that his name was Jesus of Nazareth, Redeemer of the worlde, the Sauiour and glorifier of men. And the better to declare vnto him his signes, he shewed to him an image or picture that he had of his, the which was giuen him such time as he was baptised, printed in paper : and of Iesu Christ when he ascended vp into heauen, the which, for lacke of churches and other of greater volume, hee should haue continually with him, and make his praiers thereunto. This sicke man tooke it, and fixed his eies thereon with so great deuotion and faith, in requesting him to giue him his health, and that he would presently beleeue in him and bee baptised. At the same instant, in the sight of them all, he felt himselfe whole of the infirmitie that he had suffered so many yeares before, and neuer could find any humaine remedy for the same, although he had prooued an infinite number. He straightwayes willed the Christian to baptise him, vnto whome hee gaue a great summe of monie, the which hee receiued against his will, and spent it in workes of mercie; and with part thereof he bought a bigge barke, in the which at this day he dooth passe people thorough a riuer, whereas they were wont to passe great perill and danger, and hee doth it for Gods sake, and receiueth nothing for the same.

A fewe dayes after, in another part of this kingdome, there happened another myracle of no lesser substance then the first, that is, there was a Cochinchina in the said citie of Machao, who did aske to bee baptised of a barefoote frier, which after that hee had catechised sufficiently, hee gaue it vnto him: and after a great time that hee had beene in his company, and had experience of his Christianitie and deuotion, he gaue him licence for to returne vnto his countrey, with a good token, that at his comming thither he would procure to augment the desire of Christianitie, the which God had begunne to kindle in their brest. This good neu Christian did procure the same with so great care, that he did profite very much (being holpen with the fauor of God, who made him his instrument), hee healed certaine infirmities, in shewing vnto the patients an image of our ladie, the which he had continually about his necke, and had therunto great deuotion, and woulde declare to them with great zeale the Lords Prayer or Pater Noster. His fame was so much spread abrode in all parts of this prouince, wherein he dwelled, that it came vnto the ears of a mandarin, or principall iudge of the same, who was many dayes in his bedde a leaper, both of handes and feete, and neuer coulde finde any phisition nor medecine that could giue him his health, nor any other humaine remedie: who being verie desirous to bee healed, hee sent for the saide Christian, and asked if hee would take vppon him to heale him of that infirmitie, as it was affirmed that hee had done by others of greater importance. The Christian saide hee would; then the iudge did promise vnto him for the same great giftes and rewardes, but hee made no account thereof, but onelie requested of him for reward, that after hee should bee hole, that he would be baptised and become a Christian: the which he did accept, and principally he shewed vnto him the image that hee had of our lady, saying: If thou wilt beleeue in this lady, that is heere ingraued, and in her most holy sonne Iesus Christ, the Redeemer of the whole world, thou shalt presently be made hole. This mandarin or iudge did beholde the same with great attention, and thought on the words which he had heard spoken, and in determining with himselfe to beleeue the same, at the very point that he did put it in execution, he was healed of al his infirmitie, a thing which caused great admiration in all that prouince.

These myracles and that of the crosse, in a short time being knowne abrode, haue caused such a desire vnto the inhabitants of that kingdome to become Christians, that by all manner of meanes possible they do procure the same: the which is not followed for lacke of ministers, as aforesaid, and is no smal griefe vnto them that Christianly doo put themselues to consider how the diuel our aduersary doth carry vnto his infernal mansion those soules which seeme to bee well disposed for to enioy the benefite of God, and his eternal goodnesse: all the which is for lacke of ministers, and not for any other default. God remedie the same for his mercies sake.

The said father Ignacio (whom, as I haue said, I do follow in many things of this itinerario) did tell me, that as he passed by this kingdome for to go vnto Spaine, he saw the deuotion of the people thereof, and the great desire they had to bee Christians, and how that the people were ready and bent for to receiue the holy gospell, very humble and of good vnderstanding. Hee would haue tarried for to baptise them, and would haue done it onely for charity and compassion, seeing with what deuotion they did demand the same, and the great number of soules that were condemned; but hee was constrained by force to go vnto Malaca, and againe it seemed vnto him, that amongst so many people his smal force might do little good: and that it were better for him to go vnto Spaine, and to procure more companions to helpe him, as he did, and returned with him, and with many other rewards, of Pope Gregory the thirteenth receiued: and he also receiued great fauours of the king of Spaine, and with great hope, that his maiestie will giue his particular aide, for to go thorow with this enterprise, which will not be of small effect. I do beleeue of a truth, that in small time all that kingdome shall be subiect vnto the Catholike faith of Rome, and to be the gate whereby to enter the lawe of the gospell into the mightie kingdome of China, for that this of Cochinchina is vpon the same firme land, and their language and customes are almost in one manner.

Their womenn are honest and shamefast.

They are verie white people of this kingdome, and are apparelled like vnto those of China: their women are verie honest and shamefast, and their apparell is very curious and gallant. The men weare their haire dispersed, and doo combe and trim it with too much care. In all the countrie almost, all of them are apparelled in silke, for that they haue there verie much, and excellent good: the countrie is verie holesome, and full of old folkes and children, which is a sufficient proofe for the goodnesse thereof.

They neuer had plague, pestilence, nor hunger.

They say that they neuer had amongst them neither pestilence nor hunger, which is the like as we haue said of the kingdome of China.

Let him that can, do it in such sort that so great and infinite number of soules that at this day are vnder the tyranny of the diuell, may see them in the Christian libertie, and in the other life inioy their creator.

CHAP. XXI.

In this chapter is declared of such kingdomes as are adioyning vnto that of Cochinchina, and of some notable thinges in them, with the rites and customes of the inhabitants.

Nigh vnto this kingdome of Cochinchina there is another called Champa, that although it be poore of gold and siluer, yet is it verie rich of drugges and gallant wood, and great stoare of prouision. This kingdome is very great and full of people, and they some what whiter than those of Cochinchina; they are as nigh and as willing to become Christians as their neighbors, but for the performance thereof they doo lacke that which the other doo. They haue the same lawes and ceremonies as well the one as the other, and are all idolaters, and doo worship the second causes, in the same order as the Chinos do, vnto whome likewise they do make one manner of acknowledging. *The kingdome of Champa rich of drugs.*

From this iland you may go with ease vnto Malaca, leauing on the right hand a kingdome which is called Camboia, the which is great and very full of people, and all of them affectioned to go to sea, and nauigation, by reason whereof they haue an infinite number of vessels. It is a very fertill country, with great stoare of prouision: there are elephants in great number and abadas,[1] which is a kind of beast so big *The kingdome of Camboia.*

[1] The Spanish word for the rhinoceros.

as two great buls, and hath vppon his snowt a little horne. At this day there is one of them at Madrid, the which was brought out of the Indians to his maiesty, and many do go to see it for a strange thing, and neuer the like seene in Europe, whose skinne is so hard (according vnto the report) that no man, although he be of great force and strength, can passe it with a thrust. Some haue saide that it is an vnicorne, but I take it for the contrarie, and they are of my opinion almost all those that haue beene in those partes, and haue seene the true vnicorne.

In this kingdome there is a religious man of the order of S. Dominicke, called frier Siluester, whome God did carrie into those parts for to remedy the soules that are therein: hee dooth imploy himselfe to learne their natural language, and to preach the holy gospell in the same tongue, and hath them likewise prepared, that if he had any companions for to help hym, they should obtayne much fruite for the heauens: he háth sent and requested for some vnto the India of Portingall, but they would neuer send him anie, peraduenture by some sinister information, by men which the diuell doth marke as instruments, for to stay and let the saluation of those soules for euer to remayne in his tyrannicall power. This fryer did write a letter vnto Malaca vnto fryer Martin Ignacio, and vnto other religious men, intirely requesting them for the loue of God to giue such order that hee might be holpen with some religious men, of what order soeuer, with certification that therein they shall doe great seruice vnto God, and put remedie in those soules whome he dare not baptise, for feare that after lacking the euangelical refreshing, to water and cherish them, they returne to bring forth that euill fruit of idolatrie. This petition did not take effect according to his desire, for that there was not to serue his turne, nor any that was vnoccupied. They vnderstood of him that brought this letter, that the king of that kingdome had in great veneration the sayd father

Siluestro, in so ample manner, as was the patriarck Ioseph
in Egypt: hee had in all that kingdome the seconde place,
and euery time that the king would speak with him, he gaue
him a chaire: and gaue him great priuiledges, and licence
for to preach the holy gospell throughout all the kingdome
without any contradiction, and for to edifie the churches and
all other thinges whatsoeuer he thought necessarie: this
king himselfe helping thereunto, by giuing of great gifts
and charitie: he said also that in al the kingdome there were
erected many crosses, and were had in great reuerence. And
for the confirmation of the truth hereof, the aforesaid frier
Ignacio did see in Malaca a present that the king of this
kingdome of Camboia did send vnto another friend of his:
and amongst many things contained therin of great riches
and curiositie, there were two crosses very great and wel
made, of a gallant wood and very sweete, and all garnished
very richly with siluer and gold, with their titles enamiled.

Nigh vnto this kingdome is that of Sian, in the hight of fourteene degrees from the pole artike, and three hundred leagues from Machao, wheras the Portugals do go to trade: it is the mother of all idolatrie, and the place from whence hath proceeded many sectes, vnto Iapon, China, and Pegu. It is a flourishing countrie, and well replenished of all such things as be requisite for to merite the name to be good. There be in it manie elephants and abadas, and other beasts that are nourished in that countrie: besides this, it is very rich of mettals, and gallant sweete woode. The people of this kingdome for the most part are faint-hearted or cowards, for which occasion, although they are infinite in number, yet are they subiect vnto the king of Pegu, who ouercame them long time since, in a battell (as afterwards shall be declared): and they doo pay him ordinarily great and heauy tributes. They would be conuerted very easily vnto the faith of Iesu Christ, and would leaue their idols, if they had any to preach vnto them: yea and would subiect themselues vnto any king or

VOL. II.

lord that woulde fauour them, and not vnto this whom now they do obey, for that hee dooth intreate them tyrannously. They haue amongst them many religious men after their fashion, who doo liue in common, and leade an asper and sharp life: for the which they are had of al the rest in great veneration. The penance which they do is wonderfull and strange, as you may iudge by some things that I will declare here: amongst a great number that be tolde of them, there are none of them that can marrie, neither speake to any woman, and if by chance he do, they are without remission punished by death. They go alwayes barefoote, and very poorely apparelled, and do eate nothing but rice and greene herbes, and this they do aske for charitie euery day, going from doore to doore with their wallet at their backes, alwayes with their eyes looking on the ground, with such modesty and honesty, that it is to be wondred at: they doo not craue their charity, neither take it with their hands, nor do any other thing but cal or knocke, and stand still, till such time as they giue them their answer, or put something into their wallets. It is told of them for a truth, that many times for penance they do put themselues starke naked in the heate of the sunne, which is there very great, for that the country is in twenty sixe degrees of the equinoctiall, whereas they are much troubled there with gnats, whereof there is an infinite number, and is a thing that if they did passe it for Gods sake, it is a kinde of martyrdome of great desert. God for his mercy lighten them with his grace, that this which they do smally vnto the profite of their soules, may bee the occasion that after they are baptised, they may deserue for the same many degrees of glory.

Likewise in secrete they doo great penance, and doo rise vp at midnight to praie vnto their idols, and they do it in quiers, as is vsed amongst vs Christians. It is not permitted them any rentes, nor any other kinde of contractation: and if they bee seene to deale in any, they are detested and hated, as an heretike is amongst vs.

For this kind of asper liuing, the which they do, according vnto the report, for the loue of heauen, and that with great zeale, they are respected of the common people for saints, and for such they do reuerence them, and do commit them vnto their praiers, when they are in any trouble or infirmity. These and many other things more be declared of them in like order, which may serue for to confound vs, that confessing we do not obserue and keepe, hauing for the same our sure reward, not of humain interest, but that which God hath prepared for the good in heauen.

The law of the gospell in this kingdome would bring foorth much fruite, for that the people are charitable, and louers of vertue, and of them that haue it. This experience had the father Ignacio and his companions in China, at such time as they were prisoners, where there were in a city certain ambassadors from the king of Syan, who were bound to the court, and there they vnderstood that the Spaniards were sentenced to death for entring into that country without licence: they went to visite them, and when they saw them with their asper habites and very poore, and did resemble very much the habit of their religious men, they had so great affection vnto them, that ouer and aboue they sent them good. charity, the which was two bags of rice, much fish and fruits: they did offer to them al the money they would desire, and to ransome them in al that the judges would demand for them: in recompence of this good wil they shewed vnto the Spaniards, they did verifie that aforesaide, that they are great louers of vertue.

CHAP. XXII.

Of many other kingdomes that are in this new world, and of their names and properties, but in especiall of that famous cittie of Malaca.

<small>The kingdome of Lugor and that of Patane.</small> Nigh vnto this kingdome of Syan there are two kingdomes togither, the one of them is called Lugor, and the other Patane; they belong both vnto one king, who is a Moore and of the linage Malaya, yet notwithstanding the people of these kingdomes are gentiles, and doo vnderstande in them to haue great good will to become Christians, if they had anie to preach vnto them the gospell. The lande is very <small>Gold, pepper, and drugs.</small> rich of golde, pepper, and of drugges, but the people faint hearted and cowards, and for little : for which occasion they are more giuen vnto thinges of contentment and pleasure, then vnto wars or brawlings.

<small>The kingdomes of Paon and Ior.</small> At the ende of this kingdome is the straite of Malaca, in the which there are two small kingdomes, the one of them is called Paon[1] and the other Ior :[2] the people of the first are the most traiterous that are in all the whole worlde, as the Portugals haue many times experimented; and those of the second kingdome, sometimes they are in peace, and sometimes in warre with the said Portugals. They will haue peace when they do see themselues in necessity of the same, but war ordinarily. These two kingdomes are halfe Moores, by reason whereof it seemeth that with an evil wil they wil be reduced vnto the law of the gospel, if that by the help of God they be not mollified of their hearts.

<small>The Straight of Malaca is vnder the line.</small> This straight of Malaca is vnder the equinoctiall line, and is accounted from the kingdome of Cochinchina vnto it three hundred and seuenty-six leagues: this is an euill straight and very dangerous for ships that passe thorough it, for very few times it is without stormes or some other greater danger,

[1] Pahang.   [2] Johore.

as it happened vnto a verie great shippe in the mouth of the straight, in the presence of frier Martin Ignacio, the which in verie little space was swallowed vp with the sea, and in it more then three hundred thousand ducats in merchandice that was within her, although the successe thereof our people did attribute it more vnto the iust iudgement of God than vnto the storme, for that according as they were informed, they had committed grieuous offences, at the time when she sanke: for being very nigh with his shippe in the which he went, and many other more, they felt not, neither had any suspition of any danger. From this straight to go vnto Malaca, you coast alongest the sea, fiue and twentie leagues: all which coast is full of great, mightie, and thicke woods, by reason whereof, as also for that it is not inhabited, there are many tygers, elephants, and mightie great lysards, and other furious beastes.

The citie of Malaca, in our pole articke, is eleuated from the equinoctiall onely one degree: of ancient time it was the most principallest citie of all these kingdomes, and resident therein a mightie king, a Moore, but after it was conquered by the Portugals, who in these wars did wonderfull things of great force and courage: they did driue foorth all the Moores out of the same, and out of all the borders, and made of their Mezquita or temple (which was a singular peece of worke) a high church, as it doth remaine vnto this day: there are also three monasteries of religious men, one of S. Dominicke, an other of S. Francis, and the third of the companie of Iesus, or Iesuites. It is a verie temperate countrie, being so nigh the equinoctiall line: the reason is, for that euery weeke ordinarily it rayneth three or foure times (which is the greatest cause of health in all that countrie), and thereby is made woonderfull fruitfull, and with great abundance of prouision; but particularly of fruites, for there is great store, and some sortes neuer seene in Europe, amongst the which there is one that is called in the

Malaca tongue *durion*,[1] and is so good that I haue heard it affirmed by manie that haue gone about the worlde, that it doth exceede in sauour all others that euer they had seene or tasted: it is in forme like vnto a mellon, whose ryne is somewhat harde, and hath vpon it little white prickes which seemeth like haire, and within the fruite be partitions, which be of the colour like vnto *maniar blanco*,[2] and of so good sauour and tast is it. Some do say that haue seene it, that it seemeth to be that wherewith Adam did transgresse, being carried away by the singular sauour. The leaues which this tree yeeldeth are so bigge that a man may couer himselfe with one of them, which mee thinketh is but coniecture or defining: but there is cannafistola[3] for to lade fleetes, very bigge and good, and of a singular effect, one of the notablest things in this kingdome, and is a maruellous tree of an admirable vertue, the which putteth foorth so many rootes of so contrarie vertue, that those which grow towards the orient be good against poyson, agues, and many infirmities that do war against humaine life; and those rootes that growe towards the west be ranke poyson, and in effect, all cleane contrarie vnto the first. So that it seemeth here to be founde two contraries in one subiect, a thing which, in philosophie, they were woont to count impossible.

This citie is of great contractation, for that there come thether all the kingdomes that we haue spoken of, and from many other more that are nigh thereabouts: but in particular a great number of great ships from the Indians, Canton, Chincheo, and from many other places, likewise the Iapones carry thether their siluer to sell, and those of the kingdome of Syan carry many things very curious, but especially cloues, and pepper of the Iland Malucas, and those of

---

[1] The Durio Zibethinus of Kœnig.   [2] Blanc mange.
[3] From the name the cassia fistula is probably meant, although the author is silent respecting the purgative properties for which that plant is so remarkable.

Burneo bring much sanders and nutmegs, and those of Iaba and Pegu bring the wood of Aguila, and those from Cochinchina and Cham bring great store of wrought silke, drogges, and spicerie; and those of Samatra, or Trapouana, much golde and wrought things, and fine cloth of Vengalas and Coromandel. All these, and other thinges, make this citie famous and plentifull, as also very much enlarged of the Portingals that go thether ordinarily euery yeare and traficke there.

CHAP. XXIII.

Of some kingdomes of the newe worlde, and of particular things that haue beene seene in them; and treateth of the citie and riuer of Ganies.

Ouer against this famous citie, of which so many thinges may be spoken of, is that mightie kingdome and Iland of Samatra, called by the ancient cosmogrofers Trapouana, which is (as some say) the Iland of Ophir, whether the fleet which King Solomon sent, of which there is particular mention made in the Scripture, in the third Booke of the *Kings*,[1] cap. 9 and 10, and in the *Paralipomenon*,[2] cap. 9, that went and returned again laden with gold and rich tymber for to adorne the temple of Ierusalem, and of many other curious things, whose memorie doth remaine vnto this day amongst the naturall people, although diffusedly, but not so much as those that haue it out of the Holy Scripture, neither so true. This iland is vnder the equinoctial line, so that the one halfe doth extend vnto the pole artick, and the other halfe vnto the poole antarticke. It hath in longitude 230 leagues, and in latitude three score and seuen leagues: and

(marginal note: The Iland of Samatra supposed to be the Iland of Ophir.)

[1] The first book of Chronicles.
[2] Chronicles,—the second book is here referred to.

is so nigh vnto Malaca, that in some parts it is less than ten leagues. In this kingdom there are many lords and rulers, yet he that hath the greatest part thereof is a Moore, and is called Achan; it is one of the richest ilands in al the world, for that it hath many mynes of fine golde, of the which (although there is a law that they cannot take out of them more than is necessarie) yet there is great abundance carried from thence to Malaca, Turkie, and many other places. There is gathered vpon this iland great abundance of pepper and beniewyn[1] of Boninas, in great quantity, out of whose trees (whereof there is great woods) there come foorth so sweet a smel that it seemeth an earthly paradice, and was wont to be smelled twenty leagues at sea, for which respect the ships that saile that way do come so nigh the lande as they may to haue the comfort of that smell. There is also much camphora, and all kinde of spices; by reason wherof there commeth vnto this kingdome to traficke, many Turkes that come in ships and foystes[2] out of the Red Sea. Also there doth traficke thether those of the kingdom of Sunda, Iaua the great, and Ambayno, and others that are there nigh vnto them. Vnto this iland came certaine Portingals to buy and sell, whereas they were all slaine, and some for the profession of the faith; for the which they are holden for martyrs of Iesu Christ, by the opinion of Christians that doo dwell nigh, when they vnderstood the cause. The most part of this kingdome are Moores; and therefore they do abhor the Christians, and do make with them all the warre they can, but in especiall with them that dwell in Malaca, whom many times they haue put in great danger of their liues, and losse of their goods.

Running from this kingdome of Malaca by the north and northwest cost is the mightie kingdome of Pegu, the which is in bignes greater then Samatra, and equall in riches, especially of pearls and al sorts of stones, and very fine christall:

[1] Benzoin.   [2] A small boat, from "fusta", Spanish.

there is great store of prouision, and an infinite number of people, and the king thereof is mightie: to whom (as we haue said) the king of Cyan doth pay tribute, because he ouercame him in a battaile which he had with him in the yeare 1568, according vnto the common opinion: the occasion was, that, vnderstanding how that the saide king of Syan had in his power a white elephant (whome those of the kingdome of Pegu do worship for god), the king sent to buy the same, and to giue for it so much as he would esteeme or value it: but he utterly denied the same, and saide that he would not let him haue it for all that he had in his kingdom: the which caused so great anger vnto the king, that hee called together all the souldiers that he could make, with determination to get by force of armes that which he could not by faire meanes and great ritches: in the which he did so great diligence, that in a fewe dayes hee had ioyned together an armie of a million and sixe hundreth thousande of men of warre, with whome hee departed vnto the saide kingdome of Syan, which was from his kingdome two hundreth leagues, and did not onely performe his pretence in bringing away the white elephant, but did also make the king tributarie, as he is vnto this day, as hath bin declared vnto you. <small>An armie of a million and sixe hundred thousand men.</small>

The rites of the people and priestes of this countrie, doo resemble much those of the kingdome of Syan: they haue amongst them many monasteries of men that liue honestly, solitarie, and with great penance, and people verie apt to receiue the holy gospell. For ouer and aboue that they are docible and of a good vnderstanding, they are men which do studie philosophie, and are well inclyned and charitable, and haue a particular affection vnto vertue, and vnto such as they do knowe that haue vertue, and very friendly to remedie the necessitie of their poore neighbours.

Going from this kingdome towardes the north is the kingdome of Arracon, verie plentifull of prouision, but few things <small>The kingdome of Arracon.</small>

of contractation or marchandice, which is the occasion that it is not well knowen to the Spaniardes, for that they haue not gone thether. They doo vnderstand of the naturall people and of their customes, that they are very apt to receiue the holie gospell.

The kingdome of Vangala. From this kingdome alongst the same coast, you came vnto the kingdome of Vangala,[1] through the which doth passe the riuer Ganges, one of the foure that comme foorth of paradice terrenall, the which being vnderstood by a certaine king of this kingdome, he determined to cause some to ascend vp that riuer till such time as he had found the head spring or head thereof, and therewith paradice: for the which effect he commanded to be made diuers sortes of barkes, both small and great, and sent in them vp the riuer certaine men (of whose diligence hee had long experience), and were prouided with victuals for many daies, and gaue commandement that presently after that they had discouered that which hee desired, that they should return with great speede, for to giue him particular and true relation, with pretence foorthwith to go himselfe to inioy the things which he thought necessarie to be seene, and woorthie to be desired, of his trauaile, and in a place so delightfull.

These men did nauigate vp the riuer many monethes, and came vnto a place whereas the water came foorth so softly and with so small noyse, which gaue them to vnderstande that they were not farre from the first head thereof, which should be paradice, that which they went to seeke. They gaue to vnderstand that in this place, after they had seene so many tokens, and comforted themselues with maruellous sweete smels, and aires of great delight, they thought verily that they had bin in the paradice terrenall. And more, when as they came vnto that place, where as the riuer did runne so peaceable, and the ayre so delicate aud sweet, there entred into the hearts of them all, so great and extraordinarie ioy,

[1] Bengal.

that they seemed to be in the true paradice, and forgot all the trauaile that they had passed for to come thether, and of any other thing that did signifie paine or griefe. But when they did intend to go forwardes with this their pretence and intent, and thereunto did put all diligence possible, they found by experience that all their trauaile was in vaine, and howe that they remained alwaies in one place: and coulde not vnderstande from whence did come or proceede that contradiction, they could not find in the waters by reason of the peaceablenesse thereof.

This experience being done, attributing it vnto a miserie because they could not get a shore, they returned backe againe by the same riuer, till they came to their owne kingdome, whereas they arriued in a very short time, and gaue their king to vnderstand (who sent them) all as aforesaide, and many other thinges more, the which I do leaue out for that I do take it *apocripha*. They hold it for a certaintie that the riuers Eufrates and Tygris are not far from this riuer Ganges; and it seemeth to be true, for both of them doo discharge their currents, or water, into the Persian sea, the which is not farre distant from this kingdome.

The people of this kingdome haue this riuer in great reuerence, which is the occasion that they neuer enter into the same but with great respect and feare. And when they doo washe or bath themselues in it, they haue it for a certaintie that they remaine cleare from all their sinnes. Likewise this kingdome, with great ease, might be conuerted vnto the Catholike faith as it seemeth, for that they haue amongst them many morall rites, ceremonies, and vertues.

CHAP. XXIV.

Of the kingdome of Coromandel and others his borderers, and of the citie of Salamina, whereas was and died the glorious apostle S. Thomas; and of the power and riches of the king of this kingdome, and the order of their buryinges, and other thinges of great curiositie.

Running alongest the coast from Vengala, is the kingdome of Masulapatar, and certaine other kingdomes nigh vnto the same: they be all gentiles, as the rest of their borderers, yet it is vnderstood, with great facilitie they would leaue their opinions. It is a kingdome that hath great abundance of prouision, and lacke of things of contractation or marchandice, which is the occasion that they are little knowen.

Trauailing a little forwardes, is the kingdome of Coromandel, whose chiefe citie is called Calamina, and nowe vulgarly Malipur,[1] and is there whereas was martyred the happie apostle S. Thomas. And they say that at this day there remaineth some of his relickes, by whom God did many myracles. The naturall people therefore haue a particular memory vntill this day of that saint.

This citie at this day is populared with Portingals and with the naturall people: there is in it a church, wherein is comprehended the house whereas was, and died, the holy apostle: this countrie belongeth vnto the king of Visnaga, who although he be a gentile, he hath great reuerence and respect vnto the house of the holy apostle, and for particular deuotion he doth giue euerie yeare a certaine charitie. There is in this citie two couentes of religious men, the one of the companie of Iesus, and the other of the order of S. Francis.

From this citie of Calamina to that of Visnaga there wheras the king is, it is fiue and thirtie leagues by land. This king is mightie, and his kingdome very great and full

[1] See note, p. 290.

of people, and hath great rentes. They say that onely the rent he hath of fine gold, is worth vnto him three millions, of the which he spendeth but one onely, and doth keepe euerie yeare two millions in his treasorie, the which according vnto the report and fame, is at this day with many millions. He hath twelue principall or chiefe captaines, and euerie one of them hath the gouernement of an infinite number of people and hath great rent for the same, for he that hath least rent hath sixe hundred thousand ducats yearely. Euerie one of them are bound to giue the king to eate, and all the people of his house, one month in the yeare; so that by this account the twelue captaines which are the lordes of the kingdome (and as wee might say) dukes, doo beare his cost all the whole yeare. The million the which he doth spend, is in giftes and in extraordinarie thinges. The king hath in his house, what with wiues, seruants, and slaues, nigh about fourteene thousand persons, and in his stable ordinarily a thousand horse, and for his seruice and garde eight hundreth elephants, of whom he doth spend euerie day eight hundreth ducats. The garde of his person is foure thousand horsemen, to whom he giueth great wages. He hath also in his house three hundreth wiues, besides a great number of concubines: they goe all gallantly apparelled, and with rich iewels, of the which there are of great estimation in that kingdome, they do almost euerie three daies change newe colors of apparell. They do ordinarily vse colors of precious stones, such as are called in Spaine *ojo de gato*, cats eies. They haue great store of saphires, pearles, diamonds, rubies, and many other stones, that are in that kingdome in great abundance.

Amongest all these wiues there is one that is as legitimate, whose children doo inherite: and if it so fall out that she is barren, the first that is borne of any of the other doth inherite: which is the occasion that they neuer lacke a successor in that kingdome.

When the king of this kingdome doth die, they do carrie him foorth into a mightie fielde, with great sadnesse and mourning apparell, and there in the presence of those twelue peeres afore saide, they do burne his bodie with wood of sandalo, which is of a great smell, with the which they do make a great fire.

After that the bodie of the king is burned and consumed, they throwe into the same the wiues that hee best loued, with seruants and slaues, those that he most esteemed in his lifetime: the which they do with so great content, that euery one dooth procure to be the first for to enter into the fire, and they that are last do thinke themselues vnhappie. All these do say that they go to serue the king in the other life, whereas they shalbe with great ioy. This is the occasion that they goe with so good a will to die, and carrie with them the most richest and festiuall apparell they haue. Of this is gathered that they do beleeue the immortalitie of the soule, for that they doo confesse there is another life, and that thither they do returne and liue for euer without ende. They are people that would be conuerted with the like facilitie vnto the holy gospell as their neighbours, if there went any thether to preach.

Three score and tenne leagues from this citie, there is a pagode or temple of idols, whereas is a rich faire euery yeare: it is a very sumptuous building, and edified in a place so high, that it may be seene many leagues before you come vnto it.

It hath ordinarily foure thousande men of garde, who are paid with the rent of the temple, the which is rich and verye good. There is nigh vnto the same many mynes of golde and precious stones, and that is taken out of them is rent vnto the temple. There is in it a priest of the idolles, whom they call in their language Brama, and is as the high priest in that countrie. All the people of the land do come vnto him, to vnderstand the doubtes of their manner of liuing,

KINGDOME OF CHINA.   327

and he doth dispence with them in many things that be prohibited by their lawes, the which he may do according vnto the sayd lawes, and manie times he doth dispence certaine of them. But here one to be laughed at, which is, that when a woman cannot suffer the condition of her husbande, or is wearie of him for other occasions, she goeth vnto this Brama, and giuing vnto him a peece of golde, which may be to the value of a ducat in Spaine, he doth vnmarry them, and setteth her at libertie that she may marry with an other, or with many if she please : and in token of this she is giuen a marke with an yron vpon her right shoulder, so that with that alone she remaineth at libertie, and her husband cannot do vnto her any harme for the same, neither compell her to returne againe to his company. *A strange custome.*

There are in this kingdome many mynes of verie fine diamonds, and are had in great estimation, and very well knowen in Europe. There hath beene found in them a stone of so fine and of so great value, that but few yeares past, the king did sell the same vnto an other mightie king his borderer, called Odialcan, for a million of golde, besides other thinges of value that hee gaue him ouer and aboue.[1] It is a healthfull countrie, with very good and fresh ayres, rich of prouisions, and of all other necessaries, not only for the humane life, but also for curiositie and delightes that be therein. It is in fourteene degrees towardes the pole artico. All the people therein are faint-hearted and cowards, and for little trauaile, which is the occasion that they are nothing affectionate vnto warres, and is vnderstoode with great facilitie they would receiue the gospell. *A diamond sold for a million of gold.*

Nigh vnto the same there is an other little kingdome

---

[1] This is in all probability the great diamond mentioned by Tavernier, vol. ii, p. 249, as being in the possession of the Great Mogul. It was found in the washings near Caldore, to the east of Golconda, about the year 1550. Professor Tennant, in his lecture on "Gems" before the Society of Arts, expresses his opinion that the Koh-i-noor formed a portion of this large diamond.

called Mana, in the which there is a towne with Portingals, the which is called in their language Negapatan; there is in the same a conuent of the order of S. Francis, whose religious friers, although they are but few, do occupie themselues in the converting of the naturall people thereof, and it is to be beleeued that they shall reape much fruite and doo good, for they haue giuen showes of the same: for that about three yeares past the prince of that countrie was conuerted by the preaching of the same fryers, who went now to receiue the holy baptisme with great and incredible ioy vnto the Christians. All the rest of the kingdoms (as it is beleeued) will shortly imitate him. In this iland there are many pearls and aliofar, al very good, round, and fine.

CHAP. XXV.

This chapter treateth of manie kingdomes of that newe worlde, the rites and customes of the inhabitants, and of some curious thinges.

<small>Ilandes of Nicobar.</small> The afore saide father Martin Ignacio, departed with his companions from this cost, and went towards the Ilands of Nicobar, whereas are many Moores and gentiles, al mingled the one with the other. They did not stay there, but presently passed to the town of Cuylan, which is inhabited with Portingals, and from Malaca foure hundred and sixteene leagues. This iland is situated from sixe vnto ten degrees vnder our pole, and hath in longitude three score and sixe leagues, and nine and thirtie of latitude. Of old time it was an iland much celebrated, and in those partes had in great reuerence, for that it is saide that there dwelt and died there in times past, men, whose soules are in heauen, and are celebrated and honoured by them of the countrie as though

they were gods, with many sacrifices and orations, the which they do ordinarily. There come from other kingdomes bordering thereupon, vnto this ilande, many pilgrimes; but our people could neuer vnderstand the ground and occasion thereof, neither how they liued, whom they doo hold for saints. There is vpon the same iland a very high mountaine, which is called Pico de Adan, which father Martin did see, and did heare the naturall people thereof say, that it had that name, for that by the same Adam went vp into heauen; but what Adam it was they could not declare.

There is on this Pico like a monasterie, the which the naturall people doo call pagode: at one time they had therein an apes tooth, the which they did worship for their God: *An apes tooth for a god.* and there came thither vnto that effect some two hundred and three hundred leagues. [It so happened, in the yeare 1554, the vizroy of India, called Don Pedro Mascarenas, sent an army vnto this kingdome, with many Portugals, with intent to reduce them vnto the obedience of the king of Portugall, all of that country, as they were before, who few yeares past did rise against them, and tooke away and denied their fewter.[1] The souldiers did sack that pagoda or monastery, and thinking to finde some treasure therein, they broke it, and beat it downe vnto the foundation: and there they found the aforesaid apes tooth, the which they did worship, put in a chest of golde and stones, and carried it vnto Goa, vnto the said vizroy. When that this was vnderstood and knowne to other kings their borderers, and vnto him of Pegu, of this losse (the which of them was iudged to bee great) they sent their ambassadors to the said vizroy, that they might in the name of them all, demaunde the saide tooth, the which they

---

[1] The passage inserted between brackets is supplied by the translator from the French of De la Porte. The clause of the sentence thus strangely translated is as follows: " pour le reduire à l'obeyssance de la couronne de Portugal, comme il estoit auparavant et de la quelle il s'étoit soustrait depuis peu d'années par une rébellion générale."

did worship, and to offer for the ransome thereof seuen hundred thousand ducats of gold. The viceroy would haue giuen it them for that quantitie of gold which they did offer, and would haue done it in effect, if it had not bin for the archbishop of Goa, who was called Don Gaspar, and other religious men, who did disturbe him, putting great scrupulositie, and laide vnto his charge the hurt that come by their idolatrie, in giuing them the same, of the which he should giue a straight account vnto God. The which did so much in him, that he dispatched away the ambassador, without any regard of the gold that they would haue giuen him in their presence: he did deliuer the same vnto the said archbishop and religious men, and they before their eies did break it, and burnt it, and threw the dust thereof into the sea, which was not a little woonder vnto the said embassadors, to see how little they did esteeme so great a quantitie of golde, and for a thing which they esteemed not, but threw it into the sea with so great liberalitie.]

This ilande is fertile, peaceable, and healthfull, and all full of woods, and there are mountaines very thicke of orange trees, siders, limas, plantanos, and palmas, and many synamon trees, which be the best in all the world, and of most strength and effect, for the which they go to buy, for to bring it vnto Europe, and they giue it for a small price. Likewise there is pepper, but the naturall people did pull vp certaine hils that were ful of it, and of sinamon, because they saw there came from farre to buy these two commodities, and fearing that it would be an occasion that their country would be taken from them. It is a countrie of great prouision, and doth bring foorth mightie elephants, and they say that there is many mynes of diamonds, rubies, and other stones that are called girasolis. In no part of this Orientall Indies, there was none of so good a beginning in the conuersion of the soules, as was in this iland: for that certaine religious friers of the order of S. Francis did labor very much, and did baptise in a few daies more than fiftie thousand soules, which gaue to vnderstand that with a verie good will they did receiue the law of the gospell, and had edified many churches, and fourteene monasteries of the same religion : but few yeares past, a king of that kingdome, being weary of certaine things, which in all that Indians are very publicke, he forsooke the religion and faith he had receiued, and did raise and destroy many Portingals that were there inhabited, thrusting forth all the religious men that did baptise, and minister the sacraments. This euill king was called Raxu. Many of them that were christened, and content with the faith of Iesus Christ they had receiued, detesting that which this tirannous king had done, they went and dwelt in the company of the Portingals, and others did build a town, the which is called in their language Columbo, whereas is a great number of them : vnto this day do indure throughout al that kingdom the crosses, in token of their ancient Christianitie : alongst all the coast they doe vse many galiotas or gallyes, and goe with them, robbing and spoyling al thereaboutes. The naturall people doo say, that with a good will they would againe returne and receiue the law of the gospell, if they had it there preached. From this iland, after they had passed a little gulfe, they came vpon the coast of a kingdome called Tutucurin, and ran all alongest the cost of the same, running from the cape of Comerin to Cuylan. Here there is a pagode or temple of their gods very great and rich, thether come all the gentiles of that kingdom, at certain feasts in the year with great deuotion : there is in it a triumphant chariot, so great that twentie horse cannot mooue it, they bring it foorth in publike vpon their festiual daies, and is carried by elephants, and by an infinite number of men, who voluntarily do hale and pull at certaine roapes that are made fast therunto. Upon the highest of this chariot is made a tabernacle very richly adorned, and within the same an idol, whom they do worship : then immediately vnder the same are the kings wiues that go singing. They doo bring it forth with much musicke and reioysings, and do carry it a good way in procession, and amongest many thinges of honor that they doo vnto it, they do vse one so brute and beastly as the reader may well iudge thereof, which is, that many of them doo cut peeces of their owne fleshe and doo throwe it vnto the idoll, and the other, not contented with this, doo throwe themselues on the grounde that the chariot may passe ouer them, and there they remaine all to peeces. Those that do die in this sort, they account them for great saints, and are had in singular veneration. Many other maners and fashions of idolatrie is declared of this kingdome, and more beastly than this we haue spoken of, the which I let passe because I would not be tedious in this itinerario. All the people of this kingdom be very bad and ill inclined, for which cause the fathers of the company of Iesus, that are in certaine townes nigh vnto the same, cannot as yet bring them out of their errors, although they haue put therein great care and diligence.

Upon the same cost, and a little distant from this kingdom, there is a towne of Portingals called Coulan, and twentie-fiue leagues further a citie which is called Cochin, in the which there are religious men of St. Francis, of S. Dominicke, and of S. Austin, and of the companie of Iesus, who haue there a very good studie or seminarie, whereas they do bring foorth much fruite. Nigh vnto this citie is Santo Tome, whereas are many baptised and good Christians, very abstinent and chast, vnto whom the patriarkes of Babylon doo prouide them of bishops: the authoritie where with they do it is not knowen, nor whence they haue it, for that as I do vnderstand, seat apostolicke did neuer giue it them. About the same matter, at this present there is in Rome a bishop of this kingdome, and one of the kingdome of Pimienta, with whom I haue talked diuers times, and is come thether to giue his obedience vnto the pope, and to knowe of him the order that his pleasure is should be obserued, in receiuing of those bishops which come thether by the commandement of the patriarke. In this kingdome there are many kings, but the principallest of them is he of Cochin, and next vnto him, he of Coulan, and nigh vnto them are many petie kings, as is hee of Mangate and Cranganor, and are all gentils, although amongst them there are mixed many Moores. There hath bin found in this kingdome certaine Iewes, that haue gone from Palestina and those parts. There is in this countrie vniuersally, a lawe verie strange and little heard of, which is, that the sonnes doo not inherite after their fathers, but his brothers sonne, and the reason they giue for the same is, for that they haue no certaintie of their children, for that they haue no wiues proper nor appointed to themselues, I promise you it seemeth to me, their reason to be as barbarous as their law, for that the like inconuenience doth folow their brothers children. They haue many rites and blindnes amongst them, but one aboue all the rest, which is, that in certaine feastes amongst them, they do vse bathes, and after that they are bathed, they say that they remaine free and cleare from all their sinnes. They haue many augorismes, of whom I will not intreat, for that they are not worthy of memorie. In this country is gathered most of the pepper that is brought into Europe, for which cause this kingdome is called that of the Pimienta.

CHAP. XXVI.

The chapter doth treate of many kingdomes of the Newe World, and of the particular and curious things of them.

<small>The kingdome of Cananor, Tanaor, and Calicart.</small> The aforesaid father went from Cochin to the kingdome of Cananor, and passed by Tanaor and Calicut, which is called of the naturall people Malabar, they are like kingdomes, but in them much people. In that of Cananor, there are inhabited many Portingals and religious men of the order of S. Francis: it is a countrie in all things like vnto Cochin, for which cause, and for that they obserue and keepe one maner of customs and rites, I remit the touching of this kingdome to the other aforesaide.

Then forwards on there are other two small kingdoms, the one is called Barcelor, and the other, Mangalor; there be in them some Christians: it is a good countrie and rich, and hath it for certaine, that within a little time they will be all baptised. From this kingdome they went vnto Goa, a principall citie, and inhabited with Portingals, and is as the metropolitan of all those kingdomes: it is in fifteen degrees of height, and is set from Cochin vnto it a hundreth leagues, this citie is situated in a little iland, compassed round about with water, and in compasse but onely four leagues, and is diuided from the firme land of Odialcan by a mightie riuer. It is a good countrie and peaceable, and doth inioy a very faire and pleasant riuer. In this citie ordinarily is resident the viceroy of the India and the archbishoppe: there are many churches and conuents; and besides the high church, there are fourteene parish churches, besides fifteen hermitages that are within and without the citie: there be four conuents, all very sumptuous, of S. Dominicke, of S. Austin, of S. Francis, and of the company of Iesus. And without the cittie there is another of *Recoletos Franciscanos*, reformed Francis friers.

Nigh vnto this iland are those of Salcete and Bardes, there *Ilandes Salcete and Bardes.* whereas the religious men of S. Francis, and the companie of Iesus haue certaine Christian townes. Few yeares past, the Gentiles of Sancete[1] did kill certaine fathers of the company of Iesus, in abhorring the faith, who died with great spirite and strength: so that I beleeue they went into ioy with God.

Beyond Goa, on the same coast towardes the north, is in eighteene degrees and a halfe from the towne of Chaul, and beyond that Basayn, and nigh thereunto Damaun; all these three townes are inhabited with Portugals; and the farthest is the prouince of Cambaya, subiect vnto the grand Tartar, or Mogor, by an other name. Two and fortie leagues beyond that is the cittie called Diu, whereas is a very faire and good fortresse of Portugals, with a very great hauen and sure, whose name doth extend throughout all Turkey. *The towne of Chaul, Basayn, Damaun, Cambaya.* *The cittie of Diu.*

Two hundred and seuentie leagues beyond that is the citie of Oromuz, on the coast of Persia, and in the same hath the saide Portugals an other fortresse, much better then that of Diu, and more inexpugnable: it is the biggest in al the Indians, but not of so great name as that of Diu. In this cittie of Oromuz they gather nothing else but salt, and that in great aboundance; yet, notwithstanding, it is replenished of all that may be imagined, for that there is brought thither from Persia and Arabia great prouision, and many other curiosities. They say, that from this place they may easily go to Venice, taking their way to Aleph, and to Tripoli in Soria. *The cittie of Oromuz.*

All this coast of the Indias vnto Persia is inhabited with many and mightie kingdomes, in which there are an infinite number of people: one of them is that of Odialon, the which is very rich, and of much people, and all Moores. Nigh vnto this is another called Disamaluco, harde by the kingdome of the great Tartar, which, in their language, is called *Odialon.*

---

[1] Misspelt for Salcete—Salsette.

Mogor. Mogor, the which, next vnto that of China (I doo thinke), is the greatest in all the world, as may be collected in that which is declared of the mightinesse thereof, both in ancient and latter histories. On the other side of Oromuz is

Persia. the kingdome of Persia, whose king is Xactamas, or Ismael Sophi, great Soldan of Egypt, descending by lyneall desent from the Soldan, Campson Guario, whom Selim, emperor of the Tartaros did ouercome in battell, nigh vnto Damasco, in the yeare 1516.

All those of this kingdome are Moores, although they and the Turkes are as the Christians and heretikes, for that the Persians do follow the interpretation of the lawe of Mahomet of certain alies, or doctors. And the Turkes go a different way, and do follow others. This contractation and different interpretation of the lawe, is the occasion that betwixt the one and the other there is ordinarily cruell warres: and it is the great mercy of God, for that the Turke may not haue any space to come and do euil vnto his Christians; or if he do come, he shall be ouertaken with the Persians, his enimy the Sophi, and intrapped with all the euill that they can do vnto him: who that although he be a Moore, and of the sect of Mahomet, yet he is a friend vnto Christians.

CHAP. XXVII.

Of other kingdomes and notable things that are vntill you come into Spaine, and to conclude, the compassing of the world.

Arabia Felix. Neere unto the straite of Oromuz is Arabia Felix, where as all the inhabitants are of the sect of Mahomet, and doo follow the same interpretation that the Sophi doth. So running a long by Arabia, you come straight vnto the Red *The Red Sea.* Sea, or Arabico, the which hath foure hundred and fiftie leagues of longitude, and in some partes it is of a mightie depth: the water thereof seemeth to bee red, although taking it out thereof it is white: the cause thereof is for that the ground vnder the water is of the same colour. By reason whereof, when as the sun doth shine thereon it seemeth red, and thereby it hath got the name the which it hath vnto this day. By this sea, and by that of Basora, the great Turk doth carrie much spicerie, silkes, and cloth of golde, and all riches out of the orientall Indias, the which may easily be disturbed, but the way how is not for this place nor time. On the other side is the land of Abexin, which is that of *The land of Abexin that* Prester John, a kingdome although it is very great, yet it *of Prester Iohn.* extendeth very litle on this coast. From this kingdome or poynt, going to the southwest, is six hundreth leagues to Mazanbique, whereas there is inhabitance of Portingals. All this coast is black people, gentiles, and idolaters, and is in fifteene degrees in altitude towardes the south, and in the same maner are all the rest that are inhabited from Mazan- *Mazan-biqua.* bique vnto the Cape of Buena Esperansa. They are without memorie of the preaching of the gospel; if that God for his mercy doe not take pitie on them, and put into the heartes of some to goe thither, and to procure the remedie of so infinite nnmber of soules.

So after the sayd father had informed himselfe of all that is sayde, and of many other thinges more, which is left out for to euitate tediousnes, till such time as of them may bee made a particular historie, hee departed from Goa and Cochin towardes Portingall, and passed by the Ilandes of Maldivia, *The Ilands of Maldivia* which are many, and all are inhabited with Moores, nigh vnto the which they doe enter the poole Antartico, crossing the equinoctiall from the coast of Arabia; from thence they sayled with a faire winde till they came right against the Iland of Saint Lorenso, which is very great, for that it hath *The Ilands of S. Lorenso.*

two hundreth seuentie and fiue leagues of longitude, and fourescore and tenne of latitude; all inhabited with much people, very quiet and ciuile: the faith of Christ was neuer preached amongest them; yet I doo belieue that if it were, they would quietly receiue the same. Passing from this ilande, they came vnto the Cape of Buena Esperansa, the which is another very good iland, whose inhabitants and dwellers are much like to those of Saint Lorenzo: it is in the temperate zona, and nigh vnto the straights of Magellanes. This Cape of Buena Esperansa is called by another name, the Cape Tormentorio: it is fiue and thirtie degrees large from the pole antartico. And from Cochin vnto this cape they put one thousand three hundred fiftie and eight leagues, that way which they do ordinarily nauigate. When they doo passe by this cape, they were wont to have great and strong winds. They go from thence to the Iland of S. Elena, which is beyond the cape forwards, fiue hundred and seuentie leagues. It is not inhabited with people, but full of swine, goats, and great aboundance of partriges, and in all the coast is great store of fish, the which is taken with great ease; it is but a little iland, and hath circuit no more than fiue leagues.

marginalia: The Cape of Buena Esperansa.
marginalia: The Ilande of S. Elena.

From this ilande they do nauigate foure hundred leagues vntil they come vnder the equinoctiall, vpon the coast of Guinea, returning vnto the pole artike, in foure and forty degrees in altitude (which was almost at the same place from whence he departed at his gooing forth) after hee compassed the world. They passed in sight of the lande, and from thence they sayled forwards and sawe other land, vntill they came vnto Lisborne, hauing (after they had crossed the equinoctiall) sayled a thousand foure hundred and fiftie leagues. So that after the aforesaid father, Frier Martin Ignacio, had made his account of all that he had trauelled from the time he departed from Siuel, til he returned vnto Lysborne, in compassing the world, he found that it was nine thousand

marginalia: Guinea.

and forty leagues by sea and by lande, besides many other leagues that he trauelled in China and in other parts, of the which hee dooth make no account. All these leagues are full of mightie kingdomes, and al, or the most part of them, are subiect vnto the tyranny of Lucyfer. God, for his infinite mercy, conuert them, and take pittie on them, as hee did when that he came from heauen vppon the earth to die for all, and put into the heart of the king of Spaine, that, amongst other good workes, the which, with his most Christian zeale dooth intend and do, for to procure this, which will be so much vnto the glory of God, and great desert of honor vnto himselfe, the which he may do very commodiously, being, as he is at this day, Lord of all the Indies, and of the biggest part of all that newe world.

This petition is worthy, that all we Christians doo desire of God, for that his holy name in all the world may be praised and exalted; and the sonnes of Adam, who for their sinnes are so dispersed and forgotten of God, and first beginning, they may go and inioy the happy and glorious kingdome for the which they were created.

FINIS.

INDEX.

Abexin, the kingdom of Prestyr John, ii, 337
Abulfeda, i; ignorance of, respecting China, vi
Acapulco, ii, 223, 253
Adultery, law respecting, i, 63
Agriculture, ii, 56
Aguizi, i, 72
Aguila, an odoriferous wood, i, 58; ii, 303
Alazan, i, 51
Alfaro, Pedro de, visits China as a missionary, lxxiv; arrives at Manilla, ii, 125; his desire to visit China, ii, 126; conversion of a Chinese priest by, ii, 127; opposition of the governor to his proposal, ii, 128; his unsuccessful attempt to reach China, ii, 129; his second attempt, ii, 132; his companions, ii, 134; they meet with a storm, ii, 135; arrive at an island, ii, 136; their escape from the Chinese guardships, ii, 137; they reach Canton, ii, 140; enter the city, ii, 141; an interview with a judge, ii, 144; the interpreters' version of their story, ii, 145; they are examined again, ii, 149, 152; treachery of the interpreters, ii, 155; jealousy shown by the Portuguese at Machao, ii, 158; necessitous condition of their party, ii, 161; a stipend allowed them by the viceroy, ii, 161; they are sent to Aucheo, ii, 165; their arrival, ii, 167; reception by the viceroy, ii, 168; they return to Canton, ii, 180; ill feeling of the captain-general of Machao towards them, ii, 184; his plans defeated, ii, 185; Alfaro and some of his party arrive at Machao, ii, 194; the others go to Chincheo, ii, 198; and return to Manilla, ii, 204
Alvarado, A. de, ii, 28
Amazons, island of the, ii, 301
Ambassadors, reception of, i, 157
Ameias, province of, ii, 245
Anchasi, office of the, i, 102

Anchosan, i, 72
Andrade, F. Peres d', his voyage to China, xxxi
Andrade, Simon d', sent to China with a Portuguese fleet, xxxiv
Animals of China, ii, 285
Annals of China, sketch of the early, i, 69
Anthey, i, 73
Anthrey, i, 72
Antoninus, embassy to China sent by the emperor, iii
Ape's tooth, worshipped in Ceylon, ii, 329; its destruction by the Portuguese viceroy, ii, 330
Arab merchants, early account of China by, iii
Arabia Felix, ii, 336
Aracan, kingdom of, ii, 321
Archipelago, ii, 258
Arms used by the Chinese, ii, 288
Army of China, weakness of, lxxviii, lxxx; description of, i, 90; reviews of, ii, 102; its numbers, ii, 288; its pay, ii, 289
Arracon, see Aracan
Artillery, early acquaintance of the Chinese with the use of, i, 129
Artreda, letter by, on the arms of the Chinese, i, 130
Atzion, i, 51
Aucheo, ii, 75, 78, 85, 167
Auchin, i, 75
Aucon, ii, 113
Augury by lot, i, 46; ii, 262
Ayas, xvi.
Aynao, see Hainan
Aytao, office of the, i, 102
Aytim, ii, 201, 221

Banbosa, see Barbosa
Banquets, i, 137
Barba, a Tartar chief, xv
Barbosa, Duarte, i, 33
Barcelor, ii, 334
Bardes, islands of, ii, 335
Basayn, ii, 335
Batala, an idol, ii, 261

Bausa, i, 74
Beads, used in praying, i, 57
Begging, prohibition of, i, 66
Bells, ringing of, i, 57
Bemthey, i, 73
Bengal, kingdom of, ii, 322
Benjamin of Tudela, his reference to China, vii
Bindoro, ii, 130
Blind persons, constrained to work, i, 68
Boneg, i, 75
Bonze, a word of Portuguese origin, ii, 162
Books obtained by Herrada, i, 134
Bouchier, G., Mechanical apparatus constructed by, xi
Boxeador, cape of, ii, 268
Brama, chief priest in Visnaga so called, ii, 326; his power of dispensation, ii, 327
Bridges, lvii
Buena Esperansa, cape of, ii, 888
Buliano, ii, 31
Burgos, G. de, ii, 268
Burial of the dead, i, 59; ii, 291; of the kings of Visnaga, ii, 326
Burneo, isle of, ii, 261

Cabile, ii, 15
Cabite, ii, 268
Cagayan, river of, ii, 131
Calamina, see Malipur
Calicut, ii, 334
Camels used in the Canaries, ii, 214
Cambaya, province of, ii, 335
Camboia, kingdom of, ii, 311; crosses erected in, 313
Campeachy, ii, 222
Cananor, ii, 334
Canary Isles, derivation of their name, ii, 209; description of, ii, 209, 213
Canasia, see Hang-cheou
Canfu, vi
Cannafistola, a Malay fruit, ii, 318
Cannibals, effect of a friar upon, ii, 215
Canton, vi; ii, 140
Capital punishment, i, 119
Capsonson, ii, 270
Caraci, city of the, x
Caribs, their cannibal propensities, ii, 214; effect of a Spanish friar upon them, 215
Carpini, John de Plano, Chinese described by, viii
Cassava, bread made of, ii, 218
Cattle, abundance of in Mexico, ii, 227
Cavalry, description of Chinese, i, 88
Cavendish, T., the navigator, R. Parke's letter to, i, 1

Ceremonies at a deathbed, ii, 290; at burials, 291
Ceylon, ii, 328; fertility of, 330; progress of Christianity there, 331
Chabes, P. de, ii, 21
Chacon, L., ii, 21
Champa, kingdom of, ii, 311
Characters used in Chinese writing, i, 121
Chaul, ii, 335
Chautubo, ii, 112
Cheapness of provisions in China, ii, 285
Chichimecho Indians, ii, 226
Chimbutey, i, 73
CHINA, known to the Romans, iii; early account of by two Arab merchants, iii; observations of Edrisi on, vi; reference to by Benjamin of Tudela, vii; visited by Marco Polo, xvi; by G. de Monte Corvino, xxii; by O. de Pordenone, xxiii; by Ibn Batuta, xxvi; the embassy sent to Cathay by Mirza Shah Rokh, xxvii; voyage thither of a Portuguese fleet, xxxi; failure of the Portuguese embassy, xxxvi; visit of F. Mendez Pinto to China, xxxvii; account of the customs and laws of the empire in 1555, xxxix; visited by G. da Cruz, li; described by G. Pereyra, liii; visited by Spanish missionaries, lxix; described by Herrada, lxxii; Alfaro's voyage there, lxxiv; observations on the empire by M. Ricci, lxxvii; by G. Roman, lxxix; Mendoza's description of China, i, 8; its climate, i, 11; fertility, i, 12; productions, i, 14; antiquity of the kingdom, i, 18; its extent, i, 20; provinces, i, 21; cities, i, 23; the great wall, i, 28; sketch of the early annals of China, i, 69; account of the Emperor Vitey, i, 70; the royal palace, i, 77; number of payers of tribute, i, 80; amount of tribute paid, i, 82; the army, i, 86; military strength of the empire, i, 90; law against undertaking foreign wars, i, 92; against leaving the kingdom, i, 93; against the admission of strangers, i, 94; the royal council of state, i, 96; the chief officers of state, i, 101; how chosen, i, 106; ministers of justice, i, 107; legal proceedings, i, 109; tortures, i, 111; watch kept over the conduct of the judges, i, 112; rewards and punishments awarded them, i, 115; Mendoza's embassy to China, i, 162; expedition of M. de Herrada to China,

INDEX. 343

ii, 29; his arrival, ii, 37; he visits Tansuso, ii, 44; Tong-gan, ii, 58; Chincheo, ii, 59; Aucheo, ii, 78; their return to Manilla, ii, 111; expedition of Alfaro and other Augustines to China, ii, 132; they arrive at Canton, ii, 140; are sent to Aucheo, ii, 165; they return to Canton, ii, 180; some of the party go to Machao, ii, 194; the rest return to Manilla, ii, 204; expedition of Martin Ignatius and other Franciscan friars to China, ii, 207; they leave Spain, ii, 208; arrive at the Canaries, ii, 209; Desseado and Dominica, ii, 214; two of the party killed by the Caribs, ii, 214; they reach Puerto Rico, ii, 216; and Hispaniola, ii, 217; description of Cuba, ii, 220; of Mexico, ii, 223; they visit the Ladrone Isles, ii, 254; the Philippines, ii, 258; they sail for China, ii, 268; their arrival, ii, 269; they are taken to Quixue, ii, 274; examined there, ii, 276; sent to Sancheo-fu, ii, 277; to Hucheo-fu, ii, 279; return of Ignatius home, ii, 310

Chincheo, ii, 59

CHINESE, described by Carpini, viii; by Rubruquis, xii; account of their laws and customs, related in the College of Jesuits, Malacca, in 1555, xxxix; by G. Pereyra, liii; their houses, xl; prisons, xliii; feasts, xlv; costume, l; bridges, lvii; religion, lxi; punishments, lxiii; origin of the name of China, lxiv; hospitals, lxv; their cowardice, lxviii; the navy, lxxix; complexion of the Chinese, i, 11, 20; their dwellings, i, 27; dress, i, 30; description of the Chinese women, i, 31; the porcelain manufacture, i, 33; the currency, i, 34; the idols, i, 36; the principal saints, i, 41; augury by lots, i, 46; devil-invocation, i, 49; Chinese mythology, i, 50; doctrine on the immortality of the soul, i, 53; the temples and religious orders, i, 54; their beads and bells, i, 57; funeral rites, i, 59; mourning apparel, i, 61; marriage customs and ceremonies, i, 62; law of inheritance, i, 63; punishment of adulterers, i, 63; singular marriage custom in Tartary, i, 63; marriage of the emperor, and princes of the blood, i, 65; maintenance of the poor, i, 67; condition of the blind, i, 68; payers of tribute numbered, i, 81; no subjects allowed to travel without a license, i, 93; jealousy of foreigners, i, 94; legal proceedings, i, 107; tortures, i, 111; prisons, i, 116; punishment of criminals, i, 119; characters used in writing, i, 121; the same characters common to different languages, i, 121; schools, i, 122; knowledge acquired by all classes, i, 122; paper and pens, i, 123; examination for the degree of Loytia, i, 125; how it is conferred, i, 126; early use of artillery in China, i, 129; art of printing early practised there, i, 131; books obtained by Herrada, i, 134; banquets, i, 137; festivals, i, 139; modes of salutation, i, 141; courtesy to women, i, 144; seclusion of their women, i, 145; courtesans, i, 146; shipping, i, 148; fishing boats, i, 151; breeding of ducks, i, 153; birds used for fishing, i, 155; reception of ambassadors, i, 156; compasses used in China, ii, 37; use of chopsticks, ii, 47; carriers of baggage, ii, 55; agriculture, ii, 57; highways, ii, 58; fruits, ii, 60; a Chinese entertainment, ii, 72, 87; a Drama, ii, 88, 104; presents to public officers forbidden, ii, 90; idols, ii, 91; a review of the troops, ii, 102; presentation of petitions, ii, 103; jealousy of strangers, ii, 139, 142; administration of justice, ii, 153; physiognomy, ii, 163; ploughing, ii, 166; invocation of devils, ii, 203; method of irrigation, ii, 279; shipping, ii, 284; mines, ii, 286; silk, ii, 287; arms and army, ii, 288; religious ceremonies, ii, 289; funeral rites, ii, 291; character of the people, ii, 293

Chop sticks, ii, 47

Christianity, conversion of Chinese to, ii, 122; of the Philippine islanders, ii, 126; said to have been introduced by St. Thomas, ii, 290

Chyley, i, 73

Cia, ii, 245

Cibao, mines of, ii, 217

Cibola, ii, 246

Cincoan, i, 73

Cinsones, ii, 229

Cities of China enumerated, i, 23

Climate of China, i, 11

Coanty, i, 72

Cochin, ii, 332

Cochin China, description of, ii, 303; picture sent to king by a friar, ii, 304; desire of king of to embrace Christianity, ii, 305; miracles wrought there, ii, 306

Cochin Chinese, description of, ii, 310
Columbo, in Ceylon, ii, 331
Comedy in China, ii, 88, 105
Compass used by Chinese, ii, 37
Compulsary marriage in Tartary, i, 63
Concham, i, 75
Congreve, his mention of F. Mendez Pinto, xxxvii
Conjurations against devils, ii, 135
Conversion of Philippine islanders, ii, 263; of Japanese, 299
Copper money, i, 35
Corchu, ii, 112
Cormorants, fishing with, i, 155
Coromandel, kingdom of, ii, 324
Cortes, Hernando, his reverence for priests, ii, 230
Cosmos, an intoxicating liquor described by Rubriquis, xiii
Costume of the Chinese, 1; of state officers, i, 102; ii, 144
Cotey, i, 74
Cotino, A., ii, 160
Coulan, ii, 332
Council, the royal, i, 96
Courts of justice, ii, 276
Courtesans, i, 146
Cowardice of the Chinese, lxxviii
Cranganor, ii, 333
Cripples, laws for maintenance of, i, 67
Crosses, erected by Mexican Indians, ii, 242; also in Cochin China, ii, 306, and in Camboia, ii, 313
Cruz, Gaspar da, visits China as a missionary, li
Cuba, ii, 220; treasures thrown into the sea by the natives of, ii, 221
Cubun, i, 72
Cuenca, N. de, ii, 34
Cumdan, vi
Cuntey, i, 72
Cuylan, *see* Ceylon
Cyan, *see* Siam

Damaun, ii, 335
Debt, law of, in the Philippines, ii, 261
Debtors, law against, i, 111
Desert beyond the wall of China, ii, 283
Desseado, island of, ii, 214
Devil worship in China, i, 41, 48; ii, 26; in Mexico, 242
Devotees, penance of, ii, 314
Diamond mines of Visnaga, ii, 327
Dignitaries of state, i, 101
Disamaluco, ii, 335
Diu, ii, 335
Divorce, law of in Visnaga, ii, 327
Dogs, great numbers of, found in the Canary isles, ii, 209

Dominica, island of, ii, 214; ferocity of the natives, ii, 215
Dowry given by the husband in China, i, 62
Drama, description of a Chinese, ii, 88, 104
Ducks, breeding of, i, 153
Duennas, F. de, one of Alfaro's companions, ii, 134
Durion, a Malay fruit, ii, 318

Eclipses, Chinese explanation of, ii, 291
Eden, Richard, his History of Travayle in the West and East Indies, ii
Edrisi, the Arabian geographer, his observations on China, vi
Education of the poor, i, 122
Elephant; war between Pegu and Siam for an, ii, 321
Emperor of China, seldom seen in public, i, 79; his concubines marry on his death, i, 65; lord of the entire soil of the empire, i, 79
Entertainment, description of a Chinese, ii, 72, 87
Espeio, A. de, his expedition into New Mexico, ii, 234
Examinations in learning, i, 125
Executions, i, 119
Extirpation of the natives of Hispaniola, ii, 218
Ezoulom, i, 51

Faxiuandono, ii, 298
Feather pictures of the Mexicans, ii, 229
Feria, J. de, ii, 268
Fernandina, ii, 10
Ferro, the water-distilling tree of, ii, 210, 211, *note*
Fertility of China, i, 12; ii, 285
Festivals, i, 139
Fires, precautions against, i, 104
Fishing, xxiv, lxvi
Fishing vessels, i, 151
Fontey, i, 74
Forster, J. Reinhold, his opinion concerning the site of Karakorum, xix
Fruits of China, ii, 60; of Malacca, ii, 318
Fucheo, i, 27
Fuco, described by O. de Pordenone, xxiii
Funeral rites on the death of an Emperor's wife, xxx
Futey, i, 72

INDEX.   345

Gahai, ii, 44
Ganges, account of an attempt to discover the source of the, ii, 332; reverence paid to its water, ii, 323
Gaspar, Archbishop of Goa, ii, 330
Gautin, ii, 112
Geese, flocks of, ii, 166
Giuzza, xvi
Goa, ii, 329, 334
Gombu, i, 75
Goyti, M. de, ii, 13
Guanser, i, 73
Guansian, i, 73
Guardships, ii, 137
Gubates, ii, 251
Guertas, ii, 216
Guetaria, S. de, ii, 259
Guinea, ii, 338
Guntey, i, 72
Gutemberg, J., i, 131

Hainan, isle of, ii, 283, 303
Hang-Cheou, described by Marco Polo, xxi; by O. de Pordenone, xxiv
Hatuey, ii, 221
Havanna, ii, 220
Hermit, a Chinese, ii, 292
Herrada, Martin de, his account of China, lxxi; books obtained by, i, 134; his desire to visit China, ii. 5; meets Omoncon, ii, 25; is sent to China with H. Martin, ii, 29; their voyage, ii, 31; arrival at Tituhul, ii, 37; adventures there, ii, 40; first landing, ii, 45; they leave Tansuso, ii, 50; reach Tangoa, ii, 53; Chincheo, ii, 59; audience with the governor, ii, 65; arrival at Aucheo, ii, 78; their difficulties, ii, 92; examination, ii, 101; return to Manilla, ii, 119
Highways, xli; ii, 59
Hilocos, the, ii, 10, 31
Hing-hoa, seized by the Japanese, ii, 75
Hispaniola, island of, described, ii, 217; extirpation of the natives of, ii, 218
Holgoi, witches so called, ii, 262
Horses, excellence of Mexican, ii, 225
Hortiz, Sancho, ii, 17
Hospitals, lxv; i, 67
Houses, description of Chinese, xl; i, 26
Hucheofu, ii, 279
Huntzui, i, 51
Hurricanes in the West Indies, ii, 220
Huy Hannon, i, 72

Ibn Batuta, his account of China, xxvi
Idols of China, i, 36; ii, 91; of the Philippine isles, ii, 261
Ignatius de Loyola, a Spanish Franciscan; his expedition to the East, ii, 207; he leaves Spain, ii, 208; reaches Mexico, ii, 223; the Philippines, ii, 258; China, ii, 269; his treatment there, ii, 270, 281; he returns by Cochin China, ii, 310; Malacca, Ceylon, ii, 328; Cape Comorin, ii, 331; Malabar, ii, 334; Goa, ii, 337; the Cape of Good Hope and Guinea, ii, 338; back to Lisbon,
Ignorance considered infamous in China, i, 122
Illocos islands, see Hilocos
Imaginary island of St. Borandon, ii, 212
Immortality of the soul, Chinese belief in the, i, 53; ii, 291
Indians, treasures thrown into the river by those of Cuba, ii, 221; their objection to meeting Spaniards in Paradise, ii, 264
Industry of the Chinese, i, 13
Inheritance, law of, in China, i, 63; singular custom concerning it in Pimienta, ii, 333
Insuanto, office of the, i, 101
Invocation of devils, ii, 203
Irrigation, method of, ii, 279

Japan, said to have been peopled from China, ii, 294; reason of the migration, ii, 295; Chinese hated by Japanese, ii, 296; kings of, ii, 297; warlike nature of the people, ii, 298; an unsuccessful expedition to China by them, ii, 299; progress of Christianity there, ii, 299; priests, witches, and women of, ii, 300; slaves in, ii, 301
Jor, see Johore
Johore, ii, 316
Josshouse, a Portuguese word, ii, 162
Judges in China, laws concerning, i, 107; diligence of, 109; their conduct investigated, i, 112; punishment of unjust, i, 115; ii, 169, ii, 275
Jumenos Indians, ii, 237
Justice, courts of, procedure in the, i, 107; ii, 153

Kampion, xviii
Kancheu, xviii
Karacosmos, a Tartar beverage, xiv
Karakorum, a Tartar city described by Rubruquis, x

INDEX.

Khambalu in China, xix
Khamchu, xxviii
Koh-i-norr, ii, 327
Kublai Khan, xv, xvi, xix

Labacares, Guido de, governor of the Philippines, ii, 15
Labrador, ii, 256
Ladrone islanders, singular custom of the, ii, 254; their knavery, 256
Laulo, isle of, ii, 111
Laupy, i, 73
Laws, of marriage, i, 61; inheritance, i, 63; the poor, i, 67; tenure of lands, i, 79; against leaving the kingdom, i, 93; against admitting foreigners, i, 94; a law of frankpledge, i, 110; concerning debtors, i, 111; on torture, i, 111; concerning courtesans, i, 146
Le, a Chinese coin, i, 82
Leachis, visiting justices, i, 113
Legal proceedings, i, 109
Legaspi, M. Lopez de, lxvii; ii, 3, 260
Leon, F. de, ii, 17
Letters, the writing of, i, 123; common use of, i, 124
Limahon, a Chinese corsair, lxviii; account of, ii, 6; his first attempt on Manilla, ii, 11; its failure, ii, 14; he burns the city, ii, 17; his fleet destroyed by the Spaniards, ii, 22; his escape, ii, 23, 115
Lincheon, i, 70
Linthey, i, 73
Lotzitzam, i, 51
Loyola, Martin Ignazio de, see Ignatius
Loytia, a title of honour, lx; examination for, i, 125; how conferred, i, 127
Lugor, ii, 316
Luzon, ii, 258

Mace, a Chinese coin, i, 82, note
Macheo, ii, 158, 183, 191, 194, 302
Magalhaens, Fernando, his discoveries and death, ii, 259
Maguay, or Macaw-tree, ii, 228
Mahomet, ii, 261
Malabar, ii, 334
Malacca, city of, taken by the Portuguese, ii, 317; provisions and fruits there, ii, 318; its commerce, ii, 319
Malacca, straits of, dangerous navigation in the, ii, 317
Maldivia, islands of, ii, 337
Malipur, ii, 290; relics of St. Thomas at, ii, 324

Mana, ii, 328
Mandarin, a Portuguese word, ii, 162
Mangalor, ii, 334
Mangate, ii, 333
Mangu Khan, court of, ix, x
Manilla, founded by the Spaniards, lxvii; ii, 4; Limahon's attack upon, ii, 17; ii, 258
Manju, or Southern China, described by Marco Polo, xx
Manuel, king of Cathay, ii, 282
Maqueda, duke of, ii, 210
Marriage, ceremonies and laws of, i, 61; singular law in Tartary of, i, 63; marriages of the princes, 65
Martin, Hieronimo, accompanies Herrada to China, ii, 29
Mart'n Ignatius, see Ignatius
Mascarenhas, Don Pedro, viceroy of India, ii, 329
Masulapatar, ii, 324
Mattheusi, Oderico, see Pordenone
Mazanbique, see Mozambique
Measures of length, i, 21
Megoa, see Hing-hoa
Mendoza, Juan Gonzales de, sent on an embassy to China by Philip II, lxxiii; its failure, lxxvi; publication of his work, lxxxi; various editions of it, lxxxii; his return and death, lxxxiii; account of his embassy, i, 162, 168, 170
Mercado y Ronquillo, Gonsalo de, governor of the Philippines, i, 167
Mexican Indians, description of the, ii, 229; their obedience to ecclesiastics, 230; their cities, 241, 245
Mexico, the kingdom of described, ii, 223; orthodoxy of the Mexicans, ii, 224; climate of, ii, 224; rains, ii, 225; breed of horses, ii, 225; cattle, ii, 227; the Indians of, ii, 228; price of provisions in, ii, 231
Military strength of China, i, 90
Mines, ii, 286, 320
Miracles in Cochin China, ii, 306
Miranda, Arias G. de, his kindness towards the Spanish missionaries, ii, 280
Mirza Shah Rokh, sends an embassy to China, xxvii
Missionaries, their efforts in China, i, 171
Mogor, the kingdom of the great Tartar, ii, 336
Money used in China, i, 17, 34, 82; ii, 162
Monte Corvino, G. di, sent on an embassy to China, xxii

INDEX. 347

Mourning apparel, i, 61
Mozambique, ii, 337
Musical instruments, i, 140
Musk, preparation of, i, 16 ; ii, 285
Mythology, the Chinese, i, 50

Nanking, xxi
Nauala, isle of, ii, 219
Navy, the Chinese, lxxx
Negapatan, ii, 328
Neighbours, bound to reveal each others' offences, i, 110
Neoma, a saint, i, 43
New Mexico, account of the discovery of, ii, 231; expedition of Ruyz, ii, 232; of Espeio, ii, 234; Indian towns, ii, 241; Devil worship there, ii, 242
Nicobar Isles, ii, 328
Nikpha, sea of, story told by Benjamin of Tudela concerning the, vii
Nobunanga, king of Japan, ii, 296; sets up his picture to be worshipped, ii, 297
Nombre de Dios, ii, 223
Number of tribute-payers in China, i, 81

Obando, J. de, i, 165
Ochantey, i, 72
Ocheuty, i, 51
Odialon, a Moorish kingdom, ii, 335
Officers of state in China, i, 101
Oktar Khan, xix
Omens, ii, 263
Omoncon, a Chinese captain, sent against Limahon, ii, 25 ; visits Manilla, ii, 27; returns to China with M. de Herrada, ii, 81
Ontiueros, J. de, ii, 235
Orchon, the river, x
Orion, influence of, vii
Oromuz, city of, abounds in salt, ii, 335
Ortega, Francisco de, lxxiii
Orthodoxy of the Mexicans, ii, 224
Ortiz, Stephen, ii, 133
Otey, i, 74
Othey, i, 73
Outon, i, 75
Outzim, i, 75
Padilla y Meneses, A. de, i, 168
Pagoda of Vishnaga, ii, 326
Paguina, i, 36
Pahang, ii, 316
Painting, i, 32
Palace of the emperor, i, 78
Palma de Cocos, ii, 266
Panama, ii, 224
Pangasinan, the river, ii, 18, 21, 32, 34
Panzon, *see* Pwan-Koo

Paon, *see* Pahang
Paper currency in China, xii
Paper made of canes, i, 123
Pardo, J. Dias, ii, 129
Paris, William of, *see* Bouchier
Parke, R., the translator of Mendoza's work, lxxxii; i, 1
Passaguates Indians, ii, 236
Patane, ii, 316
Peak of Tenerife, description of the, ii, 210
Pearls, ii, 285; fishery, 302
Pegu, kingdom of, ii, 320; war with Siam for a white elephant, ii, 321; religion of, ii, 321
Pekin, xix, xlvii
Penance of devotees, ii, 314
Pens, i, 123
Pereyra, Galeoti, his account of China, liii
Perez, Bartholomew, his embassy to China, i, 159
Persia, ii, 336
Persian embassy to China, xxvii
Petitions, presentation of, ii, 103
Pico de Adan, a mountain of Ceylon, ii, 329 ; pagoda thereon, containing an ape's tooth worshipped by the people, ii, 329 ; afterwards destroyed by the Portuguese, ii, 330
Philippines, i, 163; discovered by the Spaniards, ii, 4, 258; Magalhaens' voyage there, ii, 258; condition of the natives there, ii, 260; their law of debt, ii, 261; religion, ii, 261; superstitions, ii, 262; conversion to Christianity, ii, 263; fertility of soil, ii, 264; products of the country, ii, 265; the Palma de Cocos, ii, 266
Pictures shewn to the dying, ii, 290
Pimienta, kingdom of, ii, 333
Pine trees planted near graves, i, 61
Pintatey, i, 72
Pinto, F. Mendez, xxxvii
Pires, Tomas, his embassy to China, xxxiii; its failure, xxxvi
Pitch used for ships, i, 150
Pintados, the islands, ii, 10
Plague, unknown in China, ii, 284
Plano Carpini, John de, *see* Carpini
Play, a Chinese, ii, 88
Plon, ii, 114
Ploughing, ii, 166
Poala, ii, 242
Polo, Marco, his travels, xvi ; imprisonment at Genoa, xvii; route to China, xviii ; description of Khambalu, xix; excursion into Southern China, xx ; description of Quinsai, xxi
Polygamy sanctioned by law, i, 63

348 INDEX.

Ponchasi, office of the, i, 101
Poor houses, i, 67
Poor laws, i, 60
Porcelain manufacture, i, 38; ii, 287
Pordenone, Oderico de, his description of China, xxiii
Portuguese, voyage to China, xxxi; i, 96; jealousy towards the Spanish missionaries, ii, 158
Posts, Chinese system of, xxvi
Prayers for the dead, i, 54
Presents to officers of state prohibited, ii, 90
Prestyr John, ii, 337
Priest, conversion of a Chinese, ii, 127
Printing, art of, i, 131; its antiquity, i, 132; description of a Chinese book printed in 1348, i, 133
Prisons, xliii; i, 116
Prophecy concerning the fall of the Chinese empire, xliv; i, 76
Provinces of China enumerated, i, 22
Puerto Rico, ii, 216
Pumps for ships, i, 150
Punishment of criminals, lxiii; ii, 276
Pwan-koo, the Chinese Adam, i, 50

Quanina, a Chinese saint, i, 41
Quathy, i, 73
Quinsai, *see* Hang-cheou
Quintero, P., ii, 160
Quioutey, i, 74
Quires, province of, ii, 244
Quixue, ii, 274

Rada, M. de, *see* Herrada
Rains, violent, in Mexico, ii, 225
Ramon, Geronimo de, his "Republicas del Mundo", lxxii
Raxu, a king of Ceylon, persecutes the Christians, ii, 331
Red Sea, explanation of its colour, ii, 337
Religion, Carpini's account of that of the Chinese, viii; Pereyra's account of it, lxi; i, 10, 35; similarity between Budhist and Roman Catholic ceremonies, i, 37; doctrine of a future life, i, 53; religion of the Philippine islanders, ii, 261; in Sumatra, ii, 320; in Pegu, ii, 321; in Aracan, ii, 322; in Siam, ii, 314; in Persia, ii, 336
Religious orders in China, i, 56
Renaudot, Eusebe, his translation of an Arabic MS. relating to China, iii
Revenues of China, i, 82
Review of troops, ii, 102
Rhinoceros described, ii, 311

Ribera, G. de, ii, 21
Ricci, Matteo, letter on China, lxxvii
Roads in China, i, 27
Roman, Geronimo, observations on China, lxxvii
Romans, China, known to the, iii
Ronquillo, G., ii, 268
Rubruquis, G. de, his mission to Mangu Khan, ix; description of the Chinese, xii
Ruyz, Austen, expedition into New Mexico, ii, 234
Rysbroeck, William Van, *see* Rubruquis

Sacrifices to idols, i, 48
Salamina, ii, 290
Salcete, *see* Salsette
Salsette, island of, ii, 335
Salutations, i, 141
Salazar, Domingo de, ii, 4
Salzedo, J. de, ii, 10; destroys Limahon's fleet, ii, 22
Samatra, *see* Sumatra
Sancete, *see* Salcette
Sancheofu, description of the city, ii, 278
Sandi, Francisco de, governor of the Philippines, ii, 126; opposes Alfaro, ii, 128
San Francisco, Sebastian de, one of Alfaro's companions, ii, 134
Sangley, China so called, i, 20
San Juan de Lua, ii, 222
Santo Tome, ii, 332
Sarmiento, Pedro, one of Herrada's companions, ii, 29
Schools, number and excellence of Chinese, i, 122; visitation of, i, 123
Seclusion of women, i, 145
Seres, Chinese so named by Ammianus Marcellinus, iii
Serica vestis, iii
Servants, condition of in Japan, ii, 300
Sharks, rapacity of, ii, 219
Shipping, description of Chinese, i, 148; pitch used for, i, 150; pumps, i, 150; great number of ships in China, ii, 284
Siam, kingdom of, described, ii, 313; war with Pegu for a white elephant, ii, 321
Sian, *see* Siam
Sichia, a Chinese saint, i, 41
Silk, of common use in China, ii, 286; trade in, ii, 287; the "Serica vestis" of the Romans, iii
Silvester, a Dominican friar, his efforts in the cause of Christianity, ii, 312; honour to which he attained, ii, 313

Sincapura, strait of, ii, 258
Sinsay, a Chinese merchant, ii, 24; sails to China with Herrada, ii, 31, 37, 41, 83, 97, 115
Slaves, condition of, in Japan, ii, 300
Sosoc, i, 73
Spices, abundance of, in China, i, 17; in Sumatra, ii, 320
St. Borandon, the imaginary island of, ii, 212
St. Domingo, *see* Hispaniola
St. Helena, isle of, ii, 338
St. Lorenzo, isle of, ii, 337
St. Thomas, said to have preached in China, i, 37; relics of, preserved at Malipur, ii, 324
Strangers, Chinese jealousy of, i, 94
Succuir, *see* Sucheu
Sucheu, visited by Marco Polo, xviii
Sumatra, said to be the Isle of Ophir, ii, 319; its mines and productions, ii, 320
Suntien, a great city of China, i, 56, 77
Sutey, i, 74
Sweynheim, Conrad, i, 131

Tael, a Chinese coin, i, 82
Tamos, ii, 251
Tanaor, ii, 334
Tangoa, *see* Tong-gan
Tanhom, i, 50
Tansuso, visited by Herrada, ii, 44
Tantey, i, 73
Tartars, description of, i, 9; religion, i, 10
Tartary, singular custom respecting marriage, i, 63
Tea, earliest mention of, iv
Temples in China, i, 56; ii, 91; ii, 274; at Visnaga, ii, 326
Tenerife, island of, ii, 210; the Peak, ii, 210
Tepyna, i, 75
Teyencom, i, 51
Thieves, punishment of, i, 119
Tiguas, province of, ii, 233
Tinqui, xx
Tituhul, ii, 37
Tobosos Indians, ii, 236
Tolanchia, i, 36
Tonco, i, 74
Tong-gan, ii, 52
Tordesillas, Augustin de, one of Alfaro's companions, ii, 131
Torture of criminals, i, iii
Totoc, office of the, i, 101
Touznacaotican, ii, 9
Tozo, i, 75
Trade winds, ii, 253

Trapovana, the ancient name of Sumatra, ii, 319
Trautheyco, i, 41
Triana, John de, one of Herrada's companions, ii, 35
Tribute paid to the emperor, i, 82
Tripoli, William of, *see* Rubruquis
Troncon, i, 74
Tunis, the Goletta taken by the Turks, i, 165
Tutuan, office of the, i, 101
Tuticurin, kingdom of, ii, 331; idolatrous rites there, ii, 332
Tym, i, 74
Tzentzey, i, 72
Tzintzon, i, 28, 71
Tzintzoum, i, 75
Tzintzuny, i, 72
Tzobu, i, 74
Tzunthey, i, 73
Tzuyn, i, 74

Unguen, a city described by Marco Polo, xxii
University of Mexico, ii, 227
Unthey, i, 73
Usao, i, 51
Uzon, i, 75

Vangala, *see* Bengal
Vasquez Coronado, Francisco, ii, 246
Velas, islands of, ii, 253
Velasco, Luys de, viceroy of Mexico, ii, 3, 260
Vera Cruz, ii, 222
Viceroys of Chinese provinces, i, 101
Villa Lobos, commander of a Spanish fleet, ii, 259
Villa Roel, Pedro de, one of Alfaro's companions, ii, 131
Vintoquian, a pirate, ii, 7
Visnaga, city of, ii, 324; description of the king, ii, 325; ceremonies at his burial, ii, 326; temples, ii, 326; high priest called Brama, ii, 326; his power of dispensation, ii, 327; diamond mines, ii, 327
Vitey, first king of China, i, 69
Vossius, his opinion as to the knowledge of the ancients respecting China, ii
Vozequixama, ii, 298

Wall of China, description of, i, 28
Walled cities, ii, 288
Wealth of China, ii, 286, 288

Weapons, use of, forbidden to the people in China, ii, 58
Witches in the Philippine islands, ii, 262; in Japan, ii, 300
Witnesses, examination of, i, 109
Women of China, Persian mention of, xxix; burial of ladies of the imperial family, xxx; description of, i, 31; their small feet, i, 32; concubines of the emperor, i, 65; women forbidden by Vitey to be idle, i, 71; courtesy towards, i, 144; seclusion of, i, 145; courtesans, i, 146; chastity of Chinese women, ii, 293; women of Japan, ii, 300; of Cochin China, ii, 310; divorces in Visnaga, ii, 327

Writing, Chinese method of, xiii; i, 121, 123

Xavier, Francisco, ii, 299
Xactamas, king of Persia, ii, 336

Yanqui, xx
Yanthey, i, 73

Zaguato, ii, 248
Zaitun, a Chinese seaport, xxii
Zaytzon, i, 75
Zubin, isle of, ii, 258

STANFORD UNIVERSITY LIBRARIES
CECIL H. GREEN LIBRARY
STANFORD, CALIFORNIA 94305-6004
(415) 723-1493

All books may be recalled after 7 days

DATE DUE

DOC OCT 27 1994

DOC JAN 05 1998

MAR 0 3 2000

Lightning Source UK Ltd.
Milton Keynes UK
UKHW022307240521
384312UK00002B/136